Praise for *Your First Year in Network M*

"New network marketers . . . read this book! The Yarnells, multi-million dollar income earners with twenty years experience, provide a comprehensive operational structure . . . outstanding content . . . and over 200 specific recommendations to profitably survive your first year . . . and build a long-term business foundation. I'm recommending this book to all of my network marketing students."

—*Charles W. King, professor of marketing, University of Illinois at Chicago, seminar leader, UIC Certificate Seminar in Network Marketing*

"A highly original work from two people who have dedicated themselves to the personal enhancement of network marketing distributors worldwide."

—*Lou Tice, author, chairman, lecturer, and co-founder of the Pacific Institute, Inc.*

"The Yarnells are insightful, educated teachers in the world of network marketing. This book is a joy to read!"

—*Kay Smith, Nu Skin Blue Diamond, one of ten inductees in the International Network Marketing Directory's Hall of Fame*

"Everyone involved in, or even considering becoming involved in, network marketing should read this book. The Yarnells' uncanny ability to not only perceive but offer helpful solutions to the myriad of obstacles that beset all who attempt to succeed in this industry make it an invaluable aid."

—*Greg Martin, CEO of ShapeRite Concepts Ltd.*

"Mark and Rene are two of the most powerful leaders in our industry. Their commitment to the success of others and their courage to speak their hearts and minds have transformed the lives of hundreds of thousands. Study this book!"

—*Richard B. Brooke, chairman and CEO of Oxyfresh Worldwide, Inc.*

YOUR FIRST YEAR IN NETWORK MARKETING

ALSO BY THE AUTHORS

By Mark Yarnell

Self-Wealth (PaperChase Press, 1999)

Power Speaking (PaperChase Press, 1994)

By Rene Reid Yarnell

The New Entrepreneurs Audio Program (Quantum Leap, 2000)

*The New Entrepreneurs: Making a Living—
Making a Life through Network Marketing* (Quantum Leap, 1999)

The Encyclopedia of Network Marketing (Quantum Leap, 1995)

MARK YARNELL AND RENE REID YARNELL

YOUR FIRST YEAR IN NETWORK MARKETING

OVERCOME YOUR FEARS,

EXPERIENCE SUCCESS, AND

ACHIEVE YOUR DREAMS!

THREE RIVERS PRESS
NEW YORK

Copyright © 1998 by Mark Yarnell and Rene Reid Yarnell

All rights reserved. No part of this book may be reproduced or transmitted in any form or by
any means, electronic or mechanical, including photocopying, recording, or by any information storage or retrieval system, without written permission from Random House, Inc., except
for the inclusion of brief quotations in a review.

Published by Three Rivers Press, New York, New York.
Member of the Crown Publishing Group, a division of Random House, Inc.
www.crownpublishing.com

THREE RIVERS PRESS and the Tugboat design are registered trademarks of Random House,
Inc.

Originally published by Prima Publishing, Roseville, California, in 1998.

Printed in the United States of America

Library of Congress Cataloging-in-Publication Data

Yarnell, Mark.
    Your first year in network marketing : overcome your fears, experience success, and
achieve your dreams! / Mark Yarnell and Rene Reid Yarnell.
        p.   cm.
        Includes index.
        1. Multi-level marketing.   I. Yarnell, Rene Reid.   II. Title.
HF5415.126.Y373 1997   97-35554
658.8'6—dc21   CIP

ISBN 0-7615-1219-5

34 33 32 31

First Edition

Mark Yarnell would like to dedicate this book to his daughter, Amy.

Rene Reid Yarnell would like to dedicate this book to our parents:
Lin and Helen Harrington and Duane and Patsi Yarnell
for leaving traditional jobs behind to live the life of entrepreneurs and
inspiring us to follow in their footsteps.

And to our children:
Chris Grove and Amy Yarnell
who intend to carry this entrepreneurial gene into the next millennium.
Hopefully, they will spread this spirit and touch far more lives than we did.

Three generations of family love have been the driving force behind the
many financial, emotional, and spiritual blessings we have enjoyed
during our shared lives together.

"We are at that very point in time when a 400-year-old age is dying and another is struggling to be born—a shifting of culture, science, society, and institutions enormously greater than the world has ever experienced. Ahead is the possibility of the regeneration of individuality, liberty, community, and ethics such as the world has never known, and a harmony with nature, with one another, and with the divine intelligence such as the world has never dreamed."

DEE HOCK
Founder of Visa

CONTENTS

FOREWORD

As a business reporter and self-help writer, I have been researching and writing about the network marketing industry for eight years. During this time, I have had the privilege of interviewing some of the top leaders in the industry, and listening as they revealed their hardest won and most closely held success secrets. Yet I have never found a richer lode of hard-edged, practical information on network marketing than I did between the pages of *Your First Year in Network Marketing* by Mark and Rene Yarnell. I learned more from reading this book than I have during all the years that I have spent exhaustively researching the MLM industry.

Of course, I am hardly surprised by the book's high quality. From the first time I ever spoke with Mark Yarnell, I knew that he was a master communicator. Many of the heaviest hitters in network marketing become surprisingly inarticulate when you try to get them to explain the nuts and bolts behind their success. But Mark has always possessed the unique ability to summarize and encapsulate his business wisdom in easy-to-swallow nuggets, delivered with humor and drama, and honed with a keen and subtle intelligence. The stories and insights that Mark imparted to me, through many fascinating interviews, played a big part in making my book *Wave 3* the success that it eventually became.

It is clear from reading *Your First Year in Network Marketing* that Rene Yarnell is cut from the same cloth as her remarkable and talented husband. Together, they make an unbeatable team. These two have been through the wars together. In *Your First Year in Network Marketing*, they write with brutal candor of the bad times as well as the good, imparting to readers an unusually balanced picture of what it really means to work an MLM business and what it really takes to succeed.

You won't find any loose talk in this book about getting rich quick. The Yarnells made their millions the hard way. Their formula for success is severe and merciless. It demands strenuous work and superhuman persistence. But for those who stick it out, it offers the realistic hope of genuine financial freedom.

This is a book that every first-time networker needs to read. It shows you exactly where the pitfalls lie and how to avoid them. And it does so in language that anyone can understand, reinforcing each point with inspiring, real-life anecdotes. For those networkers who take their business seriously, *Your First Year in Network Marketing* is, quite simply, indispensable.

— Richard Poe
Author of *Wave 3* and *The Wave 3 Way to Building Your Downline*

ACKNOWLEDGMENTS

Many thanks . . .

To Richard Kall, for being, undoubtedly, the finest mentor and upline anyone in network marketing could have. We love you.

To John Fogg, for creating *Upline* magazine and for persevering long enough in a highly competitive industry to see his dream become a reality, and in the process, uplifting many people who would otherwise be living lives of mediocrity. We appreciate you.

To the publishers of *Success* magazine—especially Duncan Anderson—for believing in us enough to print our articles on this industry at a time when no other periodicals were willing to risk telling the truth about our remarkable profession. We thank you.

To Dr. Charles King, for believing enough in us and in our industry to team with us in creating the first network marketing certification course ever offered. We treasure our relationship with you.

To Blake Roney and Steve Lund, who founded our network marketing company in the '80s, thus allowing us to achieve the wealth and time freedom to pursue our dreams. Thanks for the memories.

To our close friend, Richard Brooke, president and founder of Oxyfresh, for trusting us to train your distributors early in our careers (even though we were in a competing company). We try to emulate your integrity.

And finally, to the numerous and enthusiastic network marketers who have touched our lives over more than a decade. You are destined to change the course of history and to lead the way for the growing number of professionals seeking an alternative lifestyle in the new millennium. We are proud to share this incredible industry with you.

INTRODUCTION

According to *Webster's Dictionary*, "to survive" means to remain alive or in existence, particularly to live on after the death of others. The fascinating thing about network marketing is that, in many instances, survival—i.e., staying in existence after others leave the business—is precisely what leads to dramatic wealth. Attrition is a considerable factor in our business. Yet we have rarely met anyone who has worked steadily in network marketing who doesn't eventually achieve success. And those rare individuals who do not succeed are usually their own worst enemies, constantly reinventing the wheel and complicating the simplest path to prosperity in the history of capitalism.

Of course, priorities vary as widely as do people. While some choose network marketing as a means to an end (wealth), others simply enjoy it for its own merits.

These folks join Multi-Level Marketing to build their confidence, widen their circle of friends, and feel more productive. And in spite of the fact that they'll never earn huge incomes, you couldn't pry them away from this business with a crowbar. That kind of money was never really their goal, and you'll read many of their stories in this book. In fact, were we to double the number of stories of success, we still couldn't possibly elaborate on all the remarkable benefits to be derived by those who have chosen to participate in this wondrous industry.

In network marketing, you persevere or you perish. Quitting is the one sure way to fail. Surviving the first year establishes a new distributor with a good basis for success. Our analysis shows that an estimated 95 percent of those who survive ten years in network marketing become wealthy beyond their wildest expectations.

In network marketing, you persevere or you perish. Quitting is the one sure way to fail. Surviving the first year establishes a new distributor with a good basis for success.

These survivors have achieved either staggering financial rewards and/or total "time freedom," that is, having all the free time to do the things that really matter to you with the people you love most.

At this particular time in history, when traditional business offers so little security, network distribution is literally the last bastion of free enterprise. It's a system in which common people can invest a small sum and, through sheer tenacity and determination, rise to staggering levels of financial reward and personal freedom. It's a field devoid of the pitfalls of traditional business: payroll, employee benefit costs, advertising, overhead, bookkeeping, and accounts receivable. Network marketing has an entirely different set of entrapments of its own. But once understood, these problems are easily overcome. We believe success is critically dependent on awareness, from the very beginning, of what these hazards are and how to overcome them. Hence this book.

The network marketing industry traces its roots to the 1940s when Nutrilite Products, Inc., launched the sale of food supplement products and, ten years later,

Amway introduced the sale of household products. Over the past fifty years, the industry has matured into a legitimate and efficient channel of distribution ideally suited for the next wave about to break in the world of business. All we can say is, thanks to Rich DeVos and Jay Van Andel for having the vision to pioneer this industry. Network marketing annual sales are nearing $20 billion in the United States alone, being moved by an estimated 8 million people. Worldwide, more than $100 billion of a broad spectrum of products and services are being sold by an estimated 30 million independent network marketers. And keep in mind that we are still a very young industry with an expansive, promising future. Several studies have predicted that a third of all goods and services will be moved via network marketing in western nations shortly after the turn of the century, and this could be as high as 50 percent in developing nations by the year 2110.

Historically, the industry has been product-driven, selling from the traditional categories of personal care, vitamin/nutritional supplementation, home and family care, leisure and educational products. Starting in the 1980s, services became a growing component, particularly in the deregulated telecommunications industry. Other services have included credit cards, financial services, insurance, prepaid legal services, travel, self-development, and motivational programming. With the forthcoming deregulation of the public utilities industries between 1998 and 2002, network marketing companies are positioning themselves to enter this market as well.

The evolving maturity of our industry is clearly demonstrated by the twenty network marketing companies now traded publicly on NASDAQ and the New York Stock Exchange. And many others are preparing to "go public." In order to file an Initial Public Offering (IPO), companies must establish standardized accounting procedures and be open to Securities and Exchange Commission (SEC) scrutiny and control. Therefore, those companies that do go public must establish and maintain high standards of business practices, which elevates the character of the entire network marketing community.

Investors' response to the publicly traded network marketing companies has been outstanding. *Upline* magazine, an industry trade publication, maintains an "Upline Index" that tracks the financial performance of these public network marketing companies. In 1996, this index showed an increase in stock market value for the industry of more than 63 percent as compared to the Dow Jones Industrial Average increase of only 33 percent and the Standard & Poor's 500 Index increase of 34 percent. This nearly two-fold gain of the network marketing industry over traditional corporations has created considerable excitement among savvy investors.

The average person needs as little as $200 or $300 to get started in network marketing. Included in this figure is the purchase of some widely accepted products or services to be personally used and shared with others. Our industry is based on simple word-of-mouth recommendation of products and services; distribution moves directly from the producer to the consumer, which cuts out all the intermediate agents and dealers who have nothing to do with production or consumption. As goods are distributed, the network marketer then receives compensation equal to the advertising budget of most large corporations. We've all known for years that "word of mouth" is the best form of advertising. Therefore, should it not also be the most lucrative?

We have recorded a couple of dozen audiotapes during our collective twenty years in network marketing, and the one that is still the most requested is entitled, "If MLM Is So Great, Why Am I So Depressed?" We think the reason people enjoy that tape is because we dared to tell the truth about the pitfalls in this industry. We admitted that, in spite of our success, we both considered quitting many times during those first years. Unfortunately, many people heard that audiotape far too late in their network marketing careers and, while they enjoyed a good chuckle because they could identify with our admitted first-year problems, most had already lost their upstart enthusiasm so necessary for success. And once people lose the drive and enthusiasm to carry them through the tough months, once that excitement is gone, in many cases, so too is the chance to achieve dramatic wealth. There is an often quoted adage in this business: "It's much easier to give birth to a new distributor than it is to resurrect a dead one." And yet as the stories poured into our Swiss chalet from across the Atlantic, we realized that this book may indeed resurrect thousands of discouraged network marketers once they read some of the truthful anecdotes shared by so many legends of this industry.

As a prelude to these stories that we hope will impact your life, it seems appropriate to introduce to you one of the legends, Doug Wead, who is with the oldest and largest MLM company. Before we tell his story, we would like to tell you a little about the man. The night the Gulf War began, you may have seen Doug Wead interviewed on television by Dan Rather. Doug was then serving as special assistant to President Bush. He has been quoted in *Time, Newsweek, US News & World Report, The Washington Post, The Wall Street Journal*, and hundreds of other major publications, and his twenty-six books have sold over 3 million copies in fifteen languages. Except for his six year "political sabbatical," Doug Wead has dedicated his last twenty years to building his organization, as well as researching and writing about network marketing. Doug has filled auditoriums and soccer stadiums in Poland, Hungary, France, Turkey, the United Kingdom, Australia, Indonesia, and the United States with eager network marketers in just the last year.

So what does a legend like Doug Wead do with his money, credibility, time freedom, and power? In 1979, working side by side with Pat Boone and Archbishop Bernard Cardinal Law of Boston, Doug founded what is today one of the world's premier relief organizations, Mercy Corps International. Last year it distributed $73 million worth of medicine and famine relief to troubled areas of our world.

Let's now visit Doug's first year in network marketing through his own eyes as he writes powerfully and humorously about his life experiences.

"Most of us involved in network marketing are gluttons for punishment. Subconscious-sadomasochists. Basically, we hate ourselves. That's why we get into networking in the first place. We see it as almost guaranteed suffering. I need this. This will really make me feel bad—which I so richly deserve.

"Wouldn't you know that I would end up successful, making money, traveling the world, meeting presidents, feeding the hungry. See? For me, nothing happens the way it's supposed to. I can't even fail right.

"In that sense, my early anticipated struggles in network marketing were a disappointment. I had no problem with rejection. I enjoyed every one of them. I was much quicker to respect and identify with the people who turned me down than those rare prospects whom I was actually able to 'recruit.' Each rejection was only positive reaffirmation of my own negative self-image. Likewise, going without food, or sleep, or money was only what I deserved for making such an arrogant assumption that I could survive in network marketing 'dreamland.'

"No. For me the very real problem was not physical at all. It wasn't money, it wasn't people, it wasn't product, and it wasn't time. For me, the challenge was entirely between my own ears. It still is, incidentally. For me, the early struggle was only philosophical. Of course, I can do it. Anybody can do it. The question, the very real nagging, haunting question was: Should I do it? Is it right? Is this what I am supposed to be doing with my life?

"Nothing is more wearisome and draining than self-doubt. Nothing is more effective at stripping off the fine edge from everything you say or do. Nothing can empty your emotional gas tank quicker.

"For me, the challenge was entirely between my own ears. It still is, incidentally. For me, the early struggle was only philosophical. Of course, I can do it. Anybody can do it. The question, the very real nagging, haunting question was: Should I do it? Is it right? Is this what I am supposed to be doing with my life?"

"In that sense, for the first time in my life, I had met my match. Network marketing, which we see as such a sensitive machine, easily influenced by attitudes, was not a bit impressed with my emotional and psychological drama. It only seemed to crunch numbers like a mindless calculator. The secret for me, I was to learn, was simply to survive and then plod on. Above all, I couldn't quit. Over time, as I slowly fed this monster, it grew and grew exponentially.

" 'Believe. You have to believe,' They kept telling me. I didn't even have to do that. Two times two equals four. You don't have to believe it. It is four anyway. And my business grew—in spite of myself.

"Tough?

"Emotionally, maybe. Spiritually, maybe. But those battles manifest themselves in failure as well as success. Poverty is no refuge for the war-shocked, weary soul.

"And so I conquered. And with the money, I co-founded Mercy Corps International. Last year we gave away $73 million in food and medicine around the world. I found my 'why.' "

We hope this book will help you find your "why" too. It is our hope that this book will be given to new network marketers immediately after they sign up in order to warn them of the pitfalls before they lose their initial excitement, because once it's gone, the chances of ever getting that driving enthusiasm back are virtually nil. The first year in this business is not just challenging—it is more akin to going into combat. It's about survival in the midst of widespread failure. You may not even sense the impending danger, and then all of a sudden you've been ambushed and have lost an entire leg of your downline. One of our primary objectives in writing this book is to take the "stealth" out of your battles so that you can see your adversaries well in advance, instead of having them creep up and catch you unaware. But equally important is that once you see the clash coming, you are equipped with the necessary skills and tools to win each confrontation and thus survive your first year in MLM. Believe us, in year one, survival is the name of the game. We know this both from personal experience and from statistics compiled by several companies that suggest well over 60 percent of all new network marketers quit in their first year, during the most important phase in the learning curve. Given the possibility of earning more each month working from home than a pediatric cardiologist with a staff of ten earns in a year at his clinic (and it is possible), wouldn't any sane person be willing to invest a year or two studying MLM? And compared to the twelve-year learning curve of doctors, isn't a year more palatable?

While our industry's attrition rate is perhaps no higher than other professions involving overrides and straight commissions, it is nevertheless critical that we do our best to help new associates anticipate the inevitable conflicts that will arise and equip them with the weapons they'll need to win those battles.

It has been suggested that "every great MLMer was a lousy MLMer first," and we concur. Unfortunately, it's a fact of life that when any of us first begin a new endeavor, we are, at least initially, vulnerable novices. Although the educational process in network marketing is relatively brief, it can be devastating to many new associates. The main reason is quite simple to understand. We all hate rejection, and none is worse than when we are mocked by friends, family, and acquaintances. It doesn't take very long for people to become discouraged when every day for the first four or five months they are subjected to eye-rolling ridicule from everyone they know, love, and respect. However, if you know exactly what to expect and you aren't forced to appear foolish by cajoling, deceiving, or pestering those close to you, network marketing, even in the early stages, is quite fun and relatively painless. Preparation and anticipation are both critical.

In this book we will prepare you for most of the inevitable first-year challenges. We will teach you how to survive those conflicts by providing you with tactics that work—no theories, just facts. Most importantly, by preparing you in advance and sharing practical ways to survive each of these first-year challenges, we want to assist you in persevering. And if you do manage to survive the first year without quitting and without losing your sense of humor, the odds are great that you will continue long enough to become quite wealthy and successful.

We've had a tremendous resource pool from which to draw our lessons and examples. For the past several years, we have been fortunate to teach America's only college-level certification course in network marketing with Harvard Ph.D., Charles King at the University of Illinois at Chicago. Many of the top networkers from every company, both in America and abroad, as well as many network marketing CEOs, have attended our classes, and we've spent quality personal time with many of them. As course instructors, we learned a great deal from our students. The experiences we share in this book have all happened, if not specifically to us, then to other leaders who have shared them with us. You'll recognize many of their names. So, we feel confident that we have left very few stones unturned in our efforts to teach you the best survival strategies available to first-year distributors. Some of our industry's most successful international leaders survived their first year by utilizing the simple maneuvers laid out for you in this book. Survive your first year and you've got a tremendous opportunity to join those legends.

From Mark's father telling him that he is "ruining the family name by doing MLM," to a hungry reporter asking the attorney general of Nevada to investigate our company in hopes of uncovering a scandal or conflict of interest while Rene was serving as chairman of the County Commission, the two of us have survived some fairly devastating ambushes. We know what it's like to lose six of our seven best leaders to a new upstart scam, that is, a company that misrepresents its earnings and/or product efficacy, and we've endured the humiliation of a close friend stealing an entire downline leg. Both of us fell into the management trap at different points in our respective first years and wound up baby-sitting people who never would have succeeded no matter what we had done because they weren't willing to do what we did. Both of us suffered the misplaced personal guilt of signing up a close friend who just couldn't make it in this business. We'll teach you how to survive all of those booby traps—in fact, we'll show you how to avoid them altogether on your path toward achieving all

the money you aspire to earn and the time to enjoy it.

In our first book, *Power Multi-Level Marketing*, we presented the theory behind MLM achievement. We tried to provide a paint-by-numbers system for both part-time and full-time success. But in this book, we are vitally concerned with practical applications, that is, with giving specific examples of what can and does happen to cause potentially successful distributors to prematurely end their careers. Many psychiatrists subscribe to the theory that 90 percent of the solution to any problem consists in the awareness of that problem's existence. We agree. Our fervent hopes and prayers are that, by bringing to your attention all the problems that successful network marketers face in their first years, we will enable you to survive yours. We are sharing with you the practical, proven survival tactics used by many of the legends of this industry so that you also can prosper abundantly.

We're honored to have Dr. Charles King add a dimension to our book never before available: a quantitative analysis of network marketing from an academic perspective. Much of our most important data has been exhaustively researched and compiled by him. We've learned a great deal about the inner workings and technical marketing strategies of our profession from Dr. King—many of his

Network marketing is indeed the greatest opportunity in the history of capitalism, and we consider ourselves very privileged to be able to participate in the industry.

overviews are sprinkled throughout this book. His keen insights have been invaluable to us over the years, and his dynamic wife, Sandra, has directed all of our college certification courses. Nearly one thousand students have graduated from our course to become network marketing professionals. So, many thanks to Charles and Sandra King.

Network marketing is indeed the greatest opportunity in the history of capitalism, and we consider ourselves very privileged to be able to participate in the industry. So, naturally, when Prima Publishing contacted us about doing a book, not long after its marvelous success publishing Richard Poe's legendary *Wave Three* books, we jumped at the opportunity with tremendous enthusiasm.

As industry advocates, we believe that when any network marketing company fails, we all suffer. The future survival of our industry depends now on cooperation, not antagonism. Industry-wide success depends on elevating MLM companies and products rather than destroying the reputations, hopes, and dreams of our MLM competitors—only then will network marketing become the most lucrative profession in all of free enterprise. Some network marketers mistakenly believe that the systematic ruin of their competitors is their best strategy for success. Little do they know that's exactly why they haven't begun to reach their potential. Unlike pioneers of the Old West who circled their wagons to fight off attacks, whenever one or more companies in our industry is threatened, we circle our wagons and fire inward.

The old tactic of "divide and conquer" has been quite effective in the traditional business world. The traditional corporate pyramids have skillfully utilized the media and government regulators to similarly attack and stifle our growing industry; and all along they have hoped and prayed that we'd just go away. But we think it's time for them to stop fighting us. We respect all companies, not just those in our own industry, and we think they should do the same.

Spanning our collective twenty years in the field of professional network marketing, we have been blessed to speak to hundreds of thousands of marvelous people in every part of the world. And while we've heard our industry denigrated in a variety of ways, not once have we heard it referred to as "the rat race." This graphic description has been used on every continent, and translated into every language, to depict traditional business. "Rat race" literally means a sprint between the world's most deplorable rodents, those who actually wiped out half the population of England during the Black Plague. And what is it they are so steadfastly pursuing? Refuse and rotten grain in a hopeful pursuit to eat enough to see one more day. If for no other reason than to help people avoid that, we feel that this is a book whose time has come because the human condition should be a joyous flight among eagles, not a frenzied dash among rodents.

Betty Carter, formerly senior vice president for the Pacific Stock Exchange, recently shared a graphic comparison between the rat race of traditional business and the freedom of network marketing. In her own words, "When traditional business grows, an entire population can be reduced to rats. I moved to Seattle several years ago because of the quality of life. Today, as two corporations expand, the entire city has been forced into a mindless trek for several hours each day. The average speed on major highways has been reduced to 21 mph. Crime and other societal problems are rising dramatically. No one can yet predict the negative ecological impact of the several-thousand-person-influx each month, but environmentalists are clearly worried.

"The point is this: when MLM corporations experience explosive growth, thousands of people go home and soar like eagles. When traditional corporations explode, people from all over the world assume the posture of rats and take to the streets. Thank God network marketing has given me the freedom to run errands during the times when others are confined to their little cubicles, but it will just be a matter of time before I have to look elsewhere for tranquillity."

We feel we have an awesome responsibility to educate as many people as possible to the fact that they need no longer participate in the god-awful stress of traditional linear business. We wholeheartedly agree with Art Williams, the author of *All You Can Do*, when he suggests that we should all become crusaders in an effort to save the masses—at least those who will listen—from their headlong pursuit into eighty-hour weeks, mediocre incomes, and stress-induced coronaries. Because the American Dream has become a nightmare for so many, and because network distribution is such a viable alternative to more traditional business professions, it is incumbent upon those of us who have reaped so much from this industry to begin to sow seeds for others.

The book you are now holding in your hands is the ultimate survivors' manual. Thanks to the hundreds of unselfish leaders from diverse and numerous companies who rose to the occasion by contributing their stories, you will learn how to dramatically alter your life. Knowing full well that they would be educating their competitors, they all dared to tell the unadulterated truth about how to succeed in our industry. That kind of unselfishness alone makes us proud to call ourselves network marketers.

If only this book had been written a decade ago, we might not have had to witness the unnecessarily hasty retreat of so many dynamic people from our industry who were simply unprepared for the first year's battles. Because of this book, you won't have to endure the same unnecessary losses we did. And there is one promise we will make to you without reservation: There will be times when your eyes will well up with tears or you'll laugh so hard at some of these legends' anecdotes about their early challenges that, like us, you will have to put the book down until you can wipe the mist from your eyes. These stories are commensurate with ushering in a new industry. We believe the next decade will bring a noticeable decline in these types of challenges as new technology and distribution channels make way for network marketing in our world.

We received countless illustrations and anecdotes, all of which were heartwarming and inspiring. We regret that, due to editorial restrictions, we were unable to include each and every narrative. We want to offer a special thanks to those legends of network marketing who, by sharing their stories, did something unprecedented in business. They dared to admit, after becoming legends, their innermost vulnerabilities and bouts with anxiety and depression, so that millions of others, including their own competitors, might be inspired to exit the forty-year plan and share in the American Dream. Enjoy. And whatever else you do in the first year, just don't quit! Because surviving is synonymous with thriving in our industry.

Mark Yarnell and Rene Reid Yarnell
Gstaad, Switzerland

YOUR FIRST YEAR IN NETWORK MARKETING

CHAPTER 1

Ignoring the Rejection Rocket

Make rejection your ally instead of your enemy.

NETWORK MARKETING IS ONE of the most fun and rewarding businesses in the world, but eventually all network marketers are faced with certain widespread and universal challenges. No matter how long we participate in Multi-Level Marketing (MLM) and no matter how successful we become, there is always the possibility that we will be shot down temporarily by the most prevalent and dangerous weapon of all—the Rejection Rocket. It can and will strike any time, rendering us virtually immobile, thus destroying our enthusiasm and excitement, which are the essential qualities for success.

Rejection by Your Spouse

EVERYONE faces rejection in life, but what makes our form of rejection so very

devastating is that it often comes from the very people we most love and respect: our spouse, our parents, our best friends and business associates. We are convinced that rejection causes more people to fail in MLM than any other factor, and often they fail literally before they ever begin because their approach is from the head, not the heart. Here's the classic scenario.

Bob is at a transitional place in his life and open to a career change. He is receptive to listening to a new business concept. He goes to a network marketing meeting and for the first time everything makes sense. He may have considered working in this industry four or five times before, but he was never in a "change" mode during previous presentations. Now, because he's about to be laid off, he has a transitional mind-set. So, not only does Bob begin to see the wisdom in networking, but he actually finds himself enthusiastic about the earnings potential. Throughout the second half of the one-hour presentation he begins to make a mental list of the friends and associates whom he knows would be excellent at recruiting. Now let's look at two possible outcomes. Regardless of whether Bob actually signs up or not, he's about to be attacked by the first adversary in this business. And unless the person conducting the presentation prepares Bob and the others for what is going to occur, by presenting certain facts at the end of the first recruiting interview, Bob is going to quit before he ever begins. Later, we'll return to the particular details of this story, but first let's see what happens to Bob once he leaves the presentation. In fact, we'll examine several scenarios.

Because the timing is right in his life, Bob is excited. And because Bob knows several people who will be naturals at recruiting, he can hardly wait to break the news to them that he has found the "ultimate opportunity." If the person who introduced Bob to MLM is one of those folks who signs people up at the first interview, Bob may actually fill out a distributor agreement, promising to come back on Saturday for training. More than likely he won't be asked to sign up at the first meeting, but will instead promise to think about the business and call the presenter back with his answer. However, unless the recruiter carefully prepares Bob for rejec-

tion, Bob is now set up for failure. He's excited, though he may not have admitted that to anyone yet. But Bob is about to be blindsided by the Rejection Rocket, an inevitability seldom explained properly by most recruiters. Because he hasn't been trained, here's what happens.

First, Bob corners his wife. He's really excited and the conversation goes something like this: "Honey, our worries may be over. I think Phil has given us a gift from God. You remember how I explained the cutbacks at my company and how I told you I could actually be one of the future fatalities?"

"Yeah, Bob, but you don't really think after all these years that you could get laid off. I mean you weren't serious were you?" His wife finds this inconceivable.

"Honey listen, it doesn't matter. I was just over at Phil's and he and Nancy have gotten into a new business that looks really great. I can't believe how much money there is to be earned and freedom to be gained. Honey, Phil is about to get his first big check. And I brought home some samples of the products. Nancy is blown away by this creme and shampoo. Here, I brought some home for you to try. She wants you to call her!" (The Rejection Rocket is aimed directly at Bob's head and is about to be launched.)

Bob's wife takes the two packets of moisturizer and shampoo from him, looks at them, then at him incredulously. "Wait a minute, Bob. You're serious, aren't you? Let me get this straight. You've been with your company for seven years. We have a company car, health insurance, and we just bought our dream home. Your boss loves you like his own son and is about to recommend you to the Golden Acres Country Club. They lay off a few lousy executives and now you're seriously thinking about giving up a legitimate career and all of those years I suffered to put you through your MBA program to do some pyramid scheme. Please, Bob, tell me this is a bad dream. Tell me I'm not hearing you say this!"

Bob grins and reaches out to touch his wife's arm and she jerks it away, snarling like a cornered wharf rat. He hasn't seen that look on her face since he accidentally backed over the puppy last summer.

"No, honey, you aren't listening. We've got a chance here to get in early. We can be earning over $20,000 a month in a year. Do you realize how many hours I've been working? The baby cries when I pick her up because I'm virtually a stranger. They've laid off thirty-five men and women this quarter and I could be next. Honey, look, I'm telling you, Phil and Nancy are our friends. They aren't . . ."

"Oh come on, Bob!" interrupts his wife. "You yourself have said that Phil is irresponsible. He failed at that tire com-

pany. He failed at life insurance. Then he tried that stupid greeting card deal and we both laughed at how dumb that was. Bob, Bob, Bob, you're not thinking straight." She softens and launches a new tactic. "Bob, honey, we're set. You said so yourself. And, besides, what am I going to tell my parents? That you left your company to sell shampoo door to door?"

Bob has just heard the same spousal arguments that countless other men and women have heard over the years. It could easily have been Bob leveling the same objections at his wife who just returned from her first serious network marketing presentation. Often it's the wife who is bombarded by personal affronts from her husband. Had Bob simply said nothing until he could get his wife to Phil and Nancy's for a legitimate presentation, the Rejection Rocket would have never been launched. Or, had the approach been emotionally positive instead of intellectually negative, the outcome might have been different.

But keep in mind that even if the circumstances differ, the outcome is often the same. This discussion could have happened on a Sunday morning following a Saturday training session in which Bob had already signed a distributor application. It doesn't really matter. The point is this: We are convinced that as many as 50 percent of all potentially successful networkers fail before ever getting started because their sponsor does not prepare them for the spouse Rejection Rocket. The tragedy is that those very circumstances could quite easily be minimized if not completely eliminated through preparation and proactive measures. It's the responsibility of every recruiter to fully prepare prospects for rejection, then provide them with the tools to overcome rejection. Phil should have insisted that Bob bring his wife to a full-blown presentation, either at this first briefing or at another one soon to follow. In addition, he should have said emphatically, "Bob, don't try to explain this to your wife until you have more information, or better yet, bring her to us!"

Rejection by Family and Friends

BEFORE presenting solutions to the previous problem, let's first scrutinize another scenario that occurs frequently. Although the participants are somewhat different, the outcome is equally predictable and negative. We begin by assuming that Bob's wife is as excited as he is about this network marketing opportunity. Let's also assume that Bob has signed up, and both he and his wife have

been trained and prepared for any and all rejection. Initially, Bob decides to take the lead until their new infant is a little older; his wife will join Bob later. Bob can anticipate the primary objections used by prospective MLMers and has memorized a response for each one. In fact, he's quite proud of his knowledge and is even perhaps a little cocky about his ability to overcome objections.

Bob is excited about his new skills of persuasion, believing with a smug self-confidence that he can effectively counter each objection. He's convinced that in this battle of wits, his prospects are unarmed. He fully expects to win any and all debates about network marketing and prove to each of his friends that his new venture is far superior to traditional business. Equipped with that knowledge, he picks up the telephone and begins calling his twenty-five best prospects—those people whom he would love to spend the rest of his life with in a partnership. Usually, one of three outcomes is predictable, so let's evaluate all three.

Winning the Battle

The first outcome is what we call "winning the battle." Bob has just gotten past his close friend's secretary and is beginning his prospecting conversation. This is a man Bob has known since high school.

Their lives are quite different now, so they see each other infrequently but have nevertheless retained their warm friendship. The conversation begins with small talk, but let's move ahead to the actual dialogue about the business. Bob begins his approach: "You know, Steve, the other reason I called is to try to set up a convenient time when you and Sally can come over and take a look at a new business my wife and I have . . . "

Steve cuts in: "Bob, sounds like one of those pyramid deals to me. Don't tell me you and Christy have been sucked into one of those scams!"

Of course, Bob has been trained, albeit improperly, to handle objections and he's armed for battle. "Actually, Steve, I can understand your reluctance to look at a deal like this, but all I ask is that you remain open-minded for a forty-five-minute presentation. Let me ask you, Steve, would Tuesday or Thursday be better for you?" Bob is proud of his canned response, but as we'll see, his pride is very fleeting.

"C'mon Bob, you and I go way back. You can cut out the memorized speeches and shoot me straight. Sal and I aren't the least bit interested in one of those deals. In fact, my own father got sucked into some gold scam last summer and put over five grand into the deal, never signed up one person and has a garage full of over-priced gold coins gathering dust," Steve says gently but firmly.

At this point, or really before the conversation had even gone this far, Bob should have realized that Steve isn't in the right time in his life to see this opportunity. He isn't the slightest bit open to the business, and anything said from here on will only further alienate Steve and therefore hurt Bob's chances to approach his friend at a later date when he may be more receptive. In fact, unbeknown to Bob, he may actually do irreparable damage to their friendship by continuing to pursue the matter. (There's a specific "six-month" rule we'll present later in the book that will help you avoid Bob's dilemma. But for now, let's assume Bob is unaware of it.) Unfortunately, Bob is relentless. He knows he's in a great business and believes that if he can respond properly to each objection, he can perhaps sign up Steve and his wife. Because Steve is a professional who knows many quality people, Bob is absolutely convinced that, of all his friends, Steve has the greatest potential. Bob believes that all he has to do is skillfully overcome his friend's objections and he's got a winner on his front line. He's sure he will "win the battle." But it won't happen. And the reasons it won't happen are simple: Steve is not in the right time in his life for change, and Bob approached his friend improperly.

In this particular scenario, the objections and responses to them will probably continue for another five or ten minutes. In a last ditch effort to shut Bob up, Steve may actually agree to go to a presentation. Of course, the chances that he will actually attend are slim to none. In this "winning the battle" scenario, more than likely Bob's prospect will be a "no-show" and, in the long run, he will even lose the war. Unable to apply the six-month rule, the battle will never again be waged, let alone won. In other words, another potentially great network marketer is history. And you can bet Steve will tell ten other friends at a future cocktail party just how bizarre and frenzied their "former" friend, Bob, has become. Kiss ten more possible networkers goodbye!

Positive Negative

The second outcome is what we call the "positive negative." In this scenario, the very instant Bob mentions his intentions, Steve jumps in and aggressively points out how much he hates business deals with friends, detests MLM or any other home business pyramid, and adds, "by God, it better never surface again in the course of our friendship." Of course, Bob shuts up immediately and changes the subject back to small talk. He feels rejected because his good friend is so positive that network distribution is a rotten industry. And because Steve is so positively negative about network marketing, Bob decides to never again extend the opportunity to his friend. That is a serious mistake, as we'll explain later when we fully define the six-month rule.

The Good Ol' Boy

The third outcome is what we call "The Good Ol' Boy." An example of this scenario is as follows: "You know, Steve, the other reason I called is because my wife and I have become involved in a business that we want to share with you. It will take about an hour at the most and we can see you on Tuesday evening at 8:00 or Thursday at 7:30. Which is better for you?"

Steve answers pleasantly, "Gosh, Robert, it sounds great. Can you tell me just a little about it?"

"Well, Steve, I'd rather not discuss it over the telephone because it's about 90 percent visual. I'd like for you and Sally to see a brief video, then actually sample some products and take home some literature to examine. But I can tell you that this company is expanding globally and they're looking for brand new recruiters and trainers who have always wanted to earn over $25,000 a month."

"My God, Bob!" Steve excitedly responds. "$25,000 a month! Whew! I can tell you right now we are always open-minded to new opportunities, especially when there's that kind of earnings potential. I think Thursday would be our best bet. What time?"

This last scenario is actually somewhat common when new distributors are calling friends. In MLM, we refer to friends as one's "warm market." Because most family members and close friends do not want to reject you, they will often agree to things they don't want, just to be "warm," hence the terminology. But we can assure you that often as many as half of all warm market appointments—and by that we mean friends, family, and associates—who commit to coming to your home for a private business presentation will not show up. And that can be more devastating than any other form of rejection because you'll feel deceived. So remember, no matter how nice they are on the telephone, half of your family and friends may not show up for your meetings, especially if you tell them about products and brochures, videos and samples. Knowing this fact ahead of time softens the pain.

Simply put, all people detest rejection—especially rejection by friends and family. Frank Pinelli of West Linn, Oregon, had been in the business all of one week when he experienced one of the worst rejections of his life. As he explains,

"I couldn't wait to meet for breakfast with a man whom I had come to respect and admire. Like me, he was a realtor and a very successful one. Both of us were in the process of leaving real estate to start our own businesses and I assumed that would give us grounds for being mutually supportive of each other. As I began to describe my networking business to him, without a moment's hesitation, he told me that even if he was a panhandler on the street pushing a cart around, the last thing in the world he would ever do is network marketing. I grew numb. My world, for the moment, was destroyed. A respected friend had, in so many words, called me worse than a bum living on the streets!

"Two years have passed and today I truly owe my ex-friend a debt of gratitude. He so enraged me that I vowed to become hugely successful just to show him how wrong he was. His having treated me like such a jerk is to this day a significant part of what drives me." Today, Frank, together with his wife, Joanne, earns about $5,000 per month. But rather than homeless or even worse, seventy-hour-a-week realtors like their ex-friend, they are both stay-at-home parents to two young children and, in their words, "job share" the business around them. Friends are often our biggest dream stealers, and once a dream is stolen, it is not easily recovered. But Frank and Joanne turned what could have been a stolen dream into a burning desire to rise to their full potential. Today, they both love what they do and have their sights set on making it all the way to the top. And when they reach the very pinnacle, it will undeniably be because one business associate tried to smash their hopes and dreams. Perhaps once they make it to the very top, their realtor friend will decide to join them in business.

Dennis Clifton, who together with his brother David built our strongest global organization, remembers how excited he was about his future when he first signed up back in May of 1986 before any of us knew what we were doing. "As I began to go down my 'list' I quickly realized that this wasn't going to be as easy as I had hoped. Almost every person that I called was unwilling to even meet with me. But in spite of this, my positive attitude was holding up . . . until one morning. I had a 'friend' who worked as a disc jockey at a local radio station. I called him at work and began to explain what I was doing. His response was something I had never experienced before. He actually began to laugh out loud. Now I don't mean a whimsical smile or a friendly chuckle—I mean a wall-rattling, spirit-crushing, belly laugh!

"I was devastated as I hung up the phone. I had never been laughed at quite like that before. Then all the voices began to come to me: 'Why in the world am I doing this? Nothing is worth this kind of humiliation. Since nobody seems to want to do this, maybe they know something I don't. If I quit now, I'll never have to go through that again.'

"I can remember slipping into that 'black hole' that so many new distributors never come out of . . . when my phone rang. It was my sponsor, Mark Yarnell. He asked, 'Hey big boy, what's happening?' I responded, 'Mark, you're not going to believe this, but I just got laughed at . . . big time!' Then I told him everything that happened . . . and guess what he did? He started to laugh uncontrollably! After a few minutes when he regained his composure, he said, 'Dennis, don't let yourself worry about that goober. Just send him a copy of your check in six months!'

"What a great response. For the first time in my life I understood the full meaning of the old saying, 'He who laughs last, laughs best.' Today, more than a decade later, that man who almost laughed me out of the business is still a disc jockey in Austin, Texas. Me . . . I live in the mountains in Colorado with my wife and kids and run an international business with distributors in over twenty countries around the world. I have made millions of dollars since that first laugh, and I can assure you . . . it was worth it. Let 'em laugh."

Maria Perkins of Santa Barbara has been with her company for eight years and has made it to the third level of her compensation plan. She sees her role in network marketing as a conduit or bridge for people like herself who cringe at the thought of sales, and recommends that her associates approach the business like professional consultants. In order to sustain herself through these years, she plays her own mental imagery tape in her mind. "No matter if it was my forty-year-old baby brother smirking at my efforts, the people who swore they would show up and didn't, or even the friends who suddenly viewed me as some ex-con about to bamboozle them into my newest scam— they all led me to the mountaintop . . . and it is here I shall remain!" Maria is convinced that we all have to operate on our own agenda, not someone else's.

May you be as fortunate as Frank, Dennis, and Maria when you have one of your friends put you down or scoff at you. Later, we will discuss the very finest "friend approach" in order to minimize the rejection like these distributors faced. But, we hope that learning of their battles with rejection will assist you in coping with your own. Fine wine can be a by-product of sour grapes. Turn your battles into a motivational force and let that force propel you through those early rejections. Dennis is right. It is all worth it.

Preparing Your Prospects for Rejection

THE Rejection Rocket can be leveled at you anytime in your career and the problem is that you generally don't see it coming. It's a stealth weapon—it can take many different forms and is frequently unrecognizable right up until impact . . . and then, kaboom! While we certainly cannot help you anticipate every potential kind of rejection, we can definitely prepare you for those forms of rejection which are the most destructive. Avoidance of these dangerous weapons is fairly simple if you begin programming your networking professionals at the very beginning, literally during the close of the first recruiting meeting.

Let's set the stage. You have just presented your business opportunity effectively by following a specific format, one we'll explain in a later chapter, and you're convinced that three of the five prospects sitting in your living room are tremendously excited about the income potential. They've asked all the right questions and you've answered them to the best of your ability. You've played the video, very clearly and simply explained the numbers during your board presentation, handed them some samples, and finally explained that training is here at your home next Saturday at 10:00 A.M. You are ready for the closing comments—comments specifically calculated to call their attention to rejection and assist them in avoiding it before they are sideswiped. We are irrevocably convinced that most people who leave the first presentation excited but never sign up or return for training are usually fatalities of the easily avoided Rejection Rocket.

Here's how we prepare our unwary prospects. We suggest you memorize or paraphrase this for your own use, speaking in the singular or plural accordingly:

"Folks, I know some of you are excited about the numbers you've heard today. I realize that you will want to do your due diligence, as would any responsible entrepreneur. But let's face it, if I'm right, if you really can earn this kind of monthly income and semi-retire in three to four years, or at least have substantial personal and financial freedom, you'd have to be brain-dead not to take me up on this deal. But I want to warn you about the two primary causes of failure so you can avoid them while you're doing your investigating." Don't be afraid to use a comment like "brain-dead" on your prospects no matter how successful or professional they appear. We've never had anyone fail to laugh at the comment. But more importantly, you are asserting your obvious leadership, a quality they desperately need to observe in their mentor before considering joining our industry.

"The first cause of failure occurs when new network marketers listen to people who don't know what they're talking about. The second cause of failure results from their NOT listening to those of us who do know what we're talking about. Let me give you an example. It's just human nature that when we get excited about something, we want to share it with others. Whether it's a new flavor of ice cream or a business opportunity, it doesn't really matter—we want to share it, especially with the people we most care about. That's fine with ice cream or a good movie, but it's not right to share this business with anyone until you're completely trained and knowledgeable about our company. Why? Because the primary cause of failure in our profession stems from people getting excited about the tremendous earnings potential and then charging out to tell their closest friends and relatives before having the slightest idea how to do our business. It is critical that you not say anything to anyone until we have taught you a successful approach.

"If you begin talking to your relatives and friends about this industry, most of them are going to tell you that you've lost your mind. And even though you think you've got all the facts, even though you know the truth about the earnings potential, and even though your friends, neighbors, and relatives know nothing, they will still tell you you're an idiot. And if you have ten or twenty people in a row question your sanity, especially people you know and love, you will give up before you begin. So don't even attempt to sell your spouse on the opportunity: simply get him or her back here for a presentation as soon as possible.

"Now I know you think you're strong enough to avoid being influenced by people whom you know are completely ignorant about our company. Everybody thinks that. And let's say that you are . . . let's say that even if twenty friends and relatives reject you and tell you you're an imbecile, you do not collapse under the weight of their negative attitudes. The real problem is this: Once they've told you not to get involved, even if you later skillfully prove them wrong and answer every one of their concerns, they will not sign up! Remember, once they've ridiculed you for getting into MLM, they cannot af-

ford to sign up themselves because that's tantamount to admitting their own foolishness. And in this era, many folks are more interested in "impression management" than in taking responsibility for their own lives and creating financial independence and time freedom.

"So until you've been signed up, made a commitment, and been trained professionally, DO NOT, and I mean this emphatically, DO NOT approach your friends, relatives, or even your spouse with this business until we have taught you how to share this information with them. Some of your very best "warm market" recruits will never join you, no matter how successful you become, if you approach them improperly. Years of experience have taught us that the single largest cause of failure results from listening to people who don't know what they are talking about."

Here's the problem: New prospects' friends and family don't know anything about your company or the business of networking. And in their ignorance they are certain it must be a scam. Until you are involved financially, they sense you are not really committed. So they will do everything in their power to "save you" from making a big mistake. When you say, "Hey, everybody, I'm getting ready to open a new restaurant," you can count on the response: "Are you sure you want to do

> Rejection by family and friends is by far one of the biggest challenges in network marketing. But you can only change their attitudes by changing your own.

that? I've heard most start-ups go under." However, once you have already made the investment, your family and friends will do everything in their power to support you in your new venture. When you say, "Hey, everybody, I've just opened a new restaurant," the response will likely be, "Oh, good for you . . . when can we come?"

Rejection by family and friends is by far one of the biggest challenges in network marketing. But you can only change their attitudes by changing your own. After you've elevated your own self-esteem and confidence level, only then will you be able to help others elevate theirs (often altering their opinions, strengthening your family's support or interest, and opening doors to your friends and associates).

We wrap up our business presentation by discussing the second cause of failure: not listening to those who DO know what they're talking about. "If any of you do decide to sign up and become my frontline associates, you must also be willing to duplicate exactly what I teach you. This business is totally different from traditional business, and if you are going to

sign up and then try to reinvent the wheel, you're going to fail. So promise me you'll follow our system or, frankly, I'd rather not even have you sign up. Fortunately, we are in an experienced organization and we know what we're doing. Your first ninety days are critical, and we start the clock today as you begin your decision making."

That dialogue is the way we close our in-home recruiting presentations, nearly verbatim. In fact, as prospects are preparing to drive away, we will frequently remind them one last time: "Don't forget, please don't attempt to explain this business to anyone, especially your spouse, until after you've been trained!" As they depart, we are already beginning to visualize them as partners.

The Rejection Rocket can be deterred quite effectively if it is anticipated and fully understood by new networkers and prospects. Actually, if you train new frontline people properly based on the systems we will advance throughout this book, rejection will be the least of your worries. In fact, once new distributors finish with their "warm market" prospects and enter the "cold market," rejection is one of their greatest allies. Why? Because the sooner it can be determined that a prospect is not receptive to a network marketing opportunity, the sooner the distributor can file her away for a six-month follow-up, and move on to viable prospects without wasting time.

Like so many network marketers, Paul Del Vecchio and Jennifer Taloe of Berkeley, California, are still struggling to build their group. And because of their positive outlook, it is growing . . . slowly. But rejection has been their single biggest hurdle to overcome, especially that first year. In Paul's own words, "I'm sure there are people who breeze into MLM and skate their way to the top, but this was not my case. I'm a college dropout who spent my young adult years pursuing poetry, the classical guitar, and Eastern philosophy. I had no background in business, spent most of my time in seclusion, and drove an old '76 Chevy pickup with a snaggle-tooth bumper that I couldn't afford to have repaired.

"Being somewhat introverted by nature, I'd have to describe my first year in MLM like the South American diplomat who, at an elegant embassy function, tried to explain in his halting English why he and his wife had no children. 'My wife, shee eez impregnable.' But when that clearly didn't evoke the response he had expected, he tried again, 'I mean, shee eez unbearable.' Puzzled by their shocked expressions, he tried one more run at it with, 'No, no . . . what I meen to say eez, she eez inconceivable!' I felt just as inadequate as that diplomat in my communication skills as I loaded up my truck and went down to the business district to approach strangers in suits about big money and free time and, let me tell you, they were not at all amused!

"And so I systematically tried everything under the sun to avoid the pain of rejection including the art of managing a nonexistent downline, but it always comes back to taking action and maintaining a positive open attitude. Napoleon Hill, the author of the classic *Think and Grow Rich*, helped me understand that my state of mind must be one of absolute belief . . . in what I am communicating to others and in my ability to deliver the message—not just a mere hope or a wish. For me, this business has been the greatest self-development course in the world. As I leave the house to prospect, I have learned that I can create one of two mind-sets. I can strive to be well received by those I approach and that is a one-step process called perseverance. Or I can try to avoid the pain of rejection and that is a three-step formula: say nothing, do nothing, be nothing." Persistence, coupled with absolute belief, can never be defeated, and that is precisely why we know that Paul and Jenny will prosper abundantly.

Call Reluctance

OFTEN the mere fear and anticipation of rejection will keep new networkers at home. Fear of getting started is one of the primary causes of failure in our industry. It is an obvious but unspoken phenomenon. New marketers will hide behind the need to study the products more, or attend a few more meetings, watching how you do it over and over, even though they've already seen it ten times. They will gladly attend training meeting after training meeting, invest time in their new business by listening to audiotapes on how to prospect and overcome objections, and generally do anything and everything possible to avoid actual prospecting. They will become involved in all manner of unproductive activities just to avoid having to, in the words of the great Nike, "Just do it!" Then after days, weeks, and sometimes even months of such busywork, they will decide that this business just doesn't work. After all, they haven't succeeded in building an organization.

The reason is clear to everyone except them. The mere anticipation of rejection leads to "call reluctance," which can and often does lead to failure. Often, a week or so before they quit, we hear the essence of their failure in the remark, "If something doesn't happen soon, we're going to have to get a job to make ends meet." In traditional business, *things* may just *happen*, but in network marketing, success comes to those who *make* things happen.

And by the way, "call reluctance" is not an experience limited to nonprofessionals. Often it's the most sophisticated executives who carry this secret phobia, not of actually *being* rejected, mind you, but of the fear that they *might* be. Mark recruited the mayor of a major southern city and after six months of virtually zero activity, he asked the mayor for his warm market list. He reluctantly handed over his top twenty-five names, but Mark couldn't find one person whom the mayor had actually called. In the final analysis, the mayor had to admit that he was afraid to call those friends because an election year was approaching and he didn't want to risk damaging his reputation with his constituents. He quit, having never called one prospect because of his fear of rejection. He later had the audacity to state publicly, after failing in a second network marketing company for the same reason, that "MLM is a scam." He came to that conclusion without ever having called a single prospect.

Not Being Taken Seriously

THOSE who make it past the initial fears of getting started will often be assailed by other elements of the Rejection Rocket. Common among women is not being taken seriously—one of the most degrading forms of rejection. It is common for an interested male prospect who is shown the business opportunity by a professional woman networker to think something like: "I'll have to talk to my wife about this little home business." It's not a case of the woman being ineffective or the man being demeaning; it's just that most men cannot identify with having a woman recruiter who is working at home. And if she is distributing cosmetics or some other product or service with which he cannot relate, that only serves to compound the problem.

No matter how strong a female leader is, in some cases the male ego cannot be assuaged by her alone. On these occasions, the potential rejection can be sidestepped by having a male upline or male partner assist her in closing such prospects. This is not codependency, but rather part of the intrinsic nature and value of what we call "double gender" closing because ours is a team-based business. First-year associates need not close prospects alone. It's teamwork that earns leaders the right to receive multi-level compensation.

In some situations, women have discovered that their gender challenges come from within rather than from without. Historically, men have had more self-confidence while women still struggle with poor self-esteem. For years some women have been financially dependent on their husbands and frequently overlooked for promotions in the workplace. We realize this is changing in America, but this phenomenon is still prevalent in Eastern cultures and among older generations. Women have so very much to offer this industry, their companies, their husbands and male partners, and certainly the members of their own organizations. The problem has stemmed from an industry-wide lack of awareness about just how much women have to give and how needed feminine qualities are in today's global marketplace. The role of women is on the threshold of explosive change, along with their image.

If you suspect that you are being rejected because of an attitude you project, then take some time to work on your own personal growth before attempting to build an organization. Read books, attend seminars, and listen to audiotapes to enhance your self-image. Surround yourself with positive people who constantly remind you of your worth as a person and the contributions you are capable of making. Shake off any residue of negative self-esteem, any emotional baggage that you may be carrying around, and take pride in yourself. It is important to understand that you have a greatness and an unlimited potential to elevate everyone around you. Practice exuding your inner strength with your head held high and you will see an immediate difference in your general acceptance, your leadership success, and your income. Perhaps no woman in network marketing's forty-five-year span has better exemplified the transition that can occur in a woman's life once she begins to accept and project her strength than Kathy Denison.

At the age of thirty, Kathy Denison awakened to realize that she was living a nightmare. She was in an abusive marriage and her twelve-year-old daughter was suffering the pain of seeing her mother mistreated. She decided it was time to take action. She left her husband and moved to the tiny town of Basalt, Colorado, where she began cleaning houses to support herself and her child. While her personal life improved dramatically over the next few years, her finances were in shambles. But without a degree, there were few options available to her. Kathy had always believed that she had the talent and mind-set to become a millionaire, but her introduction to MLM was the very

first time she'd ever been exposed to a business with no limits and no major capital investment. Within five years, she would be relaxing on the beach in San Diego in her dream home with a husband, Mark Rogow, who shares her goals and dreams.

Many people were first introduced to Kathy Denison and her remarkable story in Richard Poe's bestseller *Wave 3*. But no one can write as dramatically and accurately about Kathy as Mark Yarnell, who personally sponsored her and served as her mentor for her first years in this business.

"When I first met Kathy Denison in Aspen, Colorado, in 1987, she was a single parent living in a tiny one-bedroom apartment doing her best to support her family on her meager maid's income. I had begged our realtor to help me find a housekeeper because we were entertaining so many friends, and our home rapidly became like a bed-and-breakfast. (By the way, move to Aspen and you'll learn just how many of your friends love you!)

"Kathy agreed to meet me as a favor to her best friend, the realtor, but had actually decided not to accept the job. At that time, she was already cleaning numerous houses and felt burned out. On the other hand, she really needed the money, and she owed the realtor a debt of gratitude for the numerous jobs she had arranged for Kathy after she left her abusive marriage.

"When Kathy walked into my home that first day I was immediately impressed with two things: First, she was obviously an extrovert. Second, she had enthusiasm, a very warm smile, and, although she was working as a maid, she was definitely a 'people person.' Naturally, the old 'recruiting Yarnell' came out as he generally does whenever I meet a strong personality.

"But in Kathy's case, I suppressed my enthusiasm as rapidly as it surfaced, mainly because I wanted to devote a solid year to snow skiing, hang-gliding, and writing the first edition of my book *Power Multi-Level Marketing*. And truthfully, even though I teach new distributors not to 'play God,' that is, never to qualify prospects and always assume that everyone has the potential to succeed, I violated my own teaching. I decided that in spite of her enthusiasm, I wasn't going to sponsor my housekeeper in a town of 2,000 because the chances of her success were minimal. What a fool I was. After finally awakening from my stupor and signing her up, Kathy promptly signed up every possible prospect in Basalt and Aspen, then moved to San Diego and gradually built a business that transformed her into a millionaire. After recognizing my own stupidity in prejudging a maid, I made the

decision to never again violate the one definitive precept in our industry: 'There's a seed of greatness in everyone. Never qualify prospects for any reason.' "

Nearly a decade later, Kathy Denison is one of network marketing's true heroines. As more women like Kathy join our industry, and we continue to hear more financial and emotional rags-to-riches stories, women will continue to occupy positions of importance in increasing numbers. And as Richard Poe so correctly pointed out in *Wave 3*, "Denison's stripped-down approach served her well. She rose from a lowly maid to a millionaire in just a few years." In 1997, Kathy was named one of the top ten "Women of Distinction" in Jerry Hoffman's *International Directory of Network Marketing*.

We spent an afternoon skiing in Switzerland during the winter of 1997, and when we returned home we saw the familiar red light on our answering machine signaling that we had a message. That simple two-minute message meant as much to us as any other achievement in either of our lives. Mark flipped the on-button, the machine rewound, and there, in a broken voice, was our frontline associate Kathy Denison. Her message was a simple: "Thank you for believing in me!" That afternoon Kathy and her wonderful partner/husband, Mark Rogow, had received their Millionaire's pin from the home office signifying that they had earned over a million dollars, thus inducting themselves into the company's elite Millionaires' Club. So overwhelmed and appreciative was Kathy, so moving was her message, that we sat down and silently shed tears of joy. In that brief moment, the purpose that most forcefully drives us in network marketing was fulfilled. To this day, we can write without equivocation that you could take away everything we own—our income, our entire downline, homes and cars—and our involvement in network marketing would be justified in its entirety because of the joy we felt for Kathy and Mark on that afternoon. Seldom, if ever, has one of life's experiences so touched us at the very core of our beings as did Kathy's short message.

Kathy has an inner strength, a personal belief, and an unmistakable self-worth that allowed her to rise from maid to millionaire. We believe there are thousands of women out there just like her, and every one could succeed if they could shake off their limited programming. To any woman who may feel assaulted by the Rejection Rocket because of her own self-imposed struggle with a negative self-image, we suggest that you select another successful woman as a mentor. Allow her to coach you every step of the way, and duplicate her steps to success.

Don't Take Rejection Personally

NEW associates must be taught that a "no, thank you" is not a personal rebuff. A waitress pouring coffee in a coffee shop might be told "no, thanks" by one, "no more for now" by another. She might be told "I have plenty, thanks" or even "I don't like coffee." But none of these responses sends her running to the lady's room in tears because all of her customers rejected her. And yet that is comparable to what happens to brand new distributors. They take *no*, however it is said, too personally. In our industry, a decline to participate in the opportunity most often means "the timing isn't right for me now." Occasionally, it means "I don't like direct selling." But it never means "I don't like you." Think of prospecting in MLM as a sifting process. Like the waitress walking around with a coffeepot, we are merely searching for those who *would* like to have what we have to offer. Accepting *no* is merely part of the process of finding those who say *yes*.

Consider this fact: Of the first sixty-seven individuals whom Mark first approached about joining his organization, sixty-six said *no*. This slow start was mainly because Mark abandoned his

Accepting *no* is merely part of the process of finding those who say *yes*.

warm market. He was a minister at the time and felt that it would be a conflict of interest to call on his church members. So he began in a predominantly cold market. Later, he finally recruited a few parishioners after he was himself certain of his company's long-term stability. However, his first prospects were cold calls and all but one rejected his offers to even see a presentation. Mark felt like quitting right then and his sponsor actually did that week. Instead, Mark called Richard Kall, his upline mentor, who persuaded him to remain in the business. Had Mark's original upline sponsor not become discouraged by rejection and stayed involved, he would have, after five years, been earning over a million dollars a year off Mark's downline alone. By the time we married and merged downlines in 1991, it had exceeded twice that amount. That's what the Rejection Rocket can cost a person.

Personal rejection is one of the toughest human emotions anyone can experience. But as we all know, life is about balance, and where there is rejection there must also be acceptance. Dealing with it is an ongoing task. At one point, rejection nearly drove Phil Mims of Grapevine, Texas, out of networking. As he explains,

"I'd had a good career with seventeen years in the wholesale jewelry business prior to getting involved with network marketing. That career gave me a good lifestyle, wonderful friends, and a professional ego.

"Making the transition into MLM meant starting over, forcing me out of my comfort zone. As I approached friends, family, and jewelry associates to be either my customers or to join me in business, I watched personalities change. Friends became cold and distrusting. My family began to snicker. Jewelry associates responded with concern for my sanity. It hurt me when they appeared to feel that I was taking advantage of them and abusing our relationships. I wanted to just say, 'Okay, never mind,' and head back into my comfort zone and 'secure' jewelry life. I almost quit network marketing entirely. Those feelings continued for my first eighteen months in MLM because my friends were important, and their acceptance was crucial.

"Then it hit me. Some members of my downline began thanking me. They expressed their gratitude for my help and for leading them to great changes in their lives. Wow! The acknowledgment made my heart pound and my eyes tear up. It dawned on me that if I were to quit and return to my jewelry business, I would perhaps lose my new friends and business associates whom I really liked better. Networkers are such caring, sharing, giving, and excited people, who, like me, are seeking success, peace, and freedom. Traditional business offers these things for a few people, whereas success is possible for so many in network marketing.

"To remember now that I almost quit because of my wounded pride helps me to understand what my new downline reps face. Shedding my old self and becoming a new person was indeed a painful transition. The hardest thing I ever did was to leave the comfort zone of my jewelry business. But as a result of my newfound personal freedom, personal growth, and feelings of appreciation, I've found a bigger and better comfort zone. I'll always be a networker, thankful that God opens doors, provides the courage to go through them, and furnishes the light to guide my way."

Not Talking to Enough People

IF we only talk to a dozen people in the course of a week, the act of rejection by those few becomes bigger than life. If we contact a few dozen people each week, rejection is no problem because a few will always get involved! Remember this law of balance: Increase the number of approaches and decrease the impact of rejection.

Susan averaged ten contacts a week in her business because she was working part-time and had an extremely busy schedule. Because she was working from her warm market list, she had a high ratio of positive responses. Five promised to come to her Tuesday night business briefing to learn more about this opportunity. Two actually showed, but neither signed. All she could think about were the three who didn't show, and the fact that they didn't even have the courtesy to call and cancel. Four more weeks of that kind of rejection and she will be out of the business. Why? Because her prospecting numbers are too small. Susan may be a hypothetical prospect in our example, but such low-number prospecting can, and indeed has, forced would-be legends right out of business—shot down by rejection.

Unless, as a part-timer, you are approaching at least five to ten prospects per day, you are not serious about succeeding in this business. As a serious part-timer, those numbers should increase, and as a full-timer, they can grow to thirty or more per day once entering the cold market. Meeting attendance and brochure reading doesn't count as "real time." When first launching your business, if your goal is to build an organization, 80 percent of your time should be spent prospecting. All other activity is busywork until you have achieved a certain level of success. Do not become a professional audience participator! Get out of the bleachers and onto the field.

In contrast to Susan, the two of us prospected huge numbers of people when first building our individual organizations. Before marrying Rene, Mark's biggest Rejection Rocket was launched when six of his seven frontline executives bailed out and went into a vitamin deal back in 1986. He didn't just lose six out of seven distributors—he lost major leaders. That is the ultimate rejection. Again, he leaned on Richard Kall to keep him focused on the importance of perseverance. Consider the impact of Richard's inspiration. There were two major triumphs: First, the one remaining executive distributorship today earns us more than 50 percent of our income. Second, because Mark continued to approach large numbers of prospects, he had seven more qualifying executives who would soon take the place of those who left.

Remember: It is the sheer magnitude of the numbers of prospects we approach that keeps us from overreacting to those who do reject our approaches. Prospecting small numbers makes the rejection bigger than life; prospecting large numbers focuses our attention on those who say *yes*. If you make contact with a hundred people in the course of a week, twenty of whom say, "Yes, I'd be interested in looking at what you have," and eighty of whom say, "No thanks," your focus will be on the positive. Out of that twenty, you will be excited about the three who signed up, rather than the eighty who weren't interested. On the other hand, if you approach only ten people, two of whom say they are willing to take a look and then decide against it, your attention inevitably is on the entire ten who got away. Network marketing begins as a numbers game and evolves into a people business while a legitimate organization of excited networkers is being built.

Remember: It is the sheer magnitude of the numbers of prospects we approach that keeps us from overreacting to those who do reject our approaches.

The Narrow Focus Syndrome

MANY people make the mistake of inviting rejection by presenting a far too narrow focus. They often promote a single product or just one division of their company as opposed to creating wide appeal by stressing the leveraged income and free time that result from orders of commonly used products and services. Network marketing is intrinsically designed to appeal to everyone. It is not meant to be an elitist club, nor is it effective if you promote just a single product line. And yet newcomers and old-timers alike often make this mistake.

Some people failed to earn as much as they should have when their company added an exciting new nutritional division in the early '90s. And the reason is obvious: Even liberal estimates suggest that less than 30 percent of the population used vitamin supplements back then. Thus, seven out of ten people approached with only the new division just weren't interested. They couldn't relate to nutritional products and were unwilling to change their behavior. The original division upon which the company was founded consisted of personal care products. One hundred percent of our population bathes, shampoos, shaves, moisturizes, deodorizes, and brushes their teeth with reason-

able regularity. So success would have been more widespread had the distributors offered *both* lines of products in their presentations, thereby avoiding the needless problems created by limited focus.

Even more significant, they should have been selling prospects with the American Dream: big money and free time. Nearly everyone is interested in ways to achieve wealth. So focus your presentations on personal and financial freedom, making certain to call your prospects' attention to all your products, services, and divisions. This comprehensive approach is how legends ultimately build large and dynamic organizations.

Turning Rejection into Positive Motivation

JOHN Corkill worked for a large title insurance company for ten years, the same one his father had been employed by for over forty years. They enjoyed working together and shared a track record of success. When corporate politics became unbearable, John, with his father's understanding and support, went to work for a competitor and tripled his income during the first year. Over the next five years he created a six-figure income; then, due to a merger, he was laid off. His father, still with the original title insurance company, was now in charge of starting a new division and offered his son a full-time position, but the company could only pay him a pittance of his previous income.

One week before he was due to start the job, John was introduced to network marketing. He found the right company and chose to go full-time immediately. After receiving the news, his father's comment was "John, I guess everyone has to do something. However, if you fail at that one, you can always sell makeup since one of the largest companies is based right here in Dallas. But whatever you do, I just hope you're not going to come over to my house and try to push your products on your own dad. I know all about network marketing. Those people make $200 a month and nine out of ten of them fail." John assured his father that his disapproval of the new career path he had chosen was understandable and that he just didn't want to rely on his father for normal family support.

When John did not become defensive, something clicked in his father, who seemed to realize that he was treating his son like a carpetbagger. He asked John to sit down and began inquiring about his goals. When his father was convinced that his son was fully committed to becoming the one out of ten who succeeds, as he had done with the company in which they both worked, the father-son relationship was back on track.

For John, the story of his father's "rejection-turned-acceptance" became a driving force that motivated him to stick with his new network marketing business. Not only is he well on his way, appreciative for his father's rejection and eventual acceptance, but John plans to retire at the same time as his father so that they can enjoy the wealth together, grateful for his father having started him off on the right foot. Reaction to family rejection can often be redirected, becoming a positive force for building your business.

SUMMARY

- Failure in network marketing often results from two problems:

    1 The new distributor's argumentative approach in recruiting frontline people who have already made it obvious that the timing isn't right in their lives.

    2 The mistaken belief that the goal is to overcome objections, sign up people at all cost, then drag them across the finish line through motivation and management systems.

- If warm or cold market prospects are approached properly, they will only reject your offer if the timing is not right, in which case you want to gently back off and re-approach them every six months.

- Rejection is your ally, not your adversary, and if handled properly it will expedite your recruiting activities and actually set you up for a positive outcome.

- Don't talk about this business with friends or relatives until *after* you have made a commitment and have been trained. (Make it a point to teach this at the close of your presentation.)

- As you begin talking to prospects, you have the choice of creating one of two mind-sets:

    1 You can strive to be well received by those you approach by setting yourself up for a friendly callback.

    2 You can try to avoid the pain of rejection by saying nothing, doing nothing, being nothing.

- Persistence, coupled with absolute belief, can never be defeated.

- When you are not getting the support that you desire from family and friends, begin first by focusing on your own attitude and changes in their behavior will naturally follow.

- Once you are trained, begin immediately by picking up the phone and calling the people on your list.

- Don't let "call reluctance" and the fear of rejection stop you before you start on your adventure in network marketing.

- Rely on the credibility of your upline leaders.

- Remember, you are in business for yourself, but you are never in business by yourself.

- As their sponsor, prospects look to you as their mentor and leader.

- If you are feeling low self-esteem, read, study, listen to tapes, attend seminars, and do all that you can to continue working on your personal growth.

- As you grow personally, so will your networking business; and, as your business grows, so will you.

- Building too slowly is discouraging, and often results in networkers focusing on those who rejected the opportunity rather than on those who accepted an invitation to look at the business.

- The growth of your business will be in direct proportion to the numbers of people you are prospecting on a regular, daily basis.

- Network marketing is a numbers game after the first ninety days of "warm marketing." It becomes a people business once distributors begin interacting with their sponsors to build their organizations.

- Rejection is not to be taken personally, but merely as an indication that the timing isn't right in people's lives.

- Persevere with every ounce of enthusiasm in order to give yourself the necessary excitement to do this business correctly.

- Prospecting small numbers makes the act of rejection bigger than life; prospecting larger numbers focuses your attention on those who said *yes*.

- Don't make the mistake of presenting too narrow a focus, that is, by promoting a single product or just one division of your company. Create wide appeal by stressing leveraged income and time freedom based on generating orders of commonly used products and services.

- When retailing:

  1 Offer your customers the opportunity to redirect their spending on commonly used products they are already using.

  2 Educate your customers about all your new products or services, thereby undertaking to change their behavior.

- Rejection can be redirected to become a force for good in building your business.

CHAPTER 2

Avoiding the Management Trap

Reinforce self-sufficiency rather than dependency.

NETWORK MARKETING IS BASED on a team-building philosophy rather than a supervisory one. Perhaps the single most frequent cause of failure in network marketing is the mistaken belief that we must manage our downline distributors. Typically, after new associates spend their first month or two recruiting ten or fifteen friends, they end up devoting the rest of their time attempting to make those few people successful—that's what we call the Management Trap. Let us quickly point out that there is a significant difference between *managing* and *supporting* a downline organization. Playing caretaker to their organization causes new networkers to spend a disproportionate amount of time on a particular leg or legs of their downline to the exclusion of everyone and everything else. It creates a false codependency, doing for others in-

stead of teaching and encouraging them to do for themselves.

The Management Trap creates two serious problems for a business builder. First, it produces weak and lethargic distributors because someone else is doing their work for them. Second, while managing others, that networker loses valuable time that could be more wisely invested in prospecting and recruiting new frontline distributors. And remember, "New blood is the lifeblood of any organization." Continually sponsoring new associates adds vitality to an entire business. If you stop recruiting before you are earning enough to live comfortably, then you lose valuable ground. And worse, since ours is a business of leading by example, your leaders will emulate you, so that everyone ends up managing and no one is prospecting or recruiting. Supporting an

"New blood is the lifeblood of any organization." Continually sponsoring new associates adds vitality to an entire business.

organization, on the other hand, is part of the team approach inherent in network marketing. It involves responding to legitimate requests on the part of any and all of your associates to help close a serious prospect or give them encouragement when they are feeling down. In this chapter, we intend to describe the difference between creating dependency in your organization and reinforcing self-sufficiency. It is critical that novice network marketers recognize the difference between productive activity and ineffectual, time-wasting practices.

Sponsoring Family Members and Building for Them

MARK discovered the pitfalls of supervising his family's line the hard way when he recruited his own father. As he tells the story, "It really hurt when my father said, 'Son, you're embarrassing me and ridiculing the family name in Missouri by

selling snake oil in one of those damn pyramid scams!' It hurt because I had always loved and respected my father. He never made much money while we were growing up, but he did start his own advertising and public relations firm. He also wrote two novels, one of which, *Mantrap*, became a bestseller in 1948. Dad was a proud man who always told me that integrity is more important than wealth and to never do business with a man whom you can't trust with a handshake.

"By the time I was a sixteen-year-old sophomore at Glendale High School in Springfield, Missouri, Dad left the field of writing novels and magazine articles to launch an advertising agency. I was so proud when he trusted me to go out and solicit clients. He said that if I could get a client to use our agency, he would let me have a shot at writing the copy. I was so enthusiastic that I went charging out and actually obtained a client the first week. The guy's name was Jerry Vaughn, and he was preparing to launch a new pet store in a little shopping center near our home. Somehow, probably on sheer guts and enthusiasm, I convinced him to give me a chance.

"I went back to Dad's office scarcely able to contain myself, and broke the good news to him. I don't remember Dad ever really getting too excited about any of my accomplishments, but I could tell he was pleased. For the next several years, I wrote copy and created ads for clients whom I picked up along the way. Some of my ad campaigns were quite well received, while others were not so successful. But through all the years, Dad supported and encouraged me. That is, until six months before my graduation.

"I didn't realize it at the time, but Dad really wanted out of the stress. Apparently, in my ignorance, I failed to see his hope that following college graduation—an event, by the way, that never occurred—I would be interested in becoming his partner, perhaps even one day taking over the entire ad agency. I had other plans. In hindsight I suppose my pronouncement at our 1971 family reunion that I intended to enter seminary and ultimately become a minister really caused him pain. I later found out from Mom that he saw it as a real slap in the face after all the years of working together. But, that's life. I was to become a minister several years later after a series of sales jobs.

"Just about the time my father was accepting my ministry and actually be-

ginning to tell our friends with pride how his son's church was growing, I told him something that would result in our not speaking for nearly a year. I told him on the telephone that I had become a distributor in a new company in the field of network marketing. I'll never forget the uncomfortable two-minute silence that occurred when I asked, *'Dad, can I send you some shampoo and conditioner? I know you're going to love them.'* Silence.

"After a couple of minutes—minutes that felt like an hour each—I broke the uncomfortable stillness by asking him to which address he wished me to mail the shampoo. That's when it hit the proverbial fan.

"'What the hell, son. You go to seminary, become a minister, now you're quitting that too. You're a quitter. And how could you disgrace the family name by getting into a pyramid?' He abruptly hung up.

"Naturally, I was miserable with rejection. That all changed, however, when I received an apology call a year later. Dad had heard from my sister that I'd built a sizable downline and was earning more each month than he was earning in a year. He called and congratulated me for my success. Then he came clean about his health. The stress was causing him heart problems and in addition to apologizing for judging me so harshly, he also intimated that maybe I could help him get out of the rat race of public relations.

"That was all I needed. The next week I was on a plane to Missouri to sign up my father and get him out of traditional business. I was very excited about the prospect of helping my dad change his life. And the reason I explained our backgrounds here in such detail is to help you understand my reason for wanting so desperately to help him. You see, this was my first experience with the formidable Management Trap, that is, the supervision of one's downline. Before pointing out my mistakes, I want the reader to fully understand the situation. And I want to do everything possible to help you avoid this devastating trap because it is very counterproductive and most often leads to failure. Our parents, siblings, and closest friends are usually the ones who lure us into the Management Trap.

"I spent four months in Springfield, Missouri, helping my father build his organization. The problem was that all Dad's people looked to me for leadership because I was doing everything for him. Not only that, but the rest of my entire group was suffering because I wasn't available to respond to their questions. Those four months that I dedicated to managing my father and his entire group were the most counterproductive of my entire career in networking. The only real value to come out of it was that I learned about the devastation of playing nursemaid to one leg of my downline and began immediately to incorporate it into our training sessions in order to keep others from making the same mistake.

"When I left Springfield, everything I had built began to crumble immediately. The new people on my father's front line regarded me as their mentor, and when I no longer had time to support them as effectively as I had while living in Springfield, several became despondent and quit in the first month. Dad was frustrated because he had no idea how to lead his people and they didn't look to him for leadership anyway. I created a cripple of my own father because, for all practical purposes, I became the director of an adult daycare center. But here's the real tragedy: Dad had the ability to succeed dramatically in network marketing. He had great communication skills, loved working with people, and had the overall competence in business that would have allowed him to build and run a quite successful organization worldwide. But I ruined it for him. You see, I loved him so much and was so committed to his success that I inadvertently created a weak person out of a strong one.

"My father's gone now; he passed away last year. And sometimes, while sitting in the solitude of my study thinking of Dad, I secretly wish an angel would appear and wave a magic wand leaving behind a tiny golden plaque above his ashes which reads: 'Here lies a great man, Duane Yarnell, who could have been greater had his son not loved him too much.' But, because I didn't know then what I know now, I feel no real guilt. Dad and I had a great friendship to the very end.

"Next, I headed straight to Orlando where my sister Melissa was a very successful executive analyst for the Tupperware Company. With my sister I had a legitimate reason to enter the Management Trap, or so I then mistakenly thought, because I felt that she had a personal conflict of interest. Because Tupperware is a direct sales company, Melissa felt that for her to build a network in another company would be entirely inappropriate. I admired her decision and decided, once again, to manage my sister's entire downline. I recruited her frontline leaders, trained them, and supported them because Melissa just couldn't violate the trust Tupperware had placed in her. Once again, I fell unwittingly victim to this administrative role.

Meanwhile, all my other organizations across the country were feeling the frustration of seldom reaching me because I was so vitally focused on managing my own family's groups.

"To make a long story short, when I went back to my own home in Aspen, Colorado, I had successfully wasted over eight months building executive downlines for both my father and sister. Within a year, both relatives had quit and virtually everyone in both of their organizations had either quit or become wholesale buyers of the product. I had wasted so much time and worse, by loving them too much, had unwittingly stripped them of their leadership roles. Fortunately, Dad had managed to recruit a couple of my old high school and college buddies, Gary Turner and Jim Grundy. Over the years they did quite well, but in the end both opted to pursue other avenues and today we earn not one penny from the efforts of extensively working with relatives. Taking on the position of caretaker to my group served to lower my income, spoil both my father's and sister's chances to succeed, and throw me off

The truth is that we are empowered far less by heredity, luck, and circumstances, than by our vision of what we believe is truly possible for ourselves.

track for nearly a year. The truth is, I should have spent only one week in each city training Dad and Melissa—then they might have both been prepared to build their groups."

If you find yourself alone in network marketing, with none of your family members supporting you, there are better ways to transform them than trying to coerce them into the business and then doing it all for them. If we want to change others, we begin by changing ourselves, and alterations in their behavior will naturally follow.

The truth is that we are empowered far less by heredity, luck, and circumstances, than by our vision of what we believe is truly possible for ourselves. Jimmy Kossert of Renton, Washington, is one of the legendary "big money" earners in the networking industry. But it took an early morning self-evaluation to break an inherited cycle that had predominated in his family for over a century. He explained it to us in this way:

"It was near the end of my first year in MLM that I chose, early one morning at 5:00 A.M., to break the cycle of poverty that had been in my family for generations. Everyone I recruited had quit . . . everyone. Everyone I loved had told me no. I had no money coming in, no chance to return to a downward-spiraling real estate market with any hope of financial re-

covery, no experience in other fields, no college education, and no will to persevere. My great-grandfather had been poor and uneducated as had my grandfather, my father, and now me. Poverty, I thought, just ran in the family.

"My wife and children slept silently, and as I sat contemplating these people I so loved and our uncertain future, a blinding flash hit me. Everyone in my past, perhaps at one time or another, had probably lamented the rotten hand they'd been dealt, but unlike them I had one ace in the hole. Unlike my ancestors, I was now privileged to be in a great company where people were actually earning unlimited income. None of my forefathers had ever been given that option. I, Jimmy Kossert, had been chosen to lead the charge out of generations of servitude and mediocrity for an entire ancestry who, before me, were never so privileged as to be able to restore dignity to our family tree. As I tiptoed to the bedsides of my one- and three-year-olds, I silently affirmed, 'I will do for you what my great-grandfather would have done given the same opportunity. I will finish this race and I will win.'

"From that moment on, I set out to break the cycle of poverty. I know my predecessors might have done so themselves, had they been blessed with an unlimited income opportunity. My wealth now stands as a testament to a great-grandfather who

Those frontline recruits who demand the least attention are usually the ones who become the most successful.

---

persevered in everything he did in a generation which offered no possibility for wealth and time freedom for poor, uneducated people. None of my kids will ever have to sit in the dark at 5:00 A.M. and feel depressed because they're impoverished. Thanks to network marketing, the cycle is now broken."

The Messiah Complex

WITH both of us coming from theological backgrounds, we know what it's like to be victims of the "Messiah complex," which is very similar to the Management Trap, but with more emphasis on saving people. Given our backgrounds, at one time or another we wanted to save the entire world and every single person we sponsored. Each time we found a good person, especially one who appeared to need saving, we would end up dedicating much of our time managing that individual and his or her entire organization. But it doesn't work, as Rene and I both learned over and over.

Here's the irony. Those frontline recruits who demand the least attention are usually the ones who become the most successful. For example, let's consider Dennis and David Clifton, brothers from Texas. At the time, Dennis was a student in the doctoral program at the University of Texas and David was a detective with the Houston Police Department. After only about a month in the business, Mark recruited Dennis and taught him everything he knew, and Dennis then taught David what Mark had shared with him.

Mark initially thought he had offended them somehow when their phone calls ceased to come daily. But he discovered that they didn't need him like they did in the very beginning. They had their serious prospects call him to confirm the authenticity of this business and to be closed, but, otherwise, they understood the simplicity of recruiting and training others, and they just did it. If there's one primary lesson we learned during our first few years in networking, it's that those recruits who need us the most usually succeed the least, and those who prosper self-sufficiently deserve all the credit.

Mark recalls, "I remember it feeling like a real slap to my ego the first time Dennis Clifton went an entire month without calling for help. Yet, when I awakened from my need-to-be-needed stupor, I was astounded to discover that the Clifton boys had passed me by. Only in MLM is it rewarding to have our downline members reach the very top level of our compensation plan before us."

Kathy Denison and Terry Hill needed no "Messiah" either. In spite of the fact that neither had ever participated in MLM before, even as frontline distributors, they simply didn't need Mark to save them. Except for a few telephone calls their first month or two, and some help closing prospects in their first years, they became totally self-sufficient immediately. The new people who whined and moaned and complained were all out of the business in a few months. Those who have become millionaires did it primarily on their own. Mark gave them the support and the duplicable system Richard Kall taught him and they proceeded to successfully accomplish great things. They are all winners. The last thing a winner needs is a manager or a savior.

Remember, if new recruits finish their training and go to work without calling you every day and asking you to do everything for them, don't be offended. Be joyous! In this business everyone has the ability to do great things, but those who lean on their uplines for everything are usually the ones who fail the most rapidly. What makes our industry so much grander than traditional employment opportunities is the fact that we are compensated for our productivity. We aren't like some traditional corporations, such as TWA, who, at the time of this printing, haven't given their hardest working employees a raise in ten years, while their CEO allegedly continues to earn $3,000 a day. If new associates want to earn more than a particular leader above them, they just need to be more productive, i.e., find more frontline distributors and customers who will use and share the products. That's what we love most about our business. While we can never actually lose our downlines—unless we stop ordering products—our downline leaders can certainly pass us in earnings. And some of ours have, especially since 1992 when we chose to dedicate ourselves to enhancing this industry's image through positive articles and media reports; lectures to universities, clubs and organizations; and books such as this. We haven't actively pursued frontline recruiting nearly to the extent we did our first few years because we've elected to use the freedom earned for other causes.

Additionally, we are upline leaders to some very sizable international organizations, all of which expect us to be present in their cities at least once a year. We travel extensively in some twenty countries. From Tokyo to Dallas, and Sydney to London, we love to spend time with our friends and associates throughout the world. And even now, while we conscientiously avoid sinking into the director's seat, we do nevertheless feel a definite desire to spend quality time in each leader's city. Due to our travel agenda, several key players in our downline—some who have been in the business half as long as us—have become more prosperous. Why? Because they kept on frontline recruiting—that's the primary way to increase income. Yet, we still have a significant number of people who deserve to earn more but don't because they are bogged down in the Management Trap or caught up in the Messiah complex.

To be frank, there have been times when people earning one million dollars a month, far more than us, question our sanity for choosing to try to elevate the entire industry instead of becoming gazillionaires by continuing to frontline recruit globally. Our response to them is simple: Read *Living with Passion* by Peter Hirsch. We've found our passion. We are irrevocably convinced that network marketing is the very best, high-integrity economic system for global solutions to some very pressing problems in such places as Third

World countries. And lest you not understand what we mean by pressing problems, we'll give you just one example. It has now been estimated that by the year 2000 some forty million people worldwide will have died of AIDS, leaving behind some five million orphans, 90 percent of whom live in Africa and other Third World countries. As of this printing, not one agency has yet been created to deal with this problem. There are so many enormous global problems just waiting for us out there. Many network marketers earning millions each year have joined us in projects to make the world a better place. There are indeed things more pressing than becoming excessively wealthy and we in MLM have the money and time freedom to make a difference.

We aren't alone in being plagued with the Messiah complex. Jo Tonita is one idealistic network marketer who, like many, shares this phenomenon.

"The biggest challenge to me was figuring out who was really going to build a business once they showed an interest. To succeed, one must have belief before evidence, that is, they have to be able to picture themselves there and feel the emotions of it long before it actually happens. I didn't understand that initially, so I simply worked and managed others who were unable to see the end result and then became quite frustrated when they quit. I wanted everyone to succeed, so I tended to spend too much energy and time helping in whatever manner I could. As a result, I found myself drained of energy and taking their failures personally.

"I overcame these challenges by learning how to facilitate visionary goal setting but I'm still very selective about those with whom I choose to work. I realize that my success will be directly related to what I think about the most and where I direct my energy. It's unnecessary to fall into a management mode when what we truly need to do as a leader is provide a duplicable strategy for our new associates, then allow them to create their own success."

Jo and Rick Tonita are networkers who are among the top sales leaders in their company in Canada, having now been nearly twenty years with only one company. It is our hope that many more network marketers will be able to say that with pride over the next twenty years.

When you find yourself frustrated because your associates are not successful, teach them how to visualize the end result and direct most of your energy toward those who do.

"Just Recruit a Few and Drive Their Lines Deep"

ONE common misconception in the network marketing industry has led people down into the administration pit. Certain leaders contend that the key to success in our industry is finding four or five good people, then driving their groups by focusing exclusively on supporting them until they are wealthy, then finding five more and doing the same thing. That is the absolute antithesis of what is required to succeed in our profession. The three magic words are "GO WIDE FAST!" Recruit as many frontline distributors each month as you can, until you are earning at least $10,000 a month consistently. Then you can relax a bit until you feel refreshed, only to run right back out there into the frontline recruiting trenches.

There are indeed things more pressing than becoming excessively wealthy and we in MLM have the money and time freedom to make a difference.

Unfortunately, some well-meaning authors and leaders have done a horrible disservice to our profession by misleading new distributors into believing that success in our industry requires less effort than it really does. People who teach this philosophy do so innocently because that's what they've been taught through their upline leaders who learned to do this through books and tapes. The first ninety days of warm-market prospecting are much more personal and support-intensive since new distributors are focused on their friends and families. We will discuss this more in later chapters. But the truth is that you cannot hope to achieve a tremendous income, like those huge figures the legends in our industry earn, unless you play it as a numbers game, especially once you enter the cold market.

Ron Wiggins, who left the shoe business after eleven years to join network marketing at the age of twenty-seven, said one of the most important things he learned his first year is that "success defies all logic . . . so quit trying to figure it out. Just do the numbers! And when prospecting large numbers of people, don't try to tell them everything you know. It's a matter of raising their curiosity, not satisfying it." He goes on: "I was doing so much of the wrong, eventually it just started to add up! From all the mistakes I made, I learned and now teach from expe-

rience to eliminate logic in your own mind and simply do what's been done by the experts and authorities of the industry who have already made all of the mistakes themselves. You've got to get rid of any personal perceptions you may have and try to accept from the beginning that it's going to be a lot of hard work on a very consistent basis."

After a year of hard work, Ron had matched his previous income. Shortly thereafter, his wife, Chris, also left her job and together, working full-time, they have become one of the top network distributor teams in Dallas. It took Ron and Chris four and a half years to reach the very pinnacle of their company's compensation plan. Today they earn a five-figure monthly income. They have utilized their experience to become experts at training, and have learned to keep it simple so that their system can be easily duplicated.

If network marketers were truly doing the numbers that it takes to succeed, no one would have time to fall into the entrapment of administration. Human nature looks for the line of least resistance, and, clearly, it is much easier to work with existing distributors than it is to face the daily rejection that occurs when recruiting new people. Because this is a business of duplication, your people will do what you do. If you manage your downline, so will they. If you spend most of your time prospecting and recruiting, so will they. The secret is not managing your organization; rather it's finding leaders, who will in turn find other leaders. Generally, leaders must be found; they cannot be created. But many people have untapped leadership skills that do not manifest themselves until the timing is right. In order to "find" those leaders, you must keep prospecting and recruiting, realizing that new blood is the lifeblood of any network marketing organization. Recruiting is the only viable way to offset the inevitability of attrition. This is a numbers game that inevitably becomes a people business once distributors are sponsored into the business, often forging lifetime bonds.

It would indeed be wonderful if we could all skip to the bank each month with checks for $100,000 after merely working with a handful of frontline leaders. It is human nature to want to believe that there is an easy way to achieve this goal. We warn you against leaders and authors who grossly and unfairly mislead people by projecting concepts that feel easy and effortless to everybody, yet don't work. Don't be taken in by those who teach management as a philosophy of success because it is indeed the very cause of as much as 50 percent of the failures in our industry. Here's the scenario: A new associate is exposed unwittingly to this

system, spends a few weeks talking five friends into signing up, then the rest of his/her short career consists of attempting to drag those five people over the finish line. Then the next thing you know, our network marketer is having weekly babysitting sessions in the living room of someone's home.

Fortunately for Amway, two of their biggest leaders saw the folly of this philosophy early on. Because, as leaders, they command so much respect and loyalty from their downlines, they were able to immediately replace this concept with more realistic guidelines by removing one bestselling book from their sales tool repertoire. We truly believe that one of the several reasons that Amway has continued to grow and become a multibillion-dollar empire, while none of their competitors have done half as well, is the absence of widespread dissemination of this management philosophy. Their distributors don't try to manage everyone; they continue to place their emphasis on showing the plan, thereby adding new frontline distributors. It is the same with our own downline. Over the years, we have promoted *Power Multi-Level Marketing* (our book) and *All You Can Do* by A. L. Williams. Consequently, our most successful leaders continue to recruit large numbers of frontline distributors and teach their people to do the same.

Baby-Sitting the Downline

BEFORE we met, one of Rene's most promising groups was in Rochester, New York. It was a dynamic growing leg of her organization led by a couple, Gary and Laurie, who were self-sufficient with all of the vision, the integrity, and the enthusiasm to succeed at network marketing. They sponsored a friend named Mike, who was their strongest catalyst. For nearly two years, everything went well. Rene traveled there twice a year to work with them, and the rest of the time she supported them with teleconference and speakerphone meetings. There were generally two to three hundred people in attendance, and the number of emerging leaders was growing with each visit. It was the epitome of how a long-distance networking organization can succeed. Then, almost in a single week, it all changed.

Mike, once the best recruiter in the whole group, had secretly slipped into a management mode. His group was sizable and he felt it was time to devote his energy to overseeing their recruitment activities. Because of his strong personality, no one felt they could do anything as well as he did it. With Mike so readily available, his organization leaned on him for everything—presentations, hand-holding sessions, closings, sizzle sessions, product

clinics, and pep talks on the phone. Depressed and discouraged, Mike phoned Gary, who suggested that he talk to Rene. The phone call went something like this:

"Mike, you sound down. What's the problem?" Rene was concerned.

"I don't know. It just isn't working anymore. I'm absolutely fed up with baby-sitting my group. Isn't there anyone out there who can just do it on their own?"

"Mike, you are the best recruiter in the business. How many people have you sponsored this month?"

There was a hesitation before he answered. "I'm too busy baby-sitting. And no matter how hard I work, my group isn't growing anymore. I don't get it."

"You know the saying: 'New blood is the lifeblood of this business.' Stop recruiting and your organization dies a slow death. You want it to come alive? Go back to what works and what you do best—recruit."

"I just can't see the light at the end of the tunnel. It looks like I'll be baby-sitting the rest of my life. Ask my wife, I'm not even good at baby-sitting my own kids. If I could just find a way to do this without baby-sitting. . . ."

One month later, Mike found a new company, a wholesale buyers club. It was exactly what Mike was looking for—a deal with no inventory, no product information to learn, no training required and no baby-sitting a downline. Just sponsor people and when they order anything, the upline gets a cut . . . or so he thought. He told everyone in Rochester about this great new company. Gary and Laurie were horrified, but fearing that they would lose out, they also signed up in the new company . . . just in case. Nearly all the leaders followed Mike into this new deal, but only as a backup to our company, of course. Yet because of this distraction, many of Gary and Laurie's downline lost focus. The last time Rene went to Rochester, Gary and Laurie were out of the business, and the number of serious players had dwindled from a few hundred down to about twenty-five. Six months later, the wholesale buyers club was out of business.

When we stopped to analyze what happened, we realized it all started when Mike stopped recruiting and became discouraged with baby-sitting his group. This was the time to give extensive *support* to the Rochester group—a time for new leaders to emerge. Had Gary and Laurie been able to stay focused themselves and not let Mike divert them and their entire organization, this group could have become one of our largest legs. If the clock of time could be rewound, Rene would love to have them all back—"I had built a close relationship, both upline

and downline to Gary and Laurie, and I miss these friendships that were once a regular part of my life." But once an organization has fallen apart, it is far easier to "give birth" to new people than it is to try to "revive the dead."

Experience Abroad

ONE of our most graphic examples of the Management Trap occurred when we opened a foreign market. We sponsored one couple, taught them everything we knew, and worked through them to build a dynasty in the new country. We developed a friendship and found that we shared many things in common, including similar life values. Prior to the official launch, we did weekly teleconference calls, which is both a legitimate and efficient way to build a new market prior to a company's opening. Through our mutual effort, and to our delight and surprise, we had more than 1,500 serious prospects attend our opening day celebration at a private location hosted by us. For us personally, it was the single largest launch of a foreign market in which we had ever participated. And yet, a year and half later, our frontline couple's income continued to drop below their first executive check.

How was this possible after such an awesome beginning? Prior to the official launch, everything was kept to a simple system—no hotel meetings, just friends telling friends; no literature; not even products because they weren't allowed to be sold yet. But almost immediately after the opening, the couple we sponsored stopped building their frontline and started managing their group. In fact, they spent the next eighteen months creating sales tools and coaching those struggling on their frontline to buy as much product as they needed in order to meet monthly requirements for advancement. Although we translated our own materials for their use, they were convinced that their culture required something different. So they developed a new manual to replace ours. They developed slides for hotel meetings because they believed their compatriots would respond especially well to that kind of presentation. They worked with flip-chart presenters and overhead projectors, and then, of course, wound up continually updating all those materials because their downline leaders were never quite satisfied. They traveled all over the country spending money they didn't have to speak at hotel meetings being held by their downline.

While serving as administrators to their organization, they had no time left for such mundane activities as frontline recruiting. This couple sponsored thirty-one people their first month. They spon-sored an additional nineteen people over the next four months. But both of them working full-time sponsored only six new distributors over the next fifteen months! In other words, they sponsored fifty people the first five months and then, with so much time invested in managing their organization, averaged only one new associate every two and a half months thereafter. This couple was far more achievement-oriented than materialistic, and therefore they were more interested in setting records and receiving recognition than in making money. Their goal was to be the first in their country to reach the maximum recognition level in our company. They achieved their goal, only temporarily, but their entrance into the Management Trap ruined what should have been our greatest income-producing leg.

The couple quit in frustration. To this day they blame it all on the compensation plan, the product pricing, and the failure of the industry in that country. They worked as hard as any two people have ever worked in network marketing. But it wasn't the cost of merchandise that led to their failure, nor was it the company's re-muneration method or the inadequacy of network marketing in that part of the world. It was caretaking their organization combined with their futile need to be "first" that brought them down. Their

If you stop building your frontline before you have a solid income, you will fail in this business. No one can succeed by sponsoring only one new distributor every two and a half months.

downfall began their fifth month in the business when they stopped recruiting frontline.

The good news is that this is not the end of the story. Two other top leaders followed them out of the business, but at the request of some of the emerging leaders in this group, we are continuing to work with them. They have learned the hard way this lesson of trying to watchdog their groups and have gone back to basics: building a small customer base; prospecting; going wide on their frontlines; working a simple, easily duplicated system out of their homes. We believe in this group and in its leadership, and are convinced that this time they are on track to set both economic and industry records in their country.

It's crucial to learn from other people's mistakes, so pay close attention to this story. If you stop building your frontline before you have a solid income, you will fail in this business. No one can succeed by sponsoring only one new distribu-

tor every two and a half months. And even worse, by your example you will teach your people to do the same. Full-time network marketers recruit for a minimum of two to three years before they can slow down. For part-timers, it takes longer than that. Set your sights on the goal, strive consistently to meet the steps outlined in your business plan, and don't look for excuses. Whatever it takes, just do it!

The Piano Story

WE have a story we like to share with people early in their careers. It's a great illustration that may help you in training and supporting your own organization.

Imagine an audience of 500 people seated before a stage with a grand piano. Suddenly, out walks a person who has never had even one lesson and knows nothing about music. After the applause dissipates, he very aggressively begins to bang out horrible combinations of sounds that literally hurt one's ears. At first, the audience glances around the room in utter shock and disbelief. Following a full ten minutes of pathetic piano beating, the audience begins to boo and hiss. Within a couple of minutes, their boos drown out the performer, who calmly stands, bows, and walks off.

As the hacker exits, a pianist with thirty years experience enters from the other side of the stage. He methodically and flawlessly plays a beautiful Mozart concerto. When he's finished, the crowd leaps to its feet and gives him a thunderous ovation as he bows two or three times, then exits the stage.

In the dressing room the expert pianist notices that the first performer is gently humming to himself and adjusting his tie before leaving. Although the expert pianist is somewhat embarrassed to bring up the subject, his curiosity finally gets the best of him. He smiles in the mirror at the first performer, and asks a question:

"Forgive me for intruding, but I notice you aren't particularly offended by what just happened out there. I have to ask you, what's it like to be booed off a stage. I mean, isn't it horribly degrading?"

The gentleman turns around so that he is facing the pianist and with all seriousness responds, "Oh no. I didn't take it personally. It was the piano."

Perhaps one of the most interesting elements of human nature is our tendency—and to a greater or lesser degree we all possess it—to place blame elsewhere. The truth is, while many people criticize our industry after they fail, it's not the fault of the industry. As in the preceding story, a poor musician can't legitimately blame the piano for his lack of talent. You may want to remember this story and share it with new distributors.

The Buy-In

OF all the possible fiascoes stemming from the Management Trap, "buying in" for your downline or teaching them to do this for their distributors is the worst. Marketers who get caught spending more time managing than recruiting often get snared into this trap, which has serious legal consequences. And when law enforcement goes after a buy-in pyramid deal, we all look bad by association. Success in network marketing results from the creation of "real" volume as opposed to "promotional" volume. Real volume is produced from orders of satisfied customers and distributors who use and love the products (or services), ordering them month after month, thus creating long-term, stable sales volume in that organization. It is the most important type of volume because it represents money spent by bona fide customers for items that their families consume and then reorder. Promotional volume results from multiple product packages that are ordered by distributors who may be attempting to "buy their way" to the next level or intend to use these packages to get their new distributors started in the business. "Buying-in" will always backfire with distributors who simply cannot afford it and have no legitimate outlet for moving the products.

When new associates join your organization and have definite prospects to whom they know they can sell their starter packages, promotional volume can be a valuable tool for creating the often-needed initial volume swell to get distributors through qualification requirements. But first-year networkers often get confused by this sudden spurt of success and start thinking that they have created a solid flow of volume throughout their organization. Promotional volume does not result in a stable organization. Both types of volume serve their purpose in network marketing, but the majority of new distributors will benefit from being intro-

duced to a low-cost product starter package, consisting of products, training, or services they will personally use, which is the essence of starting people in our business.

Some people caught up in supervising their groups who are simultaneously working toward promotions and higher rankings within their companies will often purchase unneeded products and then teach their personally sponsored frontline distributors to do the same thing in order to meet requirements for advancement. However, if distributors are doing this business right, they will be recruiting enough new people each month in order to advance through the ranks properly. But if they start attempting to manage a small group of marketers, they may find at the end of the month that their sales volume requirements are not adequate. So, they simply call in an order for products they don't really need or intend to sell in order to meet promotion requirements, hence the name "promotional volume."

Front-end loading is forbidden by state and federal regulators who believe that such activities are pyramid-like in nature. We agree. In fact, we have a term for this kind of activity: "garage qualifying." We sometimes wonder how many American garages are crammed to overflowing with non-run pantyhose, 3-D cameras, home insulation, videos, and other nonconsumable products. If all of America's "garage products" were put together for one big flea market, we're sure it would stretch from Missouri to Maine.

Don't ever allow yourself to be duped into believing that you can "buy" your way to the top of a company. You can't! And if for any reason your company's compensation plan is set up to reward those who "buy in," it's just a matter of time before some attorney general or Federal Trade Commission representative slams the regulatory "cease and desist" order on the company. The process of buying-in never leads to long-term success. It only serves to bridge the gap between levels in a compensation plan. We do not know any distributors earning big money who bought their way to the top. But we know many who have garages full of products. Of course, if the leader is seen buying-in, the troops will all do the same. In a short time you've got a bunch of people with garages full of dust-gathering products, and then it's just a matter of time until they become disgusted and quit. And when they do, rest assured they'll tell everyone who will listen what a horrible scam this industry is. Many of the better companies have implemented product return policies of up to 90 percent, which precludes people from being burdened with so many products. It can be a rude awakening for a buy-in leader when his check arrives and it's minimal because his company has charged back all returns from the very angry distributors whom he "front-end loaded."

Some network marketers, in their eagerness to get off to a fast start, simply don't understand this philosophy and will make the mistake of skipping over the critical step of creating real volume in their organizations. It is vital that all new distributors begin with a solid commitment to use as much product as possible, share the product personally—especially among close family and friends—and teach everyone in their organization to do the same. As simplistic as this may seem, it must be done *before* beginning the more dramatic and gratifying process of creating large recruiting volume through your power players and teaching them to duplicate the process. It is the balance of both types of volume, *promotional*—to propel you into success in the early days—and *real*—to stabilize your volume and provide ongoing, residual income—that results in the long-term success we all desire. Promotional volume is extremely valuable, but your business can survive without it. However, failure to create real volume can lead to the eventual stagnation and collapse of your organization.

"Just Give Me Your List and I'll Do All the Work"

IN early 1990, Mark recruited a man whose father-in-law owned the largest citrus company in the South and had access to the most prestigious office address in Florida. Their boardroom, on the fifty-fifth floor, overlooked the ocean and had seating for 300. We'll call these distributors by the names of Jeff and Mary.

Jeff and Mary had a Rolodex of over 5,000 people, many of whom were small business owners and most of whom were entrepreneurs. Although Jeff and Mary had thousands of people to prospect, they fell victim to running an adult daycare center to which anyone in their organization could send prospects. Mark didn't fully understand the whole problem until it was too late. All he saw were the numbers and their volumes looked great. Unfortunately, Jeff and Mary began managing their organization prematurely and the group decreased in size from 3,000 to 500 people. Here's what went wrong.

Never tell people that all they've got to do is sign up, give you a list of potential distributors, and then you'll do the rest. It *doesn't* work. Jeff signed up ten people on his front line, then immediately told those men and women—some of Miami's real movers and shakers—to start sending prospects to his weekly meetings conducted exclusively on the top floor of their corporate building. He explained that he and Mary had the time to do the meetings and train the distributors and that his people would merely need a wheelbarrow to take to their mailbox each day in order to carry all the money!

For two months, everything went fine. Every one of the noon meetings on Tuesdays, Wednesdays, and Fridays were filled with curious prospects sent by bosses or close, wealthy friends to investigate this business opportunity. By the middle of the second month Mary also had to launch Monday and Thursday meetings, and by the end of the next month, those too were filled. Many prospects were signing up and their weekly volumes, in starter kits alone, were going through the ceiling. But everything changed the Monday that they announced that people were going to have to start doing their own presentations at their own homes in order to take care of the spillover. Just imagine the chaos.

To begin with, Jeff had trained no one to do anything except send him leads, and none of the frontline people who had signed up under his ten personally sponsored folks had been trained to do anything but send in their prospects. Simply put, in month three, Jeff and Mary were so caught up in the muck and mire of the Management Trap that they couldn't move in any direction.

Some new distributors were saying they'd been misled and demanded their money back. Some were angry that they hadn't yet met qualification requirements. After all, they'd been sending Jeff and Mary leads for eighty days. Where was this $15,000 a month they'd heard about? One small group revolted and went to another office complex to begin their own meetings, but no one wanted to go there or send their people because the leader wasn't as good a speaker as Jeff and they complained that the office wasn't as attractive. Two couples got together and hired an attorney on a contingency basis and filed a misrepresentation/fraud case against Jeff, who then had to spend countless hours preparing for depositions.

Mary and Jeff, without Mark's presence in Florida to supervise what they were doing wrong, purposefully hid from him the system they were using. They knew he deplored big recruiting meetings, that he spoke against offices, that he taught everyone to avoid baby-sitting distributors at all costs. They fully understood his "Go wide fast" advice, putting as many people on one's frontline as possible until wealth had been achieved. Yet

they fell victim to the Management Trap. Had Mark been in Florida instead of Austin, Texas, he might have been able to steer them right. Or had they been honest about their methods, he could have salvaged the situation. All he heard about were the many great people they were recruiting and all the great volumes being achieved. By the time he discovered the truth, it was too late, for they had both mentally and emotionally burned out.

Within five months of the day that Mark sponsored Jeff and Mary, they were selling everything but their clothes and leaving town humiliated. Mary's father had virtually disowned the two of them for embarrassing an "old money" family in the Deep South where image is everything. And we can tell you unequivocally that with their talent, and with all the names in their Rolodex of reputable entrepreneurs whom they knew on a first-name basis, all they had to do to succeed was teach the big hitters to begin with their twenty-five prime contacts, do in-homes and "Go wide fast." Those three magic words are synonymous with building your front line, not your depth, as quickly as you can. The depth takes care of itself with sufficient numbers in width. Jeff and Mary needed to do only two simple things in order to avoid their problems and ultimately become successful. First, look for close friends who were entrepreneurial types, ready for change and fed up with stress, and then show them, by example, the wonderful simplicity of in-home recruiting meetings. Second, do the first couple of meetings for each new distributor, then cut the cord thus enabling their distributors to become leaders themselves.

Ours is a business of leaders building their front lines and teaching their people to do the same. Those with leadership ability will seek out other top leaders to mentor them and give them help in closing serious prospects. It is in this way that genuine *support* is given. Rather than working your new associate's list, teach your distributors how to work their own. They can come to you for support, that is, assistance in closing, after their prospects have been shown the presentation. How do you support a large group, you may ask? By teaching them three words: "You call me." And when those calls come, be there for them. Be there to render moral support, coaching assistance, help in closing prospects—but don't do for them what they must do for themselves. They must prospect, recruit, and train their own frontline associates.

Quit or Take It to the Moon

THE truth is that success in our industry does not result from extensive management. Success comes from a person with leadership skills having the vision, enthusiasm, and willingness to recruit other frontline leaders who, in turn, use and share the products or services. Then, simply teach them to duplicate the process.

Larry Pepe was a new networker who experienced a series of nightmares starting up his business: His sponsor quit almost immediately; his upline executive tried to talk him out of going forward on the accelerated program; of his first twenty-three distributors, twenty-two quit and of his first three in qualification, all failed; one of his "gold stars" was arrested one month before becoming his first executive; another turned out to be a con man who was being sued for fraud; and a

---

How do you support a large group, you may ask? By teaching them three words: "You call me." And when those calls come, be there for them.

heavy hitter from Australia was diagnosed with terminal cancer—all of this in the first three months of Larry's new network marketing business!

Then came the crowning blow—the upline leader who *had* supported him called to say she would not be available for a while because of personal problems that she needed to resolve. Larry remembers sitting on the edge of his bed after hanging up the phone, staring blankly into space, thinking "God is testing me. This is it. I either quit or become a leader right now and take this thing to the moon." A few minutes later, his mother called and said, for the life of her, she couldn't understand why a talented young attorney with a master's degree in clinical psychology who owned a success-ful business would give all of that up to be a vitamin salesman!

Larry is convinced that all of those experiences, especially being left on his own, which forced him to become a leader to his organization, were the best things that ever happened to him in business. He went to work frontline recruiting and refused to slow down until he achieved his first goal. Today, he and his upline leader work closely together and she fondly refers to him as Hercules. And the best part, says Larry, is "My mom doesn't think of me as a vitamin salesman anymore! Thank God for small miracles." This story teaches us that we need not be managers, and demonstrates that people who have the will to succeed . . . will succeed . . . regardless of the circumstances.

SUMMARY

- Managing an organization is a time-wasting practice that does for others what they should be doing for themselves, thereby creating codependency.

- Supporting the members of your group means being there for them when they call to ask for guidance, moral support, or request that you talk to one of their serious prospects.

- Managing organizations for our families and friends often causes the very people we love most to fail.

- Practicing a management mode is counterproductive for both those being managed and those doing the managing.

- We are empowered far less by heredity, luck, and circumstances, than by our vision of what we believe is truly possible for ourselves.

- Don't be offended—be joyous—when new recruits finish their training and go to work without calling you every day and asking you to do everything for them.

- In this business, everyone has the ability to do great things, but those who lean on their uplines for every single thing are usually the ones who fail.

- What makes our industry so much grander than traditional employment opportunities is the fact that we are compensated ethically and generously for our productivity.

- If new associates want to earn more than the leader above them, they just need to be more productive, i.e., recruit more active frontline distributors and customers than do their uplines.

- If you become frustrated because your associates are not successful, teach them to visualize the end result and direct most of your energy toward those who do.

- Because this is a business of duplication, your people will do what you do: If you manage your downline, so will they; if you spend most of your time prospecting and recruiting, so will they.

- Baby-sitting a downline is not an effective way to build a business.

- The key to successfully building a large, dynamic organization is to steadily continue to prospect and recruit, creating a wide front line.

- Don't make the mistake that results in nearly 50 percent of the failures in our industry: building your front line for the first few months, then stopping to manage your people.

- Merely overseeing the activities of your organization is not leading them, but rather *misleading* them into rearranging their deck chairs on the *Titanic*.

- Set your sights on the goal, consistently meet the steps outlined in your business plan, and don't make excuses—whatever it takes, just do it!

- Of all the possible fiascoes stemming from the administration of your organization, "buying in" for your downline or teaching them to do this for their distributors is the worst.

- Promotional volume—that is, money spent on products, samples, and multiple kits—is initially a means of helping distributors meet volume requirements for qualification.

- Real volume—that is, products or services ordered for regular monthly usage by satisfied customers and distributors—is what ultimately creates passive residual income and is the essence of what makes network marketing a viable, ongoing business.

- Your business can survive without promotional volume, but failure to create real volume, by not acquiring legitimate customers or not using all your own products, can lead to the collapse of your entire organization.

- Network marketing is a business of distributors building their own front lines and teaching their people to duplicate that process.

- If each network marketer builds his own front line, following the advice "Go wide fast," the depth will take care of itself, and the cream will always rise to the top.

- Support a large organization by teaching them three words: "You call me."

- Be there for your downline to render moral support, coaching, and assistance in closing their prospects, but don't try to do for them what they must do for themselves.

- Success comes to people with leadership skills, a sound vision, enthusiasm, and the willingness to put forth the effort to build an organization and find others who will do the same.

CHAPTER 3

Dodging the Depression Torpedo

Maintain enthusiasm in spite of the inevitable setbacks.

ALTHOUGH THIS BUSINESS IS 90 percent fun after the "learning curve" months, the Depression Torpedo is among the more difficult challenges facing new and seasoned network marketers alike. Of necessity, successful recruiters must be enthusiastic, sincere, articulate, and believable. A depressed person cannot survive in this industry; thus, we need to prepare our newest associates by warning them of the most common causes of depression, beginning with an open admission of our own personal struggles with this formidable adversary.

As previously mentioned, one of our all-time bestselling sales tools is an audiotape entitled "If MLM Is So Great, Why Am I Depressed?" There are probably several reasons for its popularity. Obviously it's one of those titles that grabs

people, and the content was quite humorous as we presented anecdotes from our first years in the business. But the primary reason it was so well received is because everyone can relate to it. In this chapter we will discuss depression using the image of the Depression Torpedo, so named because it seems to come out of nowhere and, after it hits, can sink a person rapidly.

One prerequisite for success in network marketing, often not as critical in traditional business, is the appearance of being emotionally charged. Every weekday, millions of people climb into their cars in a state of semi-depression and fight traffic on their way to jobs and professions which, simply put, do not require emotional energy. Some people are computer experts who are involved in data entry. The computer doesn't care if they're depressed, and since their supervisor is often more despondent, there's no need to be overflowing with joy. In fact, we could probably list hundreds of examples of boring, routine jobs that require nothing more than one's semi-conscious attention. Remember the saying "Oh, I can do this in my sleep"? In the world of traditional business, that's not just a saying.

Success in network marketing, however, depends on one factor perhaps more than any other—a positive, uplifting personality and demonstrable enthusiasm and exuberance. Network marketers cannot effectively convince people to change careers or, for that matter, participate in a new part-time opportunity unless they appear to enjoy what they're doing. Indeed, no one should ever go into the community or pick up the telephone for the purpose of recruiting prospects or selling services or products unless he or she is in a positive frame of mind.

Causes of MLM Depression

WHEN friends decline the offer to come to a distributor's home for a business presentation, or worse, stand us up after accepting the invitation, it's a bit depressing. Each time a valued associate goes

AWOL by slipping into apathy, changing companies, or quitting MLM altogether, we can become depressed. The more we dwell on such things, the more depressed we become. And yet we all know that attrition is going to happen. Over time, attrition can account for as much as a 75 percent dropout rate as we move through the ups and downs of building our business. It is a fundamental reality in MLM and one from which we will never be exempt.

After years of experience and success in network marketing, Ron Wiggins has developed a philosophical attitude about attrition: The sooner someone quits who isn't serious about the business, the sooner he knows with whom he need not waste a lot of time. Unless people are blatantly doing everything wrong, Ron's advice is to "let people do what they want to do with their business and not what you want them to do. There's a place for any and all levels of participation in this business." He's right. Since we know that attrition is the wrong thing on which to concentrate, we need to focus on the positive numbers instead. The more people we have active in our business, the more successful we will be. A well-balanced organization will be made up of a large body of wholesale buyers, many retailing distributors, some part-time business builders and a few full-time, gung-ho, recruiting maniacs. So Ron concludes,

"Work with the leaders. And do whatever it takes to protect your mind-set. You must stay focused for this business to work." (We will discuss this point in more detail in chapter six, "Fending Off the Scatter Bomb.")

Whether you are prospecting and receiving a series of rejections; whether you are setting up appointments and getting no-shows; or whether you are recruiting and watching people drop like flies before they have even scheduled a personal training session—remember, that's all inevitable. Nothing is wrong with you or your business. You are no different than the waitress offering people coffee in a coffee shop. Some people just don't care for any. You are merely sifting for those for whom the time is right.

Depression results not from attrition or even rejection. Depression ensues from dwelling on those factors and taking them personally. Learn to be as philosophical as Ron Wiggins about the disappointments: "All right! I just got nine *Nos* today. I'm that much closer to a *Yes*!" Or "Thank God John quit *before* I invested any more time in him." Attrition happens. People lose their initial enthusiasm. Some people are not coachable, so move on and start working with the new people who are coming onboard. And if you don't have any new, enthusiastic associates, go find some. If you spend too much time trying to boost up people who don't want to be in this business, it will drag you down; and the deeper you sink, the more vulnerable you become to the Depression Torpedo. It is much more energizing to look for new people who are excited, interested, and willing to learn.

When You're *Down*, Go *Up*line

WE have an age-old adage in our industry: "If you are up, go down; and if you are down, go up." Each of us has upline leaders who are, theoretically, more experienced than we and who have a vested interest in our success. We should turn to them when we are feeling concern, anxiety, or depression; hence when down, go up.

David Dryden from Dallas, Texas, learned this lesson just in the nick of time. "About two years ago, my wife, Teri, and I were looking for a way to bring her home from corporate America so that we could raise our kids instead of some daycare doing it for us. I decided to work harder and start my own business, but it wasn't working out. One day my wife came home after being prospected by a young man named Al Hewitt. After sitting in a meeting with my arms crossed and my mind closed, I gave her the okay to do the business (as if she needed my permission).

Before I knew what was going on, we had products all over our home and a house full of people curious to see what we were doing. Without realizing it, I was hooked on the business, that is, until I met my first and biggest adversary: no-shows of people whom we considered good friends—folks who had promised to come to our meeting. I was so discouraged I was ready to quit. But I had thankfully heard the adage 'when we are down, go up,' so I decided to call and introduce myself to my upline. I left messages for almost all of them, not fully convinced I'd receive any calls back.

"Then one day, something happened to change my life. I had finally had it, too many 'no-shows,' too many 'Nos,' too many late nights without success happening as fast as I thought it should. I was going to take my wife to lunch—she was still working at that time—and tell her that this was her business, her idea, and that I would support her, but she was going to have to do it without my direct involvement. I was walking out the door when the telephone rang and I almost let it go for the answering machine to pick up. Something told me to answer. On the line was a strangely familiar voice with this outrageous Texas twang asking if David Dryden was in. The call was from Mark Yarnell, who was actually returning my call. We very casually discussed the business and the successes possible, but I never mentioned my immediate plans to quit. His last comments were focused on perseverance and how many people similar to me had hung in there and how successful they were now just because they didn't quit! Well, this obviously changed my plans for our lunch conversation, and it goes without saying that Teri and I are still working our way toward our goals. Thanks to upline support from Al Hewitt all the way up to Mark Yarnell, we now know that we will achieve our dreams."

David added as a postscript that it took him nearly two years to figure out why he didn't quit back then. It was only while writing out this story from his heart late one night that he completely understood why he is still in this business, and how it changed from his wife's way out of the corporate world to their shared dream. We must always remember to return calls to our downline. A simple five-minute conversation can often be the only thing necessary to protect them from vulnerability to the Depression Torpedo.

Upline support can make or break a new networker's early months in this business. Vera Holub of San Diego, California, has relied heavily on her upline and, in turn, tried to emulate them in working with her downline. As she explains, "I grew up in the cotton fields of South Texas in a tin-roofed shack with no running water or electricity. I lost my only brother to suicide at age thirty-three. I worked my way through Junior College in a kitchen cabinet factory and finished my B.S. degree in dental hygiene. I achieved the American dream/nightmare by busting my chops, working with a bunch of neurotic dentists for $50,000 a year. Finally, I realized there had to be a better way. That day in 1988 when I saw Mark Yarnell's video explaining network marketing, I knew my prayers had been answered, and that I would do this business for the rest of my life. Quitting was never an option.

"Today I have a life about which many people only dream, and I am able to take care of my aging mother who was responsible for giving me the dream to rise above our early situation. I've taken some time to enjoy life and touch other people's lives, while building my business. I am so grateful for Mark Yarnell and Kathy Denison as my upline coaches, and for their having turned me onto this marvelous industry."

Never Convey a "Down" Attitude to Your Downline

THE last thing we want to do is negatively impact our downline organization by taking our negativity down, thus when you are "up" emotionally, that's the best time to talk with your downline. This industry is so much fun that you may find yourself seldom negative. But don't ever share your negativity with anyone in your downline or you could poison a huge percentage of your entire group. You see, it's quite devastating, especially to a new distributor, to discover that their leaders are "down" emotionally.

If you have ever played the game of gossip as a child you remember how, once in a circle with your friends, one individual would whisper a quick story to the person sitting next to her. Then, after being repeated by each person, it would reach the original storyteller often distorted completely beyond recognition. If you've never played that game, let me assure you, by the time a simple story has gone through a mere five or six individuals, that story can become dramatically distorted. And that's just five re-tellings! In networking, a simple story can be told, on the telephone or in person, as many as five or six thousand times over a period of a week or less. Can you even begin to imagine the distortions that inevitably occur? If not, here's a graphic example.

Mark describes a situation that happened to him in his first six months. "Even though my group was naturally smaller in this early stage, I discovered the dramatic impact that can occur by a leader talking to downline members when he is down himself. I was angry when a pro football player on my third level decided to quit in his second month of our business. It troubled me for two reasons: First, I had invested numerous hours in personally training him. After all, how often does a simple country boy from the Boston Mountains of northern Arkansas get a chance to coach an NFL star? Second, everyone knew him and I was in ego-heaven each time I told anyone—especially my close friends and family members back in Missouri—that I was spending quality time coaching my great friend and associate Mr. NFL. So when he quit and took five of his best friends with him into the old USA vitamin deal, I was depressed and angry. I made the mistake of mentioning to a new frontline leader what he'd done and why I was so angered by his actions.

"Two weeks later, by the time I'd all but forgotten Mr. NFL, I received a disturbing message on my answering machine from a tearful downline member of another completely separate organization. This lady was not even in my own downline. I didn't know her, had not talked to her before, and have not spoken to her since this incident. She didn't tell me what was disturbing her but merely suggested that I call her immediately so I could help her make an important decision. As best as I can recall—and it's going to be reasonably accurate because it was such an emotionally charged thirty-minute conversation—here's how the dialogue played out. Following the two minutes of ice-breaking small talk, she began her story in a depressed, and at one point, sobbing manner.

"'Mr. Yarnell, I can't blame you for leaving the company and bettering your finances, if that was your problem. Your family deserves prosperity, especially considering the amount of effort you've put into network marketing. But what upsets me is that, from what your upline has told us, you were making a ton of money. It shakes my confidence that you would believe that, at your age, playing professional football in the NFL could be as lucrative and long-term as the passive residual income from this business. My husband thinks you are gutsy to go for it, but I can't for the life of me . . .'

"I cut her off. I was shocked—literally shocked beyond comprehension. 'What did you just say, Sally?'

"'I said, my husband thinks you're gutsy . . .'

"'No,' I interjected 'before that. Something about joining the NFL? Are you kidding? I mean . . . I'm 36 years old and never even played college ball.'

"There was dead silence, though I could hear her clear her throat. Then she softly asked, 'You mean, you didn't try out for the 49ers last month? You didn't really trade in MLM for NFL?'

"I must confess, it was the most comical distortion of facts I had ever heard. When I assured her of this impossibility, I could hear her let out an audible sigh. She was so relieved to find out that I was not getting out of the business. I'll run off any mountain or glacier in the world with a paraglider, the open parachute form of hang gliding, but that's a sissy sport compared to pro ball of any kind. If I were hit just once by a mediocre NFL tackle, I truly believe I'd be lucky to live through it. I tremble at the thought of being hit by a guy like Steve Bach, a former NFLer from Portland. So I decided that this misconstrued rumor was so absurd that I needed to track it back to see if I could find its source. I never could, but it does remain the most preposterous scuttlebutt about me I've ever heard."

Here's the point. Mention anything even slightly negative to your downline and you'll likely wind up on the wrong end of a highly perverted untruth! From being slightly angered by an NFL star leaving my organization to being so fed up with MLM that I had joined an NFL team in order to play professional football

as a thirty-six-year-old, 5 ft. 10 in., 155 lb., guy is a stretch. This illustration is sufficient all by itself to give you good reason to avoid sharing angry complaints with your downline. The rumors will come back to haunt you and, at the very least, the fact that their upline is depressed will cause your downline to question the business.

A Case for Optimism

THE underlying embarrassment some professionals feel after joining network marketing and the negative reactions of their peers are two causes of depression, though they aren't easily admitted. We need to especially prepare former physicians, lawyers, accountants, and other professionals for the internal conflict they nearly always experience during their transition to MLM. In their previous life, no matter how underpaid or overworked, they were seen as somebody important with a title and an office. Now they are starting over at the bottom rung of the ladder as lowly network marketers. To even consider taking on this challenge, such professionals often suffer the anguish of feeling that, in order to go forward with this new business undertaking, they must sacrifice their very identity.

In order for professionals to be successful in network marketing, they must be willing to use their reputations and credibility toward building their business. By hiding behind the pretense that it's their spouse's business or that it is just an insignificant little side business, they will set themselves up for failure by subtly denying their commitment to their warm market. It is the responsibility of serious players in network marketing to provide such professionals with a real vision of why MLM is a remarkable industry and how many people they will help avoid the rat race, and perhaps even stress-induced coronaries. Without an optimistic outlook, people are doomed to failure in this business.

One of the greatest books Mark ever encountered as a minister was entitled *A Case for Optimism* by James Dillet Freeman. Mr. Freeman is a poet, minister, and scholar from Lees Summit, Missouri, who devoted a significant part of his adult life to a prayer ministry called "Silent Unity." As a part of the worldwide Unity movement, Silent Unity receives thousands of prayer requests each day by telephone and mail and has a vigil of quiet prayers twenty-four hours a day for those who request them. Who better than a man devoted to prayer and meditation to write a book on optimism about our often pessimistic species? Read any chapter and you will feel just a little bit better about yourself, your life, and your world.

We've come to realize that in network marketing, we have literally the greatest case for optimism in the history of free enterprise. We want to share a few of the reasons for stating this and encourage you to mark this place in the book. When one of our reasons for optimism is particularly relevant to you, underline it; then come back to it when it's necessary to lift your spirits.

First, we have the only entrepreneurial home business with literally no downside risk. You see, most businesses require significant capital before you can even hang up a sign. Not networking marketing! So we are, first of all, extremely pleased with the fact that anyone can get involved with us for the nominal price of a few products and sales aids, and even that is optional. Thus, in the competitive world of home businesses and franchises, we have *no* equals!

Second, there is literally no ceiling, no limits on earnings. A lawyer can only bill so many hours in a day and a doctor can only perform a handful of surgeries a day. Some great people working in traditional business haven't had a raise in ten years. But, in our case, we can create a raise for our family every day if we choose. Since we can recruit an unlimited number of people who each can do the same, we are ultimately paid on the efforts of hundreds of thousands of individuals. We can't speak for you or any other, but we can tell you this: We absolutely love the fact that it's possible to earn one million dollars a month. There's just something appealing about life when you first catch the vision that if you apply yourself, your grandchildren will be considered "old money" in your town.

Third, and most exhilarating of all, in network marketing, time freedom is directly commensurate with wealth and prosperity. In our opinion, nothing in life equals the joy of spending quality time doing the things we most enjoy with the people we most love. In traditional professions, small businesses, sales or corporate management, everyone is struggling through eighty-hour weeks doing mundane, boring work in order to have, *maybe*, a Sunday afternoon with their family. Nothing is more precious than free time, and those of us who have achieved it are optimistic about an industry that offers this precious commodity to others, thereby improving the possibility of family values throughout the world.

Fourth, there need not be any stress at all in MLM. According to a late '80s cover story in *Georgia Trends* magazine, the number one trend in America is stress-induced coronary. And as the article suggests, it's no longer just a risk for men.

Death from coronary disease has increased 100 percent among women since 1980. In network marketing, if you aren't having fun, you aren't doing it right. We've had a blast the last few years in spite of the fact that our business required large-scale recruiting and a lot of good old-fashioned rejection. So, like us, if you pay the price in the first few years, stress need no longer exist in your life.

That brings us to our fifth reason for optimism: the Four-Year Plan. The forty-year plan is the best that folks can hope for in traditional businesses. So, what's the forty-year plan, you ask? By age twenty-five, most people have an idea of what profession they'll enter, anything from a fishing guide to a surgeon. But forty years later, out of a typical 100 people, 5 are still working, 36 are dead, 54 are dead broke (or at least earning far less than when they were employed), 4 are well off, and 1 person is wealthy. Thus, the forty-year plan means that for four decades most of us go back and forth from home to work, back and forth, back and forth, like a silly, sick, caged lion . . . and yet at the end of that time only 1 out of 100 persons has something to show for it! In stark contrast is the Four-Year Plan. Work diligently for one MLM company for four years, build an income based on the honest movement of products or services, and you're set for life. Even more exciting, so are your heirs. Every person's MLM business is fully inheritable. If trading the forty-year plan for the Four-Year Plan doesn't get your heart pumping, you may need to be checked for Alzheimer's.

It is said that "Recognition is our most sought after reward in life. Babies cry for it and grown men die for it." We are convinced that this adage is right, and no other business can hope to provide all the recognition we receive as leaders in the networking industry. The only times either of us have broken down and cried publicly in front of large audiences have been on two occasions when we were presented with recognition plaques from our downline. Such recognition awaits all those who become reasonably successful in network distribution. Nothing in life so pleases us as when other human beings, with tears of sincerity and joy, thank us for giving them the opportunity to make their lives work.

Finally, the joys of travel and stimulating cultural experiences await everyone in this business. Work hard, succeed, and then fasten your seat belt and be prepared to see the world and enjoy new adventures while cultivating international friendships. There is nothing we human beings detest more than boring, routine work. In MLM, we have a ball traveling, learning about new cultures, visiting major muse-

ums, and sampling new and unique meals from entirely different worlds. Network marketing is an incredibly diverse and lucrative profession.

So, as you can see, there are many reasons for optimism in network marketing, and we highly encourage you to periodically review this chapter and, in particular, these ideas, should the Depression Torpedo catch you unaware. To become involved in network distribution is to become one of the luckiest people in the world.

Controlling Our Attitudes

OUR attitudes are among the few possessions that are totally ours and can never be taken from us. Houses and cars come and go, but our values and attitudes are with us forever. It is only when we continually exercise control over our own attitudes that we can manage external circumstances. Real change comes first from the inside and our behavior naturally follows.

Without this personal realization, people often become depressed in their first year of networking. There's a natural tendency to feel personally rejected when a relative or close friend decides not to participate in your business, or to take it

No one can successfully perform the tasks necessary to succeed when he is depressed, especially in a business in which success results more often from attitude than ability.

as a personal insult when someone whom you've spent hours supporting and training, decides to quit the business for no obvious reason. More than likely, those events will occur, but it is up to you to determine how you react to them.

No one can successfully perform the tasks necessary to succeed when he is depressed, especially in a business in which success results more often from attitude than ability. Many people fail simply because of their attitudes. And as we pointed out earlier, it is virtually impossible to convince people to change careers if you don't show them your enthusiasm and joy. We can't expect others to join us in business if it is obvious to them that we are less than satisfied. Always remember, enthusiasm is contagious.

In our own recruiting, we freely express excitement and effervescence as key tools in convincing others to join our business. Our prospects can tell how excited we are while many of them know their lives are boring and routine. We make certain at some point in our presentation to say, "In our business if you aren't having fun, you're doing it wrong!" Now for the practical advice.

No More News!

Never before, in our long history as civilized beings, have we had so many means of completely controlling our attitudes until now. We are convinced that the old adage originally aimed at computers can also be applied to people: "Garbage in, garbage out." Because of our backgrounds in theology, both of us have participated in extensive counseling. Often we found that depression was the result of the garbage people allowed into their brains. One man, who showed up for marital counseling explained how he'd lost the fire in his relationship. In fact, his whole life was becoming increasingly more depressing. As is so often the case, as Mark recalls the incident, a brief evaluation of this man's daily activities told the tale.

"Philip was a forty-year-old computer analyst for a major technology firm who explained his day as nothing out of the ordinary. 'I get up each morning and sit at the breakfast table reading the newspaper. Because I'm in a car pool, I either pick up my two friends, or they me, for the forty-five minute commute.'

"I stopped him with a leading question: 'Once you're in the car, what do you talk about?' I wondered for an important reason.

'Oh you know, the usual small talk,' he replied. 'But we really only spend a few minutes talking; then we flip on the radio because one news station gives traffic reports every ten minutes which helps us strategize our commute. If there's a serious traffic problem ahead, we avoid it. And besides, during that time, those who aren't driving normally have business files to examine.'

"It was just as I expected. Philip then proceeded to detail his mundane day. He and his co-workers had permission to listen to the radio at work. 'That breaks some of the monotony,' Philip explained. When he got home from work, he first read the paper while sipping a glass of wine. He had dinner with his two kids and wife, during which they all discussed their days. He spent less than two hours with any paperwork he brought home; then he and his wife curled up in bed in time to see an A&E program entitled *Law and Order* followed by the 10:00 news. He again emphasized that he led a reasonably good life, but nothing extraordinary.

"At the end of forty-five minutes of reflective listening, I recommended that Philip go six months without reading one newspaper, watching one television show about crime or newscasts of any kind, and no radio news at all. Six months without news! Following two more counseling sessions in which routine marriage counseling techniques were employed, Philip and Nancy never returned. We bumped into them two years later at a conference and they both beamed. Their marriage had taken a positive turn and Philip thanked me profusely. He made a point of mentioning that he really didn't know for certain what changed, but something had surely improved his life. 'By the way,' he said as he turned to walk away, 'except for the weekend edition of *USA Today*, I don't mess with the news anymore. Not that that has helped a great deal.'"

Wrong, Phil. The entire marriage turn-around could probably be traced right back to the elimination of those meaningless newscasts. If you are troubled by depression, read this next sentence three times: "No More News!" If Martians land anywhere in the world, you'll hear about it within fifteen minutes from someone in your circle of friends. If a princess dies, you'll hear about it even if you're on a boat in the Caribbean. We did.

Of all the absurdities in modern life, nothing creates as much depression and

> **We are irrevocably convinced that putting positive information into our brains is essential to success.**

---

misery as news. We are bombarded each day of our lives with radio, television, computer, and print news. To truly understand the effect it has on us, consider the philosophy of the news media. Remember that they are in business to make money and that to be profitable, they must be interesting. And consider the often-quoted philosophy in the news industry: "Good news is no news." They know that the American public lusts for the extraordinary. A murder is more fascinating than a man who donates $150,000 to charity. Donald Trump divorces Marla Maples, so naturally the tabloids cover every angle of the story. But last year, Trump gave $2 million to programs for New York's homeless, but we would have never known had a mutual friend not told us. We subscribe to the *New Yorker* because of the great stories, but no mention was made of Trump's altruism. Why? Because the public isn't interested in and will not buy "good news."

So, what does that have to do with us? Plenty! When we sign up new frontline distributors, we give them one specific as-

signment prior to their one-on-one personal training, to which they are invited following the completion of these assignments. We'll cover them in depth in a later chapter, but suffice to say, they are quite simple:

1. Define your goals. Visualize the end result—see yourself there—then commit your goals to writing.

2. Make a list of 2,000 warm market leads—people with whom you want to share the opportunity—then prioritize your prime twenty-five family members and friends.

3. After personally using our products, find ten customers who enjoy them as well.

4. For the sake of preserving your positive attitude, avoid any and all news for six months, except magazines which are 75 percent literature and 25 percent "current event" news.

It's very easy to enforce the first three, but not the last. However, a cursory evaluation of your distributor's attitude will reveal a great deal. If he's bouncy and sincerely exuberant, he's probably not watching the news!

Create a Positive Environment from the Inside Out

We are irrevocably convinced that putting positive information into our brains is essential to success. We do that by reading uplifting books and articles, listening to inspiring tapes, and practicing daily affirmative communication with ourselves and others.

Read books that motivate you and share them with others. Uplifting materials need to be spread like wildfire. Here are just a couple of our recommendations. First, make note of the telephone number for the American Youth Foundation: 314-772-8626. They distribute two of the most important, yet seldom read, books that we encourage each new distributor to order and read. Both books were written by the late, great William H. Danforth, founder and former CEO of the Ralston Purina Company in St. Louis, Missouri. He was a wealthy, rags-to-riches entrepreneur who had a genuine interest in the personal development of men, women, and children of all ages. Although, today very few people have heard of him, Mr.

Danforth was a champion of human potential who wrote books with this timeless message: Any person, regardless of age, color, sex, or inexperience, can rise to the same levels of success as the most renowned entrepreneurs. Mr. Danforth challenges all adolescents to become the "world's greatest" in whichever field they choose. It is absolutely impossible to be discouraged after reading either of his books, *Action* and *I Dare You.* And you don't need to read them from beginning to end; you can start reading any place in the material and skip around. While they are targeted at young people about to embark on adulthood, they are critical for adults about to launch new entrepreneurial careers.

Similarly, the story of A. L. Williams is about a relatively impoverished high school coach who had a dream. His dream was to create an unlimited opportunity in which ordinary people could rise to extraordinary heights. He founded a network marketing life insurance company, comprised of former teachers and coaches, that became so successful that, in just their seventh year, they sold more term life insurance than New York Life, Metropolitan and Prudential combined. Yet those companies were, at the time, over a century old. How? Simple. Mr. Williams did it through boosting people's self-confidence. We recommend you read his books *Pushing Up People* and *All You Can Do*. Both books are remarkable but pay special attention to his chapter in *All You Can Do* about having a cause and being a crusader. During many days when we were convinced that the difficulties of network marketing would defeat us, the words of A. L. Williams touched us and wiped out our depression.

There are hundreds of inspirational and motivational audiotapes available today. Put one into your cassette player at every possible opportunity—during drive time or when doing menial work at home, for instance—to continually absorb positive messages. These tapes will assist you in achieving your full potential, expanding your belief in yourself, and achieving your highest goals.

Fifty to sixty thousand thoughts a day go through each of our minds, 95 percent of them are about the past, and frequently it is the past that holds us back. Dwelling on negative events from the past that cannot be changed will only limit our possibilities. Do you know what happens when you play a country-western song backwards? You get your dog back, your pickup back, your girlfriend back . . . and you're right back where you started. In order to move forward, we must spend more time (1) recalling positive emotional experiences from the past, or (2) focusing on the future.

The moment you feel yourself spiraling downward, play some music from your past that conjures up happy days. You can't help but feel good. Think about past situations that turned out perfectly. Just those thoughts give you warm feelings. Then, take those feelings and emotions and inject them into the present moment. When a husband walks into his house and sees the girl he courted rather than the wife with whom he now lives a routine life, he will behave differently. His loving actions toward her will often cause similar reactions from her. This example is just one way to use the past to change our emotional responses to the present. The Depression Torpedo may be looming out there, but we don't have to be struck by it. We are 100 percent in control of our own mind-sets.

When working on personal development, putting more energy into thinking about the future is equally effective. This takes effort and determination because our natural tendency is to dwell in the past. Striving to visualize ourselves as we want to be is the first step toward change and growth. If we can't picture ourselves in a positive future, we may never get there. Too often, people limit their goals by basing them on what they know to be true at the moment. But breaking out of those boundaries allows what seemed impossible to become possible.

Goal setting is simply the process of adapting to a new reality, beginning from the inside out. To gradually turn those dreams into reality, begin to visualize them long before they ever happen. Start saying to yourself, "It is possible," even though it isn't happening now. Think in the future tense and visualize goals as already accomplished. Allow yourself to feel as if your dreams were happening now. Successful people always concentrate on the end result, while others get stuck focusing on the process, the "how." People with limited thinking ask "why?" Those with unlimited thinking ask "why not?"

The skeptics among you may worry about setting unrealistic goals or an inability to make them happen. If you believe in the value of your goals, trust us, you'll find the resources to make them happen. Set big goals and then strive to meet them. Whatever you do, don't ever give up on your goals—just change your attitudes. When the belief that we are locked into our present reality is stronger than our vision of what we really want, our growth becomes stifled. Think about what's coming in order to effect change.

Use Affirmations

An affirmation is a trigger tool—a statement of belief, written and repeated as if the goal were already an accomplished fact. Affirmations have the power to effect that outcome. Many prominent behavioral scientists have documented, in several landmark studies, the effectiveness of autogenics. We can now state to the most cynical, conservative, pragmatists that self-talk, affirmations, visualization, and autogenic programming work! Prior to the release of Dr. Bandura's studies at Stanford and those of Dr. Charles Garfield at the Performance Sciences Institute at Berkeley, California, as well as the pioneering human potential research of Lou Tice at the Pacific Institute, we would lose some of our audience when we got into affirmations and autogenic commands. Now, only those who have been

Successful people always concentrate on the end result, while others get stuck focusing on the process, the "how."

living in a closet could doubt the effectiveness of visualization and daily affirmations. Today, we know that one of the best defenses against depression or any other form of mental anguish is the daily process of drafting and repeating positive statements about yourself. Write a few down on a slip of paper and keep them in your wallet or day-timer, or on your bathroom mirror for daily recitation.

Here are a few affirmations that seem to work for everyone, but we encourage you to write some of your own, related specifically to your wants and needs. Read them silently every morning when you wake up and every night before the lights go out. After reading each one, visualize the written statement as if it is transpiring right now. Read the words, picture them happening, and feel the emotions that go with the vision. As the affirmations are gradually assimilated into your daily life, creativity, positive decision making, and goal setting become free-flowing events.

"I am powerful, knowing that I alone am accountable for the results of my decisions and actions."

"I enjoy every facet of life, because I easily and enthusiastically create fun, joy, and adventure."

"I feel supported, working with a team of positive people who share my values."

"People listen to me when I talk because I have something of value to say."

"I clearly communicate my business vision to others in such a way that they are inspired to join me and become a part of it."

"Because of my high self-esteem, I feel enormous satisfaction reaching my goals."

"I value myself as a person, and know that I am worth at least $50,000 a month and more."

"I am proud to be building an MLM dynasty as I recruit dozens of excited people who rapidly duplicate my success."

What you'll notice about this exercise is this: As you visualize the new, you gradually begin to shed the old, believing with every fiber of your being that what you visualize is happening to you at that very moment. That is when change begins to

As you visualize the new, you gradually begin to shed the old, believing with every fiber of your being that what you visualize is happening to you at that very moment. That is when change begins to occur.

---

occur. Change is often two steps forward and one step back. When you do well, say to yourself, "That's like me." When you make a mistake, say, "That's not like me. I'll do better next time." We have used each of these affirmations repeatedly and have shared them with many other people who have seen dramatic results by repeating them regularly.

Dr. Bob Scharp, a dentist from Big Rapids, Michigan, fell on tough times back in 1989. "Divorce, dissolution of my professional corporation, the premature death of my partner in my new dental practice, an office building project gone sour and finally, my wife's six-month battle with cancer had left me over $1 million in debt. By January of 1996, the IRS was threatening to seize what assets I had until $90,000 in back taxes were paid in full. The moment the IRS actually withheld payment from my major insurance vendor, the situation finally looked hopelessly bleak to me.

"I had recently attended a 'Vision Workshop' with the president of my network marketing company and came away reading and repeating the following affirmations every morning and every night. 'I am sitting on my deck overlooking my pond stocked with bass, pike and bluegill. My wife, Susan, and I are free to travel wherever and whenever we wish. People seek my advice because of my talent and religious conviction. I have the time and money to help my children as they begin their careers, etc.'

"Almost immediately things started to change. My builder loaned me $200,000 to pay all my past due debts, including the one to the IRS. My dental practice began to prosper. My network marketing business, which had been stagnant, began to grow. I regained my personal confidence and self-esteem. Within five months, all short-term debt was current and all long-term debt was being paid on schedule. Most exciting of all, in October, Susan and

I bought and moved into our dream home. It is a 51-acre farm complete with a fishing pond and a swimming pond, a lighted tennis court, a barn for our horses, a 10-acre hay field/driving range and a guesthouse that we rent out. We have deer, geese, ducks, turkeys, and thousands of birds as our guests. My relationship with my company and the industry is much more than just making some extra money part-time. It is about personal development and the freedom to lead a life of choice. It is about being content with what you do every day and helping other people lead the lives of their dreams."

More and more scientists, including respected quantum physicists, have come to the realization that we cannot produce magic results by thinking away the laws of physics. However, we *can* dramatically impact our subconscious, which directly influences our daily productivity. Perhaps you'll recall that in 1969, the Federal Communications Commission became very concerned that consumers could be unconsciously manipulated by subliminal advertising. It was eventually made illegal because it is so very effective. That same kind of manipulation can also be utilized for positive productivity. Try using affirmations for a month and you'll use them for the rest of your life. When you use affirmations you will be defending yourself

against the Depression Torpedo, and no bad news or disappointments will be able to penetrate your shield.

Create a Positive Environment from the Outside In

Our final piece of advice to avoid depression—and this need not be a tough one—is that new distributors should avoid dream stealers and negative people at least through their first year in network marketing. Often the negative people are family members or even close friends! Because success in MLM results more often from attitude than ability, it is important that we spend time associating with people who support us in our desire for success. Set clear rules for those who are constantly talking negatively about our business or criticizing our dreams.

Sit down with those negative people one at a time and have a serious, authentic discussion. Let them know that regardless of their opinion of this industry, you need and expect positive, uplifting comments or no comments at all. Tell them the truth. If they persist in involving you in counterproductive, negative discussions, you've got a decision to make. Either you deserve a life of financial security and time freedom with your family or you deserve to live a mediocre life amidst negative people. It's up to you. But, in most

> **Either you deserve a life of financial security and time freedom with your family or you deserve to live a mediocre life amidst negative people. It's up to you.**

cases, if you ask people nicely to support you, they will do so if they truly love you.

Dr. Robert Neff of Dallas, Texas had received a lot of negativity from those for whom he held tremendous respect in the first year of building his networking business. Their greatest argument was that the industry was fundamentally flawed: "taking advantage of others for your own personal gain." He knew that this wasn't his experience, but their words stayed in his head and held him back from building his business. Why? Because these words depressed him.

Although he had been raised as an atheist, Dr. Neff was growing in his understanding of spiritual values. As he was coming to grips with his place in the industry and his emerging religious faith, he had an astounding realization one morning: Network marketing was modeled after Christianity. He frantically wrote down the parallels that he saw, and as he did so, the doubts he was harboring about this industry left him. He knew at that moment that network marketing was an inherently good industry that revolved around helping others help themselves. It

was the act of writing this down that was so beneficial to Dr. Neff. We love his analysis and couldn't have expressed these parallels more eloquently—even though we were both trained as professional theologians! Reading these similarities between network marketing and Christianity, it's easy to understand how they helped to alleviate Dr. Neff's depression. Here's what he wrote:

1. It is very unlikely you'll learn about it unless someone else invites you to see it.
2. You are shown something that initially sounds too good to be true.
3. You are given support for its validity, but mostly through personal stories, and hence your belief is based mostly on faith.
4. You are told that you must first believe before you can experience the incredible benefits.
5. You can measure your belief by the amount of good that goes on around you.
6. You are given a manual to guide you.

7. While you may not understand it at first, you are asked to be teachable and follow those who have already experienced what still lies ahead for you.

8. Along the way, you will encounter difficulties and you will need to ask for assistance.

9. When up, you're asked to help others beneath you; and when down, you're able to get help from above.

10. That assistance will be given in a form that will make you stronger and more self-sufficient.

11. You will not be perfect along the way, but as long as you believe, you will reach your destination.

12. You are asked to delay gratification by putting your own needs aside for the time being so you can help others first.

13. Providing this help will require dedication, persistence and hard work.

14. Do not fear people, but instead offer a hand to them even though many will say they do not need your help.

15. By surrounding yourself with other good people who also carry the same beliefs and commitments, you are protected from negatives that can hurt you.

16. You are invited to come together on a regular basis to renew your vision.

17. As a result, you will learn more about yourself, about others, and about life.

18. In the end, you will have directly or indirectly helped thousands of people to live better lives and move on to a better place.

Network marketing is the great equalizer because it is built on attitude. Charles Swindoll, a minister and bestselling author, wrote, "The longer I live, the more I realize the impact of attitude on life. Attitude, to me, is more important than facts. It is more important than the past, than education, than money, than circumstances, than failures, than successes, than what other people think or say or do. It is more important than appearance, giftedness, or skill. . . .

"The remarkable thing is that we have a choice every day regarding the attitude we will embrace for that day. We cannot change our past; we cannot change the fact that people will act in a certain way. We cannot change the inevitable. The only thing we can do is play on the string we have, and that is our attitude. I'm convinced that life is 10 percent what happens to me and 90 percent how I react to it. And so it is with you. We are in charge of our attitudes."

Programs that support personal growth through attitudinal changes are on the rise. The Edge curriculum, "Increasing Human Effectiveness," and the Pacific Institute's "Investment in Excellence" are

We are 100 percent in control of our own mind-sets.

two such programs. Many of the concepts in this section can be indirectly credited to Lou Tice, who led us to Dr. Albert Bandura, forty-five years a psychologist and arguably the most quoted expert in cognitive strategies for self-mastery and peak performance. It was from Dr. Bandura that we learned the most important new developments in self-efficacy and human potential, which today form the basis of our own personal development curriculum.

Just Believe and Keep Going!

IT seems obvious, but we'll say it anyway: The secret of survival is simply to not give up; the way to avoid despondency is to keep the faith! Of course, they're both true. Life's challenges are essential to our growth. Without them, we would fall into a comfort zone bringing our creativity to a screeching halt. Darrell Moore of Baton Rouge, Louisiana, found this to be the case back in December of 1994 when he and his wife, Mable, faced what he described as the darkest month in their network marketing business. "In August we filed our Letter of Intent (L.O.I.) putting the company on no-

tice that we were planning to pursue an executive status. In September and October we met our qualification goals, but in November, we had to take a grace month. We already had one frontline distributor who had completed his executive qualification the previous September, so we saw December as our do-or-die month in the business. If we didn't make it, we would not only have to start all over again, but we would lose our only executive who would roll past us. We were both worn down to a nub. All we had ever heard was that December was the worst month of the year because you could not get people to do anything but think about the coming holidays.

"Mable spoke to me in a tone of voice that implied we had reached the end of the line. I felt like a doctor in an emergency room who had finally emerged from tending a loved one and said, 'We've done all we can do.' There was my wife, looking forlornly at me, asking, 'So what else can we do now?' The only answer I could come up with was to keep doing what we had been doing and not give up. I believed that hard work, coupled with faith in what we were doing, would carry us through this moment of crisis.

"The very next week, on December 10th, we gained a new frontline distributor, Bryant Miller—of all things, by losing a coin toss in Jackson, Mississippi. Sharing a co-op advertisement with one of our frontline distributors, June Lyle, we flipped a coin to see who would get the first sign-up. June won and sponsored a businessman with a résumé a mile long. We got the next prospect, Bryant, though more than a week passed before he signed up under Mable and me. He was extremely well connected, highly motivated and submitted his L.O.I. that following week. That helped us reach our executive qualification volume for December and saved our business. Today both Bryant Miller and we are still in the business (although the businessman who signed under June is not), moving steadily toward our goals. Faith is the only thing that got us through those trials and kept us going when there appeared to be no end in sight. We had faith in our company, faith in our products, and faith in ourselves. Most of all, we had faith that if we were doing our part and operating from the heart, God would show us the way." He did and brought them out of depression into the Promised Land.

John Cini from Annandale, Virginia, had an extremely short stint in corporate America that ended at age twenty-three. "After two years of college, two years in the Army, and two more years as a computer geek, I discovered I'd never make a fortune working for somebody else. In the last j.o.b. (journey of the broke) I'll ever have, I was running the computers for a car dealership, putting in seventy to eighty-hour weeks for $2,000 a month. I'm no genius, but it didn't take me long to figure out I was worth a lot more than $6 an hour." John wanted his own franchise, but had no capital. He called every ad in several papers, and after looking at many networking companies, found the right company for him. "What was the biggest appeal? The successful people who were making millions in the business were mentors I wanted to emulate. And they were willing to teach me everything they knew! Here was a group of people with integrity, and a company with products that were going to grab significant market share.

"But the problem was that during that first year, I was terrified to talk to anyone about the business. I was shy, lacking confidence in myself, hoping, but not knowing, if this business would work, and feeling extremely inadequate about being so young, inexperienced, and without money. But my sponsor, Barbara Groff-Feldman, believed in me, called me every morning to encourage me to get on the phone and start sharing with others the incredible information I had. Somehow I managed to contact about one hundred people in my first few months. Most laughed at me. I actually only sponsored one of those hundred, and she quit a week later. After six months, I had only made about $1,500 total.

"But an interesting evolution had taken place right in front of me: I had observed Barbara's sponsor go from $4,000 a month when I met her, to over $20,000 a month in that same six-month time span. She was a twenty-six-year-old single mother, Lisa Fairbanks, with a journalism degree and a great attitude, who in twenty-two months went from start up to over $60,000 a month. That made her a legend in our company. And I was fortunate enough to witness everything she did first hand to make that money. You know what I learned? She didn't do anything I couldn't do. She just worked really hard and had complete confidence in the company, the products, and her ability to make millions. So even though I was very ineffective and had almost zero income, my belief level began to explode. That's when my business changed forever: when I believed I could duplicate the success of my mentors.

"In the next year, my income went from a little over $1,100 per month to almost $10,000 a month. And today, nobody believes the story of how I began—shy and broke and ready to quit. But it doesn't matter. Just remember three magic words: 'Keep watching winners!' Today we've helped so many people quit their jobs and go through the same tremendous personal growth. It would have been so easy to quit network marketing, walk away, and say; 'Those deals don't work.' But I have an attitude in my head that I love: when everybody else gives up, that's when I really go to work. And I had great role models to help me maintain my positive focus.

"Looking back, the sacrifices I made in the beginning were tiny compared to the return on my investment. Besides, how else can someone start a business that's profitable in a year or two, with little or no debt, and then consistently make a six-figure income working from home! At age twenty, I spent about $1,000 getting a real estate license that I never used. So risking $1,000 on my company was hardly a gamble. I look back at where I'd be if I could have found the capital to purchase that pizza franchise seven years ago. I might just now be finishing paying off my loan, having lived at the store twenty-four hours a day, and I'd weigh 350 pounds from eating pepperoni pizza all day, with no time for exercise. Instead, I travel the world, have peace of mind and zero headaches, and I can be a Professional Dad for the rest of my life."

At a young age, John has made it to the top of his company—all because he found an abundance of belief instead of the abundance of investment funds that he thought he needed to make his life work. Negative beliefs about ourselves are the only barriers to our success. There's an important lesson to be learned from John: Instead of yielding to depression, simply observe other successful people and recognize that if they can do it, so can you! Keep watching winners and believe in yourself!

Whatever You Do, Just Don't Quit!

JOHN and Patricia Dwyer from New York City began their networking business in August of 1991. Having just signed up, they came home and turned on the television to watch *20/20*. Barbara Walters was interviewing an attorney general by the name of Frank Kelly who vowed to put the very company in which they had just sponsored out of business, claiming it was an illegal pyramid. Absurd as it may sound, what kept them going was the fact that many friends called to make sure they knew about the program airing. What they experienced was similar to the classic joke about the assassination of Abraham Lincoln: "But other than that, how was the play, Mrs. Lincoln?" Fortunately, what stuck with many of their friends was not the attack on the Dwyers' company, but rather Barbara's closing comments ". . . but I hear the products are good."

Patricia continues the story: "With all the publicity, this was not the most enjoyable time to build a business. We could have said 'Yes,' they are right; this is too hard; nobody wants to join our business— and, believe me, they didn't join. As far as they were concerned, it was a pyramid. We felt we might as well quit. No one would blame us! But that would have been a terrible mistake. We would have missed all the great friends that we have enjoyed meeting over the six years of building our international business. One of our turning points was attending the network marketing certification course offered by the University of Illinois at Chicago. It is the first ever of its kind, taught by the Yarnells and Dr. Charles King. We met marketers from so many different MLM companies, making friends with them and coming away knowing with certainty that this industry was going to be the business of the future."

Today Patricia and John have an international business with over 8,000 distributors worldwide. Network marketing has enabled them to get out of their former restaurant business and enjoy the rewards of working together. It has given them unlimited free time as well as financial freedom. They travel the world and support their associates along the way. They are especially grateful that, like so many others who bailed out at that time, they didn't listen to the media exposé attacking their company. Rather, they used their own good judgment, and, in spite of very rough beginnings, just refused to give up! Remember, depression can't win if you are constantly learning, bettering yourself, and associating with other positive people.

Steve and Cynthia Rose of Colorado Springs, Colorado, had a similar experience. They first heard about this industry in 1987 when they were living in Austin, Texas. They were invited to meet Mark Yarnell, who they heard was very successful with an upstart MLM company. Because of busy schedules, they passed on the opportunity. After a series of failed businesses, four years later in 1991, a young attorney and his wife from Albuquerque, New Mexico, again offered them the same opportunity. Hearing that Yarnell was still involved in the industry, and with their backs against the wall, they took a second look. Selling a sofa to gather the cash to buy their starter kit, they took off like a whirlwind only to be thwarted by the same media attacks and

regulatory scrutiny with which the Dwyers had to contend.

Describing the catastrophe, Steve and Cynthia remembered, "We saw our downline of chiropractors, bankers, and businesspeople flee like rats from a sinking ship. While we remained at the helm, our belief in the company and its products grew stronger as we watched the company open international markets, build a ten-story headquarters and warehouse, and introduce a new division through all of the turmoil. All this in the first year of our network marketing experience. After the unfair coverage by the national media, we could not speak the name of our company for several months without defending our company's position and ourselves. What we learned from our experience was invaluable. To be successful in MLM requires a willingness to make internal changes because this is truly a business of transformations, inside and out." Above all else, we must never yield to depressing, outer appearances once we know deep down that our key leaders have integrity and our products or services are beneficial to all.

Jordan Adler of Tempe, Arizona, joined his company in September of 1992 with $36,000 in credit card and IRS debt, a downward-spiraling job, and one broken-down Jeep. "I chose to 'work through' whatever challenges presented themselves. I knew that long-term residual income never came to quitters. Although I knew this, I had this habit of quitting. In fact, I had quit six of the eleven other MLM companies in which I had been involved. The other five went 'belly up' before I had a chance to quit them. I now know that it's not how many times you get knocked down that matters. It's how many times you're willing to get back up that separates the winners from the losers in this business. Some people saw overnight success in me after I joined our company. What they didn't see was the ten previous years of never sponsoring a single rep and failing over and over again.

"In early 1993, I sponsored a friend in Peabody, Massachusetts. After two $1,000 trips to Boston on borrowed money to work with his organization, we built up a group of about thirty representatives. My friend and his buddy had been promoted twice. We were excited. A few months later, I put another airline ticket and rental car on my credit card to do a meeting for them back East. I flew over a thousand miles and drove through a nasty snowstorm to get to the meeting. I couldn't believe it. All the guests 'no-showed' or canceled and my friend and his buddy quit that night and were never seen again. All thirty of their downline quit as a reaction to them. I couldn't revive a single one. Half my group vaporized that cold winter, but the fire still burned in me and I went back to Phoenix and continued to build. Today, my organization has tens of thousands of representatives and continues to grow each month. Failure can't handle persistence, but clearly, persistence always wins in the end." Jordan, a living example of persistence paying off, is now a senior director and top 100 money earner with his company.

All of these stories share one thing in common: When people just like you met their darkest moments, all of which were in their earliest stages of this business, they didn't let the Depression Torpedo sink them. When they were hit by circumstances outside their control, they just

As many as 95 percent of those people who remain in this industry for ten years or longer reach the highest pay levels in their respective companies. Whatever you do, just don't quit!

didn't give up. Throughout the industry it has been observed that, statistically speaking, an enormous percentage of people quit the business in their first year. Of more interest to us, however, is this revealing fact: As many as 95 percent of those people who remain in this industry for ten years or longer reach the highest pay levels in their respective companies. Whatever you do, just don't quit!

SUMMARY

- Network marketing requires an upbeat, enthusiastic person who will in turn attract others seeking their own well-being.

- Attrition is a basic fact in the network marketing industry.

- The disappointment about those who fail to show up at meetings or, worse, those who quit, can be alleviated by putting your energy into approaching a greater number of new prospects.

- Don't waste your energy supporting those who resist you; just think "next!" and move on.

- Work with the people who show an interest and will keep your spirits up.

- If you feel like quitting, call upline for support and encouragement.

- Share your enthusiasm, never your negativity, with your downline.

- In order for professionals to be successful in network marketing, they must be willing to use their reputations and credibility toward building their business. Denying their commitment to their warm markets will only set themselves up for failure.

- These are the reasons to be proud and optimistic about sharing our business with others:

  1   We have the only entrepreneurial home business with no upside limits and no serious downside risks.

2　Total time freedom goes hand in hand with the wealth and prosperity we achieve.

3　By working diligently in the beginning, we can ultimately have a stress-free life. Better to trade in the traditional forty-year plan for a new Four-Year Plan.

4　Recognition and travel await all those who are successful in building a network organization.

5　In our industry, recognition is derived from things in life that truly matter, such as helping people make their lives work.

6　Global travel often involves bonding with new friends and sharing exciting cultural experiences with them—adventures beyond the grasp of those caught in the forty-year plan.

- If you attempt to recruit others while in a state of depression, your efforts will be futile.

- You alone have control over your attitude. If you exercise that control, adjusting your attitude from the inside, then your outward behavior will naturally follow.

- To change your attitude and eliminate depression, we encourage you to:

    1　Avoid watching or reading the news.

    2　Read uplifting books.

    3　Listen to inspiring tapes.

    4　Only speak and think to yourself in a positive, uplifting manner.

    5　Recall positive emotional experiences from the past.

    6　Focus on the future, not on past disappointments that limit your possibilities.

    7　Set goals and use affirmations to reach those goals on a regular basis. Striving to visualize ourselves as we want to be is the first step toward change and growth.

    8   Avoid negative people or at least negotiate with them to avoid acting negatively around you.

- Don't ever give up on your goals.

- An affirmation is a trigger tool—a positive statement of belief, written and repeated as if the goal were already an accomplished fact.

- As you visualize the new—believing ardently that what you visualize is happening to you at that very moment—you gradually begin to shed the old; it is then that change begins to occur.

- As many as 95 percent of those who remain in this industry for ten years or longer, working steadily at building their groups, reach the highest pay level in their respective companies—so just don't quit!

CHAPTER 4

Blocking the False Expectation Tank

Win through integrity rather than exaggeration.

OURS IS AN INDUSTRY THAT has acquired a reputation for producing millionaires. As a result, people feel they've somehow failed if they aren't earning $100,000 a month during their first year. Even worse than this false expectation of premature wealth is the notion promulgated by a number of misguided distributors that success in MLM requires no significant effort and no major time investment. The truth is, this is a work industry. Those of us who have achieved high incomes have applied ourselves diligently to succeed, and we have stayed with it for a number of years. Equally wrong is the idea that you need not do anything except send people to a weekly hotel meeting and the leaders will do all the rest. In those meetings some leaders have been known to indeed do it

all . . . including signing up your prospects for themselves. This is a home-based industry where rewards are commensurate with effort. In this chapter, we will take a close look at what we call the False Expectation Tank by exposing and carefully refuting many of the myths used to recruit unwitting distributors. We will replace them with the actual facts about your first-year efforts.

An Analogy

IMAGINE the following scenario: Basketball superstar Michael Jordan just happens to be sitting in a coffee shop in Chicago where you and a friend have chosen to eat breakfast. You recognize him immediately, of course, but the last thing you want to do is pester him on a Sunday morning. The table next to his is vacant, so you sit at that one to be near him. As you are sitting down, you notice that Michael's two companions are both in wheelchairs. One of them is a paraplegic and the other has a metal brace on his leg—probably indicative of multiple sclerosis or some other muscle disease. They are both in their late teens.

You sit down with your back to Michael, but you're so close you can hear his dialogue. You don't mean to eavesdrop, but you can't help but overhear the conversation.

"Jim, Danny, I know you both may not believe me, but many of us in the NBA earn over $30 million a year because we were willing to pay the price of hard work and countless hours of effort. I started practicing when I was your age, and I never stopped believing that one day I'd make the team. You owe it to yourselves to look at this." Michael, you notice out of the corner of your eye, hands one of the boys a piece of paper.

The adolescent looks at it closely and exclaims, "My God, Mr. Jordan, that's more than my dad made over the past ten years and he's a doctor!"

"I know," responds Michael, "and that's just one month's income!"

"Jimmy, look at this!" Danny says as he stretches just as far as he can across the table to hand him the check.

Jimmy takes one look at the $2.8 million dollar check and shakes his head in utter disbelief. He's never seen this kind of money and can hardly imagine it's possible to earn so much in one month.

As they both continue to stare at the check, Michael then interjects, "And you know what, guys? You can do it too. Why get involved with some menial job when you can get into something with unlimited potential like playing for a pro basketball team?"

You shake your head and glance back quickly to make sure your eyes have not played tricks on you. Nope, they are both in wheelchairs.

He continues: "I'm not saying you won't have it tough—we all did. I was actually cut from my high school team so I understand the pain of failure. But I didn't give up. I practiced and practiced until I could shoot from anywhere on the court and even rip the nets half the time!"

"I've seen you do some remarkable things, Mr. Jordan . . ."

"Yes, Danny, and you can too. I'm not discounting for a minute the difficulties and challenges you'll both face. But I want you to know that you can do anything that you set your mind to do. You really do have unlimited potential, and don't let the fact that you're both confined to wheelchairs keep you from trying. Make me proud. Work hard, give it everything, and one day you too can live the life you want to live, and I know you'll deserve whatever you earn."

Of course, such a scenario could never occur because Michael Jordan knows good and well that those wheelchair-bound adolescents cannot reach the NBA. Impairments of some kind keep millions of people from having the opportunity to rise to the top of virtually every field of endeavor. Physical, educational, intellectual, and experiential handicaps keep most people at the bottom of the traditional corporate pyramids—such as IBM or Coca-Cola. These are the real pyramids in our society, where workers at the bottom are the lowest paid and the first to be let go in times of crisis. While some few move up through the system, no one has a prayer of earning what the man at the top earns, much less of replacing or surpassing him.

Yet, it is conceivable for virtually anyone to reach the top in MLM because there is no challenge that can't be overcome. And every word spoken by Michael Jordan in this hypothetical scene could genuinely be addressed to these two physically handicapped young men regarding the network distribution industry. In MLM, even those who are timid, uneducated, or have no track record of success are often encouraged to believe that they can earn a million dollars a year just like so many leaders in this industry. In network marketing, everyone is given the benefit of the doubt, and has the possibility of transcending the highest earner in the company. There is nothing to hold you back but the limits imposed by your own mind-set.

Having said that, we now want to distinguish between the potential of this business and the reality of what it takes to achieve success. While it's true that everybody, regardless of their handicaps, can achieve upside earnings potential in network marketing, we are concerned about leaders who imply that great success in this business is easy. Sometimes after years of hard effort, all resulting in failure, some people who truly are not cut out for this business continue to be misled that they can still reach the top.

There is nothing to hold you back but the limits imposed by your own mind-set.

There is a place in our industry for everyone, but each will experience success in his or her own way and time, and the level of success can vary immensely. And success need not only be measured in dollars—some will develop solid, lifelong friendships, and that alone makes it worthwhile. Some introverts will come out of their shells and feel they have gained immeasurably by what this industry has done for them. Others will earn a few hundred dollars a month and be thankful that they have something of value to do, and a little spending money besides. Some impoverished ministers will earn $15,000 as early as their fourth month. Most everyone will experience personal growth through this industry and, unquestionably, that is priceless. What better way to achieve such positive outcomes—all from home at such a low cost!

The two of us met each other through this business, and later fell in love and married. If you take everything else away from us, that alone would have made our time in network marketing invaluable. There is nothing of greater significance than finding your soul mate. So, by all means, show prospects the inherent potential of this business, but allow all distributors the right to discover their own levels of success. And by success, we mean having worthwhile goals and taking the necessary steps to achieve them. As long as you are taking a step forward, you are successful.

Balance Upside Potential with the Realistic Picture

INCOMES in MLM can become quite dramatic. We believe that anyone who has reasonable self-confidence, enjoys communicating with small groups of people while sitting at home, is coachable, and has a sincere desire to make a difference in people's lives can potentially earn $100,000 a month. However, it is important to paint a realistic picture of just how much hard work is involved in achieving financial security and time freedom. Too many distributors fail to tell the truth about the necessary effort. A recent advertisement in *USA Today* offered the following description of an MLM opportunity:

No Sales, No Inventory, No monthly quotas,
No Personal or Group Sales Volume requirements,
No meetings, Just call [phone number] to get started.

This ad was intentionally misleading. We called the number to check it out and discovered that while no purchases were mandatory, in order to receive full compensation on several levels, substantial sales volumes were required. Here's the question: If a leader is going to advertise in the business section to find other entrepreneurial leaders interested in big money, why imply that no inventory or monthly sales are necessary? That's not only misleading, it's fraud. And we believe the Federal Trade Commission and other regulatory agencies are correct to go after such marketers and companies. They deceive innocent people into believing that MLM, like the lottery, is getting something for nothing. And in case you think most people are smart enough to avoid such preposterous claims, take a close look at how many men and women bet family food money on a one-in-ten-million-chance lottery.

Let's examine what is required to earn big incomes. Network marketing income is a direct result of the amount of wholesale products and/or services purchased by those individuals in your organization. Since most families only purchase as much as they need and use, a sizeable organization is necessary to provide a large income—lots of people ordering and using a little bit. Huge organizations are developed by individuals who personally recruit large numbers of frontline distributors and, as capable educators, teach them to duplicate their process. Our in-

dustry's leading company built a multi-billion-dollar, global empire one person at a time over a four-decade period. In essence, MLM is much more a teaching profession than a sales profession. Those who make it to the pinnacle of any company are usually good communicators in a one-on-one sense. Being able to deliver a speech to a large crowd is absolutely unnecessary. Duplication is what is critical. It doesn't matter how tremendous we are as individuals, but rather how great we are at teaching others to duplicate our system, as you've already read in many of our stories. But we don't want to create false expectations by waving the oversized checks in front of people without also discussing what it honestly takes to earn them.

Understating the hard work and perseverance to achieve great success is the most often utilized strategy by those who create false expectations. Most people will quickly see through the false promises in a very short time and then quit. We are irrevocably convinced that the extremely high attrition rate among first-year distributors stems directly from being bashed by the False Expectation Tank. In this chapter, we'll take time to address many aspects of this problem, including the one that catches so many newcomers to our industry completely unaware: an unrealistic assessment of how much work is required to earn the huge incomes.

Misguided Belief That This Business Requires No Effort

CONSIDER a hypothetical situation. Steve goes to his first network marketing presentation and is immediately struck by the exponential growth potential. For the very first time in his life, he realizes the possibility of unlimited income. But here is his problem: Even though Steve knows literally hundreds of excellent prospects, he is currently earning $100,000 a year in a management position with a software firm, and is spending as much as he makes. So, the thought of quitting before he has replaced his income is simply irrational. During the question-and-answer period of the presentation, Steve asks if he can stay behind and visit with the presenters, Bill and Angela. Of course they agree to speak with him privately.

After everyone is gone, Steve explains his money situation to the successful couple. Instead of telling Steve the truth, namely, that he is going to have to work very hard for a year full-time, or perhaps for two or three years part-time, in order to replace his income, they create false expectations.

Bill says, "No problem, Steve. You've got a Rolodex full of high-caliber prospects, and Angela and I can work those people for you and then stack them on your frontline."

Of course, that will never work because Bill and Angela already have their hands full building and maintaining their own front line. They might try, but experience has taught us that no one can do this business for anyone else. And we all know that friends respond best to hearing about a business opportunity from friends first. Then, a successful sponsor or upline can reinforce what the curious prospect has learned from his friend. The power of networking is at its highest peak when it is friend telling friend. But Steve cannot possibly know all of that at this stage, having just been introduced to the industry. So to him, it sounds good. Based on what Bill has told him, he signs up, makes a list of his top 200 prospects, and turns it over to his sponsor.

The False Expectation Tank hits Steve hard and fast. It doesn't take very long for him to realize that he is not going to get something for nothing in this business. Even if Bill makes good on his promise and signs up a few quality distributors on Steve's frontline, Steve will still have to roll up his sleeves and work extremely hard or the people beneath him could roll past his pay levels. But what ordinarily happens is that Bill can't convince Steve's friends to do something when Steve is not actually approaching them himself.

Here's the point: Rarely, if ever, has a person in network marketing had the time and energy to recruit, build, and train more than one large front line. We have not met anyone who has done so. Typically, after half a year of little or no activity, Steve quits. But he doesn't really go away. From that day forward, whenever network marketing is mentioned in his presence, Steve remarks, "Yeah, MLM is such a scam. I gave it my best shot for half a year and had a sponsor who was supposedly making big money, but I never saw a penny!" There are thousands of Steves out there bad-mouthing our industry because of unrealistic claims that lead to overblown expectations.

And, unfortunately, there are numerous Bills and Angelas who have been taught to be "sifters" instead of relationship builders. Their underlying motivation is to simply blast through Steve's Rolodex hoping to find one winner, instead of helping Steve build a business based on his close relationships with friends. So, what should have been done? Well, Bill and Angela should have been honest about Steve's chances. Not only would Steve have respected them more, but he would have fully understood how much effort it would take to make the business work for him.

Here's how it should have been handled. Bill sits down with Steve and looks him squarely in the eye. "You know, Steve, I can appreciate your dilemma. I know you still need an income while you grow your business. But if your corporation was to decide to enhance their profit structure by downsizing and you were targeted, they wouldn't even consider keeping you on salary until you found a replacement income. You'd be gone overnight with some severance package designed to placate you but not meet long-term needs. The truth is, in our business, it's only those of us who treat it like a profession who get to the big money. Give it all of your energy and you'll naturally get there sooner. Undertake it part-time, and stay with it steadily, and you'll get there eventually. But there is no way for you to earn big money by exerting only minimal effort, that is, by simply turning all your prospects over to your sponsor."

Steve listens but still doesn't fully understand. He responds, "Well, how do guys like me do this business? How does anyone ever get to the kind of money I've been hearing about?"

"Steve, it's true that many leaders in our industry earn over $50,000 a month and most could afford to retire on that income in half a decade. Compared to retirement on a little pension after forty years in your profession, our offer is very attractive. But I'd be doing you a disservice if I didn't tell you the truth. And

Remember, in the network distribution industry, honesty is everything. Cheat someone at work and eight office workers hear about it. Cheat someone in our industry, and 200,000 people in twenty countries know about it within a week.

the truth is, to hit those numbers, you would have to tighten your belt and do this business full-time. The other option is to work very aggressively part-time until you've replaced your income and then go full-time. If you decide to do it either way, great! Angela and I will work with you side-by-side until you reach your goals. Otherwise, let's just sign you up so your family can use our products and services at wholesale prices and I'll touch base with you again in six months to see if your circumstances have changed."

Can you guess what Steve will do? He's going to go home and give this business serious consideration. He has no illusions about how hard he's going to have to work and, frankly, he respects Bill immensely for his honesty. Bill shot him straight, thereby preventing Steve from being a target of the False Expectation Tank altogether. He's going to carefully think it through: (1) either his future is brighter in network marketing and he is willing to make the gutsy move to live off his savings for six months and give this business his full-time effort; (2) he'll choose to take the precautionary

approach and replace his income first by remaining on his job and working the business part-time, which will take substantially longer; or (3) he'll order some products or services at wholesale and become a good customer. If he chooses against all of these options, at least Bill ends up with a great prospect he can call every six months until the time is right, instead of creating an angry distributor who, because of misinformation, now bad-mouths the entire industry whenever possible.

Remember, in the network distribution industry, honesty is everything. Cheat someone at work and eight office workers will hear about it. Cheat someone in our industry, and 200,000 people in twenty countries know about it within a week. And when an upline distributor deceives a downline distributor, it is not easily forgotten or forgiven. It is the most detestable offense in our business. Think about it in terms of your own company: those who are guilty of cheating others are the most despised people. And the sad part is, no matter how many apologies you make, once it is done, you can never recover. Your reputation within the company is irreconcilably damaged. We've seen it happen in several companies, and it is one of the most easily avoidable tragedies of our business.

Our industry affords us daily opportunities to discover our true worth. There are countless moments when we are faced with situations that require moral decisions. Each one is a personal test of our integrity, and sometimes no one will know but us, but we are challenged more than anyone in any field of endeavor to raise the standards of human values. This integrity must begin with our very first presentations. Tell the truth about your marketing plan and the tremendous amount of work necessary for success. Offer your support, but never offer to do work for a new distributor that you barely have time to accomplish for yourself. The more honest we are about the hard work in our business, the less attrition we will experience and the more respect we will build for our industry.

Unrealistic Assumption About the Numbers Needed to Succeed

BEWARE of the unrealistic assumption about the number of individuals that you need to personally recruit. Some companies have joined with field distributors in an effort to further the myth that you need not be particularly prolific in sponsoring people in order to prosper. Bunk! While there are exceptions, most successful leaders have had to sign up large numbers on their front line.

Most of the truly big-time income earners in the field of network distribution have, over time, personally sponsored at least 100 frontline distributors, and many have sponsored even more. However, there are always some exceptions to this rule, and Michael DiMuccio of Keinburg, Ontario, is one such example. After struggling for thirteen months in one MLM company, Michael found another that had remarkable products with which he could readily identify. This is how he describes his experience after joining the new company.

"During the initial launch phase, I prospected about 100 people and recruited 26 frontline. By placing so much emphasis on the relationship between myself and those 26 recruits, 5 became long-term business partners. Not everyone who signed was as committed as I was or, obviously, they would still be with me. Yet their contribution in the beginning added synergy, excitement, and volume that helped produce my personal success story: $126,000 group volume in the opening month that generated about $15,000 in personal income. This success added fuel to the fire, and the momentum continued over the next three months.

"I didn't recruit for almost a year after this; instead, I put into place an infrastructure for communications and recruiting, and developed a model that could be duplicated for presenting and training. I went back to work by launching Mexico, where I recruited five new legs and produced around $150,000 in the opening month's sales, almost entirely from a cold market. Six months later, my average income had grown to $20,000 per month.

"By this point in time, I had recruited perhaps a total of thirty to thirty-five frontline distributors. I then set my sights on the Quebec market, prospected about forty-five people, and recruited five new legs—two of which have reached a monthly income of about $12,000.

"I then had the good fortune to be referred to a tremendous businessman from Manitoba. Launching his business yielded the highest return yet. Dealing only in a warm market, he recruited twelve of his thirteen prospects, four of which exploded in the first month, followed by two more in the next sixty days. His launch generated a record $219,000 in group volume and netted him $17,900 in personal income. As a result, my income rose to an average $40,000 per month.

"Success breeds success. Now, with relatively little effort, I've sponsored and recruited twelve new legs over the last eighteen months, with four of them averaging $2,000 to $8,000 monthly. At the same time, I helped my leaders expand and took my monthly income up to $100,000.

"Today, at thirty-three years of age, after nearly six years in the business, I've personally sponsored sixty frontline recruits: six of which average a monthly income between $8,000 and $45,000; three take in approximately $2,000 to $4,000 per month; and a few more are just getting started. Many people deserve the real recognition for my success, but suffice to say that I've enjoyed an extraordinary career in an incredible profession." Michael was acknowledged as Distributor of the Year by his company for these outstanding achievements. We are currently developing strategies to make stories like this become the wave of the future in network marketing. As these kinds of ratios become more attainable in our industry, we will see a flood of new associates joining our ranks over the next decade.

Those new to network marketing should have a simple understanding of the four most popular types of compensation plans: the breakaway, the unilevel, the matrix, and the binary. There are other hybrid plans that are a combination of these, but in general, these four are the most widespread. Admittedly, the following explanations are a bit oversimplified, but understanding them in-depth is not necessary for a first-year distributor. Having a basic grasp of these compensation plans is all you'll need for now.

The oldest and most traditional is the breakaway plan. It allows distributors to recruit and be paid on an unlimited number of frontline associates. When leaders emerge by meeting the basic requirements set forth by the company, they "break away" from their upline executives, thereby forming their own organizations. In a breakaway plan, leaders receive a commission on unlimited levels generated by everyone within their own circle volume and, based upon the number of "breakaway" leaders on their frontline, they are paid a commission on a designated number of levels of their breakaway groups. Even though a larger percentage is generally paid on the circle volume, the real money is made in the massive numbers generated in the breakaway groups. Since the emphasis in a breakaway plan is placed on numbers of distributors on your front line, it is difficult to mislead new associates about the fact that it takes lots of sign-ups to receive the full benefit of the compensation plan.

The unilevel plan essentially pays commissions on a specified number of levels—as opposed to generations that can run to depths of twenty or more—as designated by the company. It is comparable to the compensation paid on the circle volume only of the breakaway plan except that it limits the number of levels. A unilevel formula, of course, has no breakaway system, but it is similar in that the only way to make money is to sponsor significant numbers on your front line, thus increasing the chances for greater exponential growth. In the breakaway and unilevel plans, each level beneath you grows larger than the levels above. Your sixth level, for example, should ultimately be larger than the five levels above it combined. So, the larger your front line, the larger your sixth level will ultimately become. Because the unilevel is not as lucrative as other bonus programs, it is more often used in combination with another plan. Again, it is difficult to mislead anyone about the numbers necessary to succeed with the unilevel plan.

The matrix plan is inherently limiting as a compensation plan by its very definition. Let's consider the 3×7 matrix as an example: You are on top and have three on your frontline. Your second level is 9, third is 27, fourth is 81, fifth is 243, sixth is 729, and seventh is 2,187. Your entire organization, if it filled up, would compensate you for a total of 3,279 people. Many leaders have ten to a hundred times that many people in their organizations. It's literally a case of converting an unlimited opportunity into a limited income position. What's worse, it's very difficult for those below you to succeed in this system. Let's pretend that everyone on your seventh level has a sincere desire to succeed in filling up each of their matrix organizations. That would require a company of over two million distributors. The problems now arise, because for people to succeed on that seventh level would require recruiting the equivalent of the entire populations of China, the United States, and Germany.

Disregarding the reality of the matrix plan, the sales pitch still is: "All you have to do is sponsor three! Only three!" The company literature and the entire sales force then promotes the idea that you can be successful in their venture if you only personally sponsor three others. And that's precisely all that most people end up doing, if that. But what we want you to understand is this: Nobody, in any company at any time in our industry's history, has succeeded in earning the truly big checks after personally sponsoring only three or four people. That is false expectation "ad absurdem!" If you are working a matrix plan, be prepared to personally recruit enough associates to fill up your first four or five levels. Do that and you'll

likely prosper. A matrix plan will only work if you do.

The binary plan is the most recent hybrid in the chain of new compensation plans. If you liked the matrix, you'll love the original binary. The premise here is that all you need to do is sponsor two frontline individuals, who are called your "profit centers." Once you've got your two, teach them both to duplicate what you've done, and so on until, poof! You're rich! Not in most cases. It may be perfected in the future but as of the time of this writing, many of the binary plans we've reviewed require distributors to balance the sales volumes of both sides of their organization. And if left on their own, each side tends to grow at radically different paces. Since balanced volumes just don't happen by themselves, distributors need to focus constantly on adding enough quality people to either or both sides in order to keep volumes in balance. Otherwise, distributors are paid only on the lower of the two sides of their binary-shaped organization.

We can already hear the shrieks and screams of matrix and binary companies who don't read this chapter carefully, so please be clear on what we are saying before you react. We've met people who are dramatically successful in every kind of compensation plan in existence and we do not advocate one above the others.

Whether in a breakaway, a unilevel, a matrix, or a binary compensation plan, you must personally recruit, or play a long-term personal role in the recruitment of, a significant number of distributors to be successful. We have heard popular authors and top leaders suggest otherwise. Don't be fooled into believing that you need only sponsor two or three frontline networkers to find your way to unlimited wealth. No matter which compensation plan you choose, success requires lots of hard work.

We do not mean to pass judgment on compensation plans, but rather to caution leaders in a matrix or binary plan against creating false expectations as they present their plan to new prospects. Unrealistic assumptions tend to emerge most often from those plans that limit the number of frontline distributors.

Carol Fitzgerald of Dundee, New York, found herself a victim of false expectations with a brand-new start-up company. She felt doubly deceived because she had networking experience, and in hindsight, felt she should have seen it coming. "I had been working part-time with a large network marketing company for about three years while home-schooling two children. I was a distributor with a large, solid nutritional and household product company. I wasn't shattering any records, but for the time I invested each week, I had a nice income and it had a steady increase each month. My organization was comprised mainly of women who had careers in corporate America but wanted to be able to stay home with their children while still maintaining an income.

"All was progressing well until a friend of mine phoned to tell me about some 'incredible environmental product' that I just had to try. I asked if it was a network marketing company, and explained to her that I was really committed to my present organization and I wasn't interested in working with more than one company. She's very creative and wasn't easily discouraged, as she knew of my current success. My birthday was four days later and a large box arrived, containing a complete sampling of products and a brief explanation of an unbelievable compensation plan. Now I knew why my friend was so excited! The products were great and the money offered was staggering.

"Binary pay plans were brand new. I had been working with a matrix program and didn't know much about binaries. They seemed too good to be true. (Why didn't those warning bells go off?) This was truly an unbelievable opportunity for fast growth and quick cash! It paid weekly: for every $1,000 worth of products sold (with $500 on each leg), $250 was paid out in commissions. Sponsorship didn't matter; there was no limit on depth; and, best of all, volume was never lost, but carried over until a balance was achieved. Typically for this type of plan, distributors were qualified to receive commissions once they had purchased $100 in product and sponsored just two other people who did the same. Distributors could personally purchase up to three positions, there was no age limit, and every one in a household could have their own distributorship. I was hooked. This company had everything! The products truly were revolutionary; they could help the environment; and the money was fantastic. I could help all of my family and friends (who were still friends then). All they had to do was buy $100 worth of these wonderful products, and I could place them in my organization and build under them.

"I dived in head first. I started with three positions, placing my children (great college fund) below me, followed by my husband, parents, in-laws, grandparents, siblings, and everyone I knew. It didn't matter if they had network marketing experience or not, anyone could understand this pay plan and, besides, they were helping the environment. Of course, every one in my group did just what I did. Nearly all of them came in with three positions and encouraged friends and family to do the same. We signed up churches, schools, and other not-for-profit organi-

zations, who in turn rallied all of their supporters. My organization exploded. This was truly what networking was supposed to be.

"My products arrived the second week. We didn't have distributor kits or training manuals yet, so I wrote materials for my group to use. The company liked my tools so they used them corporately. I organized conference calls, and conducted training sessions. The money was rolling in and everyone was thrilled. Then it happened! Delivery of products started being delayed, and checks had mistakes. The principals of the company told me that it was the tremendous growth my group had caused and that it was a good problem to have. I was assured that they were hiring extra staff to clear up the problems. We continued to fax in hundreds and hundreds of applications! But I was concerned enough to start tracking my own organization. I had all of my group fax their applications to me so that I could monitor the growth. I discovered a major discrepancy in what was owed to my people, and immediately jumped on a plane armed with my charts.

"When I arrived, the corporate heads looked at my documentation and were aghast. They 'had no idea the problem was this severe!' They brought their programmers in and decided that they had a programming error and would have to re-

Network marketing is big business played on an international stage offering staggering income potential, enormous amounts of free time, travel, power, and prestige.

enter all of the thousands of applications in order to fix it. Of course, we shouldn't lose momentum, so I was urged to remain positive and keep recruiting. They claimed to have fired the person who was responsible for fouling up product orders, and I was guaranteed that everything would be back on track within two weeks. We kept on recruiting. Even though checks and product orders were sporadic, they seemed to be trying.

"Then came Black Monday. It started when my mail arrived and I found out that my last two checks had been returned for insufficient funds. The phone started to ring and people were no longer 'thrilled.' Hundreds of people had all received the same mail and they all had my phone number. The company phone number had a recorded message saying that it had been disconnected. Reality set in.

"When I finally reached the president of the company, he explained that this situation was 'all my fault.' It seems that they had never planned on someone completely balancing her organization, and worse yet, teaching everyone to do the same. My balanced group had maxed out

the pay plan after only eight levels, and my organization reached more than thirty levels totaling several thousand distributors. The company closed its doors, teaching me a lesson and giving me a birthday present I'll never forget.

"Unfortunately it also left my family and many of my friends with very negative feelings about network marketing that have taken me years to overcome. I still have a copy of my largest 'uncashable' check in my daytimer to remind me that, in network marketing as in any other business, there is no 'get rich quick' program unless someone gets hurt. Slow and steady definitely wins the race." Fortunately, Carol was able to pick up the pieces and is now working with an experienced team toward the launch of a network marketing company that she hopes will be a reflection of what our industry is meant to be. Carol adds, "For any of my friends who may be reading this, flowers, chocolate, or just a simple card make much nicer birthday presents."

The lesson for people just starting out in network marketing is this: Binary plans, by themselves, tend to reflect a short-term cash return as opposed to a long-term, steady, residual income. If you are considering joining a company that is so new it has no track record, at the very least, make certain the principals in the company do have a track . . . a good one. It is very, very risky to join a company that has not been in existence at least a couple of years. If you feel compelled to join, and don't have first-hand knowledge of the integrity of those starting up the company, do your due diligence: check them out, call their references, and if their compensation plan is untested and sounds too good to be true, it probably is. At the very least, call the Direct Selling Association in Washington, D.C., and find out if the company under consideration is a member. If not, watch out!

If you are in your first few years in this industry making a decent living with a solid company, and, like Carol, an overzealous sponsor shows you big checks or a comp plan too good to be true, hopefully, you'll have the common sense to stay where you are. Network marketing is big business played on an international stage offering staggering income potential, enormous amounts of free time, travel, power, and prestige. To hit the big numbers is to be treated like an international rock star playing to large audiences and standing ovations on every continent. You'll be treated to the best cuisine in every location and interact with the most powerful people in industry, medicine, and law. Remember, as you are trying to appeal to various professions in corporate America and throughout the world, each one has its malcontents and frequently the most successful among them are the players who can relate to these kinds of earnings. As you move from your warm market into your cold market prospects, you need to understand that this is a numbers game and not be intimidated by it.

MLM is the "great equalizer" in which former blue-collar workers are allowed to compete with, or even bypass, doctors and corporate leaders. Perhaps from the standpoint of workloads and maybe with respect to the number of people you actually have to sponsor, you were falsely induced into MLM, but no one can truly tell you about the joy of earning five- or six-figure monthly incomes until you yourself experience it. So, don't whine, get to work! What's it going to be—four years or forty?

Inaccurate Perception About the Time Needed to Succeed

THE next problem area—time investment—is certainly worth mentioning because it so often misleads prospective distributors about one of the most important aspects of the business. While we've seen many of our associates reach five-figure monthly incomes in only a few months, ourselves included, not many do. We believe new marketers should set realistic objectives ranging from one-, two- and three-year, to five- and ten-year goals. Then, track upline until you find a person in your company who is earning the amount you wish to earn by your tenth year. Ask that person to help you set realistic goals based on the amount of time and effort they were expending at each of these monthly and yearly mileposts. It's quite reasonable to assume that if another person was able to achieve what you desire, if you can visualize yourself doing that too, and if you are willing to put forth the same amount of time and effort, you can earn the same. An average earnings report can and should be issued by your company. The way to set practical goals is to base them on incomes at varying levels actually earned throughout your existing distributor force. Remember to be realistic about the amount of time it will take, but also be expansive in determining the right goals for yourself. It is by unleashing your limited thinking that you will be able to rise to your full potential.

With respect to the amount of time required to succeed, part-timers in network marketing earn substantially less than do those working the business full-time. If a full-time person is earning $200,000 a month, a new person might quite logically assume that if she works half the time, she could earn $100,000 a month. Not necessarily true! The most Rene ever earned as a serious part-timer—who, because of her elected position to a four-year term in public office, could not quit until she had completed her commitment—was not even 10 percent of the amount we've earned together working full-time. It's because this is largely a business of duplication. Part-timers attract part-timers. If you are the leader and part-time effort is good enough for you, then part-time will seem appropriate to everyone you recruit. On the other hand, if you are working very aggressively, treating this like big business, so too will more members of your downline. Ask yourself a simple question: When was the last time you met a person who became a millionaire in his spare time? Prosperity is a full-time venture.

Our book *Power Multi-Level Marketing* is dedicated to teaching how to build a large, dynamic multi-level marketing

It is by unleashing your limited thinking that you will be able to rise to your full potential.

organization and the inevitable differences between working part-time and full-time. We have researched numerous companies with respect to average part-time and full-time incomes. You simply cannot accomplish full-time goals on part-time effort. Obviously, those who give this business their "all" should arrive at their goals more expediently. If this is an option for you—and if you have six months of staying power on the money you have in savings, then we highly encourage you to carefully select your company, and give it everything you've got.

There has never been a more lucrative time to get involved with this industry, nor has there been better public receptivity to the concept of networking as a viable business. If you believe in yourself, the organization you've joined, your company, and the industry, then simply tell the world of your discovery! That's what Mark did—sometimes putting in sixty- to seventy-hour weeks on fire with enthusiasm—and within three and a half years his efforts earned him his first $100,000 monthly check.

If responsibilities, financial constraints, doubts, or just good, common sense hold you back from beginning this business on a full-time basis, then Rene may be someone for you to emulate. Although only part-time, while serving full-time on the Board of County Commissioners in Reno, Nevada, she treated her network marketing business like a real business. As she explains, "I stayed with a consistent regimen, prospecting twelve to fifteen people every single day, holding a presentation in my home for at least fifteen prospects a week, gathered in two to three separate meetings, all of which resulted in my sponsoring a minimum of five people a month. With extra time invested on the weekends, the number of people I sponsored could sometimes run as high as ten. By never letting up, even though I had a busy professional schedule, I reached $100,000 annual income after one and half years in the business." Consistency is critical, whether you are approaching five or thirty prospects a day.

There is nothing wrong with telling people the possibilities in this industry. The true stories are intrinsically strong in themselves. There is no need to exaggerate, but everyone needs to know the amount of productive time and focused effort we invested to accomplish these goals. We weren't attending someone else's meetings; we were conducting our own. We weren't managing our downlines; we were supporting our frontline associates by helping them close their prospects, and thus building organizations that duplicated our efforts.

Faulty Premise That Upline Will Do It All for You

MANY new distributors are recruited by being told they need not work hard. All they have to do, they are assured, is send their prospects to an upline's hotel meeting, and their sponsor or upline will do the presentations and close everyone for them. But let's get back to the basics—the definition of *networking* is "friends telling friends." But *you* must be involved—talking with your friends, sharing your excitement about this business.

Networking is absolutely no different than telling friends about a good movie or a new restaurant you've discovered. You don't have to be an expert. You don't know who directed the movie or where they went on location to film it. You don't know who choreographed it or who wrote the musical score. You may not even remember most of the actors in the movie. All you know is that you loved it. It made you laugh or cry or just feel good. So you tell people. No one expects you to know everything about it. Based on your word, they will probably go see the movie the next time they are in the mood, just because you recommended it. Hearing about it friend to friend is the essence of

what makes network marketing an effective method of distribution.

But what would you think if a close friend called you and said, "Hi, it's me. I've got a lady on the line who introduced me to a new movie last week. We went and saw the movie and liked it so much that we've both called you. I'd like you to speak with her. She's on the line to answer any questions you might have about the movie because she's seen it more times than I have." Get the picture? There is a place for upline support. It comes *after* they have seen the "movie," that is, *after* they have seen the presentation, when bringing in an authority to help get them involved makes sense. Whether you introduce your prospect through an audio-visual business briefing or an in-home presentation, use your upline to add credibility after the initial exposure.

You don't have to be an authority on MLM or your company or your products to make the initial introduction. Nor do you have to deliver a polished speech or have your upline on the phone with you. Our experience has been that a little less refinement goes a long way in this business. As you share your enthusiasm about what you've learned, particularly at the presentation, you want people to walk away thinking, "I can do that too," not "Wow, what a brilliant presenter she was!"

Steven Friedberg of Parkland, Florida, learned this lesson by being thrown directly into the fire for his first meeting. Believing that his sponsor was going to do his first meeting for him, Steven invited several of his friends and encouraged them to bring a friend. Five minutes before the meeting, with nineteen people gathered in his living room, Steven found out that his sponsor couldn't make it. "At that point I came close to having a massive heart attack, I was so scared. I was sweating so much that my glasses fell off my face. I was shaking so hard that, for the life of me, I couldn't draw a straight line on the board. The meeting that was supposed to last an hour took only nineteen minutes because I had told them everything I knew.

"To make matters worse, someone I had already sponsored filled the empty minutes by taking over the floor, shouting to everyone 'you can do it' while striding from one end of the room to the other. All I could do was pray that the floor would suddenly open up and swallow me, sparing further embarrassment. It was my worst nightmare, until the next day. Three people signed up and my business was off and running." Although we do teach sponsors to do the first couple of meetings for their new associates, this story shows what can happen when people are left

with no options but to go out and, in the words of the great Nike, "just do it!"

This is a business of teamwork. Don't be misled by the false expectation that somehow your upline is supposed to take you by the hand and do everything for you. But at the same time, the reason we are compensated multi-levels is because, as we plant the seeds with our prospects, our upline mentors are there to water those seeds for us. Then, as your people bring in interested prospects, you are there to help close their people for them. It is not a matter of upline doing it all. It's about all of us doing our parts, making the whole organization function as one healthy body. Remember, you don't need colossal support nearly as much as you need to *be* a major support for others. When that sinks in, you'll truly begin your march toward wealth.

But you will argue, "I'm not making the big money yet." It doesn't matter. Most people only need to hear the same thing reinforced—the old one-two punch. If the subject comes up, "How much are you making?" let them know that you are still in the early building stages, but give them the private number of a specific person in your upline who is making big money. Our experience is that only a small number of them will follow through and call. What they really need is to hear that what they've been told is being accomplished by someone beyond their friend, someone to whom they will also have access. But when they do follow through, the big earner needs to be accessible.

Clarification of Retirement

THE definition of *retirement* is "the total withdrawal or separation of oneself, thereby indicating the end of a career." Have you noticed that the topic of retirement comes up at virtually every opportunity meeting conducted by a leader? This is a false expectation often promised and seldom realized in network distribution. This business is just too much fun and can even be conducted by telephone from an easy chair. Many of us use the word *retirement* loosely in our first approach with prospects, but what we mean is that after a certain period of time invested in the business, we can ease up dramatically. At a certain point, we no longer have to spend our lives prospecting people to achieve wealth and independence. But we must find an appropriate means of sustaining our support and accessibility to those who count on us.

When any network marketing company allows vesting, retirement without any further production requirements, few distributors choose to actually retire completely. A real leader makes plenty of time for his family, most often creating a lifestyle that blends quality free time with quality work time. But that leader usually continues to be accessible by telephone and never allows the rumor to circulate in his downline that he has fully retired. That could be a mistake, and should be avoided. But don't allow this retirement issue to disturb you. Here's why.

First, there is no other business in existence that has such universal application but also offers the rewards of network marketing. Not everybody can be an athlete or an actress. Not everyone has the funds to purchase their own franchise. But almost anyone *can* do network distribution on some meaningful scale. And once it's in your blood, it is nearly impossible to do anything else. Twice we've tried to retire and both times we've convinced ourselves that no other productive endeavor is nearly as fun. According to the eminent psychiatrist William Glasser, all of us have two fundamental needs in life: the need to give and receive love, and the need to feel worthwhile to ourselves and others. The two times we cut back considerably, we quickly discovered that we missed the interactions with friends and acquaintances we've made through our business. We soon discovered that recruiting and training new distributors is more fun, challenging, and rewarding than most other productive endeavors. Whatever we tried, we always ended up coming back to network marketing.

Perhaps we're hooked because this industry involves such a variety of experiences. When we write, speak to groups, or work one-on-one with people on the telephone, we are involved in personal growth, marriage counseling, family values, company politics, integrity issues, small businesses, global businesses, and a variety of different cultures from all over the world. The personal goals and entrepreneurial dreams of every single person with whom we interact are of paramount importance to us. Given both of our backgrounds, it has proven impossible to find another profession with such a dramatic impact on so many people.

We don't care how often you've heard about network marketing retirement, the truth is, our downline will always strive to duplicate us and the last thing we want is a downline of retired leaders. Craig Bryson, a major international player in networking, has always warned leaders in this industry about the trickle-down effect: Any company that allows vesting or retirement without any monthly production requirements could eventually destroy itself from the top down. We concur. In fact, many of the top MLM companies

offer 1 or 2 percent of total profits to be shared among its leaders, or, in lieu of that, have created an addendum to their compensation plan that provides its leaders with the incentive to continue being productive. This is not only valuable for the leaders, but also for the downline distributors who tend to duplicate their uplines' activity . . . or lack of it.

Remember, whether you are speaking to groups of five or five hundred, don't dangle the retirement carrot in front of prospects without qualifying it. Better yet, focus on MLM's ability to bring about self-determination in their lives. Most people would be very pleased if they could just spend ten or twenty hours each week at home with their families, hours they currently must spend in the office. Because we love what we do, it is sometimes difficult to know when work stops and play begins. Instead of twelve-hour days, we now spend a few hours in productive work and the rest of the day in activities with our family, playing tennis, snow skiing, paragliding, and reading or writing books.

Because of the freedom allotted us in this business, we are able to take time out to write or teach classes, like the certification course we teach in America and Asia with Dr. Charles King. But our outside work is not limited to network marketing. Mark is currently writing a love story, and Rene is writing a self-help book based on

Think of network marketing not as a career but as a vehicle to help you do the things in life that really matter to you.

her own life experiences. Mark is spending time developing a prison program and Rene is the board chair of a homeless project.

In other words, prospects should be told that they may look forward to unlimited freedom in a very few years—the freedom to do what they want when they want to do it while continuing to act as role models and support to their downline. Think of network marketing not as a career but as a vehicle to help you do the things in life that really matter to you. This explanation is much more in line with what actually occurs in the lives of successful networkers.

Erroneous View That No Product or Service Need Be Sold

NETWORK marketing is the orderly word-of-mouth distribution of products and services directly from the producer to the consumer. As products or services are purchased, the distributors responsible for those orders are compensated through multi-levels in their organization. This is the definition of network marketing and why it is often referred to as Multi-Level Marketing. With this as the very basis of our industry, we find it difficult to understand how anyone can stand before audiences and say, "In our business, you sell zero products. All you need to do is present the compensation plan and sign people up." Of all the false expectations created, this one is the most inaccurate because it denies the very essence of our business and makes government regulators suspicious of the industry.

We understand why some well-intentioned leaders say this, but it doesn't make it any less hurtful to our industry. Network marketing is often avoided by great prospects who fear that they will have to peddle products—lots of them—perhaps even door to door. Some men and women worry that they will actually become door-to-door cosmetic salespeople. To offset that erroneous notion, many aggressive leaders will suggest that new prospects need not sell anything.

The truth is this: Network marketing is about a lot of people using and sharing a little bit of product. For the system to work, each of us must do our part. Our homes should be filled with our products and services. To novices we teach a battle cry: "Just Get Ten!" After personally using the products or services, we insist that our new frontline distributors begin by finding ten customers among their immediate family and close circle of friends. That's all—just ten. Everyone should be responsible for finding ten legitimate retail customers before building a sizeable network organization. It doesn't take months to do this. It can be dealt with in a matter of days, but it must be done before they are ready to begin the more dramatic and lucrative part of the business: recruiting others who will do the same.

Simple math makes it easy to understand the importance of each person creating product movement. If you sign up without ordering or sharing the products with others, you have created zero volume. Duplicate your process and sponsor a hundred people who in turn each sponsor a hundred people, and you can brag to everyone that you have 10,000 people in your organization. The downside is that if they all duplicated your effort, 10,000 times 0 is still 0. There are two kinds of product movement that are up to each of us: personal use and customer orders.

Based on your company's compensation plan, we encourage you to set specific goals and duplicate those throughout your organization. For example, we encourage our distributors to strive for $500 a month of personal sales volume—that includes the personal use of the distributors' immediate family and customer orders from the rest of their family and friends.

For those men and women who are completely business-oriented and simply can't envision conducting product demonstrations and clinics, here is what we suggest. Once you have begun using the products and/or services yourself and have found your ten customers, put all of your energy into prospecting for business builders. As you sit down with small groups of prospects to show them the business presentation, you will inevitably have people who don't sign up to become business builders. However, they may be interested in the products or services your company offers. Without having gone out of your way, or exerted extra energy, you simply service those people as retail consumers. Others will sign up, interested only in getting the products at wholesale. Instead of joining Sam's Club or Costco and paying an annual membership fee, busy consumers are learning that, through our industry, their products and services can be delivered to them directly.

Teach your people who are resistant to product sales how easy it is to create customers out of those prospects who come to the recruiting meetings but decide not to participate in the business. This method appeals to executives and other businesspeople who are intimidated by the fear that they will lose their identity as professionals and be looked upon by their peers as product peddlers or door-to-door salespeople. That's the honest way to address this problem, instead of creating the false expectation that no products or services need be purchased in our business.

Mistaken Belief That Success Can Be Achieved Exclusively Through Retail Sales

STEVE and Jeanette Baack from Portland, Oregon, joined the world of network marketing with no prior business experience. Both were scholar athletes. Steve played professional football with the Detroit Lions for five years, and Jeanette still teaches peak performance aerobics. As they explain, "The attraction for us was big money and free time. We embraced the product line wholeheartedly, but made the fatal mistake in the beginning of not seeking out upline mentors who had

previous success in the business. We built a retail base of more than 100 customers and looked at our check after one year in the business and said, 'There's got to be a better way.' There was! Our new focus was on duplication, keeping it simple, and constantly adding new recruits to the pipeline. Once we instilled these principles into our personal business, it was easy to teach others. When you stay busy looking for people who are at the right place and time in their lives, you don't worry about the ones who say *No*. Today, our life works. We've replaced our NFL income and, more importantly, our time is our own."

So many people come into this business hearing about the upside potential, and believing that all they have to do is sell some products to get to the big money. Not true. Ours is a business of each of us doing our little part of moving products or services. As with Steve and Jeanette, the money comes once you successfully recruit a large downline and duplicate that process.

The Average Person Will Not Be Responsive to Hype

PEOPLE today are much more sophisticated than they were two or three decades ago. We've all been bombarded with millions of slick, Madison Avenue advertising campaigns before we reach adolescence. By the time we reach maturity, we've seen our share of carnival barkers, sales professionals, and pushy, arrogant marketing reps. A twenty-year-old today is more jaded and cynical than a sixty-year-old in 1940. The very last thing people want is a high-pressure pitch on an MLM opportunity. Most people today can smell a rat the minute it emerges, and can easily see through lies and fabrication. Our business already seems too good to be true. There's absolutely no reason to attempt to make it even better with false statements about exaggerated income, early retirement, or zero sales.

We suspect that most professionals avoid our industry because it doesn't make sense that an ordinary person with only a high school degree can become a millionaire in three years with virtually no risk and no capital. When a thinking person is exposed for the very first time to network marketing by a competent leader who simply articulates the facts honestly, one of two things will occur. Either that prospect will walk away shaking her head in total disbelief, or she'll lose sleep for a week from the excitement of our potential earnings and lifestyle. No one need ever exaggerate nor falsely explain our indus-

try again. The facts are sufficient in and of themselves.

Think for just a moment about how preposterous these facts must seem to a prospect who knows very little, if anything, about our industry. Although we all say it in a multitude of diverse ways, here's essentially what we are presenting to people. We are asking them, first of all, to believe that network marketing is much more lucrative than most franchises, yet to begin it costs less than $100 or $200. If the owner of a great franchise like McDonald's earns more than $200,000 a year after having invested $1 million in the franchise, how on earth does an MLM distributor earn $200,000 a month on an investment of a couple hundred dollars? It doesn't compute. The franchise owner has to acquire property and build a large structure, but the network distributor works at home. The franchise owner pays out $10,000 a week to employees. The network marketer needs no employees. For the first six years the franchise owner is nothing more than a shift-change supervisor for a bunch of pimply faced teenagers before he breaks even. In half that time, the multi-level marketer is working twenty-five-hour weeks and thoroughly enjoying her life. We could go on and on *ad infinitum* because the life of a successful network marketer seems preferable to the life of anyone in traditional business. You get the point: MLM seems too good to be true already. There is simply no need for hyperbole.

We urge you to present this business opportunity honestly and professionally. False expectations can literally ruin would-be great distributors. If people are led to believe falsehoods, once they figure out the truth, they quit. We've actually seen people quit while earning over $10,000 a month because someone had filled them with the false notion that they should be earning three times that amount. It sounds ridiculous, but it's absolutely true.

This is the only business in the world in which former blue-collar workers can earn more each month than some pediatric cardiologists do in a year. So why tell folks they can do that in four months? Four years would satisfy most people. Nothing works better to convince a person to join our industry than the following honest dialogue following your presentation:

"You know I think you and your wife would make remarkable partners in this home-based business and I don't want you to go out of here today with false ex-pectations, so please remember my closing comments. This is the most lucrative and fun profession in the world, but it's also the hardest work you'll ever do. This isn't like a lottery and it's certainly no get-rich-quick scheme. But if you are willing to put in long hours and long days for just a few years, you could end up earning over $100,000 a month and enjoying all the free time you've ever imagined. I say it's tough because you may have to prospect a lot of people to find just one who's willing to work. But remember, one good frontline distributor can easily earn you $50,000 a month or more!"

Your prospects will appreciate your honesty, and you'll never be accused of creating false expectations.

Yale-educated lawyer Ray Faltinski, our good friend and cofounder of a major network marketing company, once told us that, by far, the majority of lawsuits and regulatory hand-slapping that has occurred throughout our industry's history has most often resulted from exaggerated claims about income and products. For our children's sake, let's join together and stop these exaggerations, which could pose a significant threat to our industry's longevity. Besides, if we just tell the truth, it already sounds "too good to be true."

SUMMARY

- Don't be misled by false expectations. Success in network marketing takes hard work and persistence.

- There is no one to whom we could *not* present the MLM opportunity as a chance for success, but be cautious to distinguish between the fact that, while everyone *can*, not everyone *will*.

- Along with references to the oversized checks, distributors will also want to discuss the amount of effort required in MLM.

- The more honest we are about the hard work required to succeed, the less attrition we will have and the more respect we will build for the industry.

- Whether in a breakaway, a unilevel, a matrix, or a binary plan, the greater the number of personally sponsored distributors, the larger the income.

- Network marketing is the "great equalizer" in which former blue-collar workers are allowed to compete financially with doctors and corporate CEOs.

- With respect to the time it takes to do this business, set realistic goals based on real achievements of upline distributors or average earnings published by your company.

- Part-time effort will virtually never produce full-time results.

- There is nothing wrong with telling people the uppermost possibilities in this business, but there is no need to exaggerate because the truth is plenty remarkable in itself.

- As you bring others into this business, support them without promising that you will do it all for them.

- *Networking* is "friends telling friends," and it simply won't work unless you are willing to share your enthusiasm with your friends personally.

- There is no better way to get started in the business than to just do it: Set up your first home meeting and begin.

- In network marketing, *retirement* means that we can ease up dramatically, no longer needing to spend our lives prospecting in order to achieve wealth and independence, while still finding an appropriate means of sustaining our support to those who depend on our accessibility.

- Think of networking not as a career but as a vehicle to help you do the things in life that really matter.

- Simply defined, network marketing is the word-of-mouth distribution of products and services for which distributors who are responsible for those orders are compensated throughout multi-levels in their organization.

- Even the most serious business builders are responsible for creating a small customer base, but you will not earn the big money by merely retailing products.

- Network marketing is about a lot of people using and sharing a little bit of product.

- Once you have built a customer base, the rest of your focus can be dedicated to building your organization by duplicating your upline mentor's system and teaching others to do the same.

- Additional customers and wholesale buyers will inevitably come to you as a by-product of your business presentations.

- Network marketing is much more lucrative than most franchises, yet is only a fraction of the investment with no building, no employees, and no time spent away from home.

- False expectations can literally ruin would-be great distributors and destroy the credibility of the entire network marketing industry.

- Be honest and professional when you present network marketing as a business opportunity, and help put an end to the exaggerations that could pose a significant threat to the health and longevity of our industry.

CHAPTER 5

Attacking the Warm List Warhead

Overcome your reluctance to offer a quality lifestyle to family and friends.

THE FIRST SIX MONTHS IN the career of a new distributor are critical. Much like the first six years in the life of a child, the first months in network marketing are formative times. And it is during these impressionable months that patterns of success must be firmly established in each new distributor's mind. Very few people will survive the first year if their first few weeks are misspent, and we believe our industry's high attrition rate can be traced back to seeds of failure sown in these very early stages. Apply what we teach you in this chapter and you are far more likely to find yourself among the first year survivors and thrivers rather than a part of that attrition statistic.

Fundamental to the establishment of a network marketing business is the creation of what we call the "warm list." In fact, it's so critical to success that we've allocated this entire chapter to define, explain, and teach you step-by-step how to utilize your most powerful resource. A "warm list" is a group of individuals from your past and present whom you know well enough that were you to pick up the telephone and call them, they would recognize you once they heard your name.

The value of a warm list is that for the first few months, new distributors are able to speak with people they know, and more importantly, those with whom they would love to forge a lifetime business relationship. Indeed one motive for our recent partnership with other experts in the think tank, consulting firm 21st century Global Trust is to educate network marketers how to prosper in the coming century by focusing on "relationship marketing" rather than merely sifting through huge numbers of prospects. We are currently working on a simple, easily duplicated systyem which will allow many more distributors to capitalize on their own warm market relationships, as opposed to the past process of just "throwing mud on the wall" and hoping some sticks.

Furthermore, it matters little to this group of family and friends that distributors are new or that their presentations are mediocre. By beginning with this inner circle, what we call "warm contacts," new distributors will be prepared to enter the more judgmental world of "cold marketing," attempting to recruit professionals whom they've never met, should they have to do so. That's when approaching large numbers of prospects becomes crucial. Your warm list is what sets you apart from everyone else in the business. It is your edge for success. Without it, your approach to this business is not terribly different from standing on a street corner selling newspapers.

Creating a Large Warm List

THE larger your warm list, the more solidly you will establish your business. By age thirty, social psychologists have noted, the average person literally knows 2,000 people on a first-name basis. One of the first steps for new distributors is to begin making a 2,000-person list of people they know personally. We can hear the gasps and sighs already. Why do we recommend such a large warm list? If distributors are asked to create a 200-person list, they will average sixty or seventy names and feel proud. If they are urged to target ten times this many, they will generally come with hundreds of names and apologize for being short of the goal. Once you are well on your way with your list, select your top twenty-five people, those with whom you would most enjoy being in business. Since we believe so strongly that the warm list is the key to starting every network marketer on the right track, we are going to devote some time to it. We want you to know what objections you will hear and how to overcome them, as well as how to create and use your warm list as a tool for building your business.

Everyone has a warm list, but most don't know how to identify and record the names. Two thousand is a shocking number, but even more shocking is our inability to recall a mere 10 percent of those

The larger your warm list, the more solidly you will establish your business.

acquaintances without a specific triggering device. A triggering device is any list
of people, places, occupations, directories,
or things that allow us to recall people
from our past. At the time we first became
involved with network marketing, we
each had a very extensive warm list and
have since recruited others whose lists
far exceeded ours. We used telephone
directories, old high school yearbooks,
and books of vocations to help us create
lists of several hundred people. The next
section consists of a memory jogger to
help you develop your own warm list.

MEMORY JOGGER TO HELP
MAKE YOUR WARM LIST

Who Do You Know Who(m) . . .

you respect; shows genuine concern for other people; is active in their church;
people always seem to like; does personal counseling (such as church leaders, doctors, lawyers, etc.); is a professional; is in clubs and various group organizations
or active in civic affairs; is in a teaching position in a school or business; deals
with the public (such as police officers, firefighters, mail carriers, city officials); is
in a management, supervisory, consultant, or trainer capacity; is looking for more
out of life; is ambitious, assertive, and "on the go"; is considered a leader; attracts
leaders; has children just starting junior high, high school, or college; has children
with special talents that should be developed; wants to set a good example for
their children to follow; owns a business; holds a very responsible position that is
causing stress and pressure; wants to have freedom; is considering a new profession, changing jobs, or has recently changed jobs; is unable to advance in her job;
has talents but is held back; just started selling or is an experienced direct salesperson; relies on ideas for his livelihood (authors, designers, promoters, advertis-
ers); has never been able to get started or failed in business but still has strong
desires; is going to college, business school, trade school, etc., or just graduated;
was recently married and is just "starting out"; knows everyone in town; has international connections; exudes credibility; is elected to office; works with you
now; you see at the gym; is looking for a job; you play tennis with; you know from

Memory Jogger (continued)

the old neighborhood; appraised your home; already has a great job; takes care of your car; is on your Christmas card list; you take your cleaning to; is your accountant; you do civic work with; does your hair; runs the spa; you see at the copy shop; delivers your mail; seems to change jobs often; did your home repairs; is concerned about her skin and hair; is concerned about his weight; is into sports fitness; wants more time with the family.

Who Are Our Relatives . . .

parents, grandparents, sisters, brothers, aunts, uncles, cousins, children, step-relations.

Who Is Our . . .

mail carrier, newspaper deliverer (parents), dentist, physician, minister, florist, lawyer, insurance agent, accountant, congressional representative, pharmacist, veterinarian, optometrist.

Who Sold Us Our . . .

house, car/tires, television/stereo, fishing license, hunting license, suit, tie, shoes, business cards, wedding rings, eyeglasses/contacts, vacuum cleaner, boat, camper, motorcycle, bicycle, living room furniture, air conditioner, kitchen appliances, lawnmower, luggage, Avon products, Tupperware, carpet.

Do You Know Someone Who . . .

lives next door/across the street; is my spouse's barber/hairdresser; teaches our children at school; was best man/usher/maid of honor/bridesmaid; was the photographer who took our wedding pictures; is the purchasing agent where I work; is the finance director at school; goes hunting or fishing with me; was my Army/Navy buddy; is the architect who drew up house plans; goes bowling with me/us; is president of the PTA; was my spouse's college fraternity brother/sister; we met camping; is the credit manager of the store where I shop; is my spouse's old high school teacher/principal; repaired my television; upholstered my couch; we knew on our old jobs; went with us to the races; is in my car pool; installed our telephone; has a laundromat; teaches ceramics; owns a taxi service; cuts the grass (parents); painted the house; owns the pet shop where I bought our dog; installed our refrigerator; renewed my driver's license; owns an apartment, is in Rotary/ Lions/Kiwanis with me; is Jaycee president; plays bridge with me/us; is in garden club; is in book club; is my child's kindergarten teacher; is a deacon in my church; owns a slipcover and drapery business; manages an athletic club; gave me a speeding/parking ticket; does our income tax; cleans our clothes; hung our wall-paper; taught our children Driver's Education this summer; works with the rescue squad; owns beach/mountain cottage where we vacationed; sells us gasoline and services our car; sold my wife her wig; owns a nursery; delivers parcels; works with an exterminator/pest company; stores my wife's winter coat; sells ice cream in the neighborhood; owns and manages the jewelry store downtown; sells aluminum awnings; works for the travel agency.

Who Do You Know Who Is a Professional . . .

nurse; golf pro; student; fashion model; security guard; sheriff; fire chief; secretary; welder; crane operator; candy salesperson; police detective; music teacher; art instructor; typesetter; forester; seamstress; carpenter; pilot/steward; mobile home salesperson; bank cashier/teller; tailor; garage mechanic; editor; lab technician; restaurateur; PBX operator; social worker; lifeguard; race car driver; paper mill worker; brick mason; draftsperson; printer; officer manager; bakery owner; plant supervisor; dietitian; mechanic; anesthetist; surgeon; librarian; mortician; missionary; real estate agent; railroad ticket agent; newspaper press operator; bulldozer operator; bus driver; airline ticket agent; computer programmer; motor home dealer; business machines salesperson; soft drink distributor; air traffic controller; interior decorator; swimming teacher; typewriter salesperson; grocery store owner; insurance adjuster; warehouse manager; moving van operator; rent-a-car representative; professional baseball player; professional basketball player; professional football player; television anchor/producer; tool-and-die maker; cookware salesperson; dance instructor; sawmill operator; industrial engineer; research technician; telephone lineperson; lithographer; fisherman; bench machinist; waiter/waitress; furniture dealer; notary public; farmer; actor/actress; land clearer; horse trader; statistician; cement finisher; antique dealer; brewery salesperson; engineer; contractor; chiropractor; podiatrist; auctioneer; electrician; dental hygienist; shoe repairman; physical therapist; motel owner/manager; highway patrol officer; judge.

Take the time and use the resources to develop your list. All new distributors should sit down in a quiet room with several triggering devices and attempt to create a warm list of 2,000 people. It should take two or three days to get a good start and, by the end of the first month, you should be well on your way to hitting the target. You will never regret starting your business with this tool. Network marketing, by its very nature, requires you to talk to large numbers of people. The longer your warm list, the better your chances for success.

The Warm List Warhead Strikes

GENERALLY, the Warm List Warhead strikes after you have given this assignment to your new associates—this is when arguments between sponsors and new distributors first begin. Sometimes objections aren't even verbalized because your new associates would often rather keep them to themselves. Most new network marketers are able to come up with a dozen good reasons why they don't know 2,000 prospects and why they can't possibly "go after" friends and family first. We've heard all the arguments over the years and none of them are valid. It is vital to the success of your newest distributors that they not ignore this warm market phase of the business.

Let's review a few of the rationalizations and excuses used by new distributors so that you know how to respond to them in this first stage of recruiting. And remember, not all new associates will be honest with their sponsors and declare that they have no intention of working with their warm market list. There are many reasons people are inclined to hold back from calling on their families and friends. And it is this resistance we are referring to when we talk about watching out for the Warm List Warhead. When it strikes, it can be a killer of many would-be great distributors.

First Warhead: Lack of Conviction

Network marketing is the process of sharing one's belief in a marketing concept that is so unique and about which you are so enthusiastic that you can't hold it inside. You lose sleep at night. You can hardly wait to tell people of your discovery. When this level of conviction is lacking, people tend to hold back. It's a Catch-22. If you wait for the belief level to come, you run the risk of missing the opportunity. If you try to go forward without it, your friends can hear the reservation in your voice. So first do your best to try to work through whatever reservation is holding you back: "It just sounds too good to be true"; "Maybe it has worked for others, but I can't be sure that it will work for me"; "What if I'm wrong and I mislead my friends?" Discuss these concerns with someone in your upline whom you trust.

Whatever you do, don't make the mistake of waiting to share your discovery with friends. A common excuse is: "I don't want to call my friends until after I'm making the money." Of course, the solution is to rely on the support of your upline leaders, those who have a track record of success in the business. It is that team approach that makes network marketing so effective. What happened to Mimi Joy Swenson of Los Gatos, California, can happen to you if you use this excuse. Mimi Joy explains, "I was building my business part-time my first year and had made my list of 2,000 names. I felt like I just had to create sections on my list, and one of those categories was called my 'chicken list.' These were names of people whom I felt were already successful in their present jobs and with whom I had better wait to speak until I was more educated, making more money, and working this business full-time.

"I was attending a company function in San Francisco and, as I walked into the gathering, I experienced a scary vision. I saw the person who was number one on my chicken list. I calmly walked over thinking to myself that he was probably just there as a guest of someone. 'Hello, funny meeting you here . . . by the way, why are you here?' I asked him, puzzled. He proclaimed, 'I have just recently been introduced to this great opportunity and have made the decision to build the business and replace my income!' I proceeded to turn a deep shade of green/yellow and gulped, saying, 'Well, isn't that just wonderful. I know you will be very successful.' I wished him luck and like a sad, hurt lil' puppy, I moped to the back of the room to find a seat. I got myself situated but was feeling quite sick. As the meeting began I noticed the woman principal at our daughter's school . . . and she wasn't even *on* my list! The moral of this story for me is to never, ever pre-judge people for this business because they could end up sitting right in the same room with you at your next meeting!" Having learned the importance of working with those on her warm list, and not letting anything hold her back from calling them, Mimi Joy has now made it more than half way to the top of her compensation plan, loving the work and lifestyle of a network marketer.

Until your belief level is 1,000 percent, you might try this script when you approach those on your warm list:

"I've just gotten involved in a new business that has me so intrigued I just had to tell you. There are people making more money in a month than most make in a year, but what got my attention was the lifestyle. They are all working out of their homes, and at their own pace, and creating an ongoing, residual income that is staggering to me. I don't know if this is for real, but I can't stop thinking about it. When I saw the caliber of people coming into it, I thought of you and your [wife/husband] right away. I can't think of two people I'd rather be in business with. Besides, you two know everyone in this community, and they all respect you so much. I really think I'm on to something, but I'd like you both to look at it and tell me if I'm crazy. A few close friends are coming over Wednesday night and I would love to have you both join me so I can show you exactly how this works. Or would Thursday during the day be better for you? I really value your opinion."

Until you have replaced your income in this business, it is understandable that you may have some reservations. But don't try to solve the problem by avoiding your warm list. Approaching strangers is much more difficult than reaching out to your family, friends, and acquaintances. Find the words that are comfortable for you, but whatever you do, begin calling those on your warm list. You want to be in business with those people you most enjoy because your network organization is for life. So approach your favorite twenty-five people first. If you let your doubts stand in the way of beginning your business, you are guaranteed to fail. If you can find a way to go forward with honesty, you may succeed. Believe us when we say, "With success comes conviction."

Second Warhead:
Lack of Self-Esteem

Many people avoid their warm market because of their poor self-image. It's a delicate issue, and one that must be approached with sensitivity. Some people do not feel that their friends and relatives respect them. In fact, many people believe that the friends they approach will laugh at them and ridicule them for attempting to be an entrepreneur.

Let's look at a classic scenario: Bob is a bus driver who loves to play poker on the weekends, and he belongs to three different groups of men who also love to play cards. As Bob makes out his warm list, he writes down the names of twelve men whom he knows well from the poker clubs. The only problem is that Bob is lowest on the socio-economic totem pole. The other men are white-collar professionals and while they respect Bob's skill as a poker player, Bob just naturally assumes that they wouldn't consider listening to him about a business deal. But Bob is totally wrong. Unless you address this issue in general terms during training, Bob will not approach those men. Here's what we suggest you say because there will always be someone similar to Bob in your group:

"Folks, the biggest challenge you're going to face just as soon as you succeed in this business will be the anger of people to whom you never even showed this opportunity. You may have a group of friends, even physicians and attorneys, whom you're afraid to approach. But they won't be your friends any more when they find out that you got involved with a business that's now paying you $30,000 a month, while they're still going into an office sixty hours every week. Why would they be upset with you? Because you didn't think enough of them to show them this business. If they do resist even attending your presentation, tell them right up front that it's their choice whether they get involved or not. But you wanted to make absolutely sure that they won't turn on you in a year because you didn't give them a chance to see this opportunity as soon as you knew about it."

Notice the strategy here. We keep it a soft approach and refer to professions like law or medicine. Most everyone who isn't a lawyer or doctor looks up to those professionals. And in our business it's really not uncommon for a student or maid to sponsor an accountant or CEO of a corporation. On a scale of 1 to 10, if you think of yourself as a 5, once you sponsor a 10 into this business, you become a 10. Move past your comfort zone and offer everyone on your list this opportunity. The truth is this: We are all 10s in potential, we just need to seriously buckle down and recruit as many frontline distributors as we can. Don't let this Warm List Warhead hold you back.

Third Warhead:
Fear of Losing Credibility

As more professionals enter the network distribution industry, it is natural that they will want to postpone acknowledging their participation until the time is right. For example, some will pretend that it's their wives' business. The problem is that if you're a professional and people sense your doubts or uncertainty about the industry, they will also be suspicious. Some will choose not to join and others will join but build through someone else, such as their spouse. But the reality is that once someone of stature has joined our industry, the floodgates start opening for everyone. And more often than not, it's the ordinary, everyday people who make it to the pinnacle, not the "big hitters" of traditional business, law, or medicine, though they certainly can earn enormous wealth while pushing their sponsors into the stratosphere.

We can relate countless stories of people who have failed at this business because they were afraid to let their peers know how very serious they were about building a networking organization. One story goes back to 1990, when Rene sponsored a couple, Susan and Richard, from the San Francisco Bay area. She was a corporate executive on maternity leave, highly motivated because she wanted to stay home with her baby and not return to the office. Susan was a competent, organized, self-starter. Richard was a high-level salesman for a food manufacturer who admitted that he was no longer excited by his job, even though he was well established with a Fortune 500 company that was strong in the global marketplace. Richard was concerned about how his reputation among his corporate peers might suffer by joining network marketing. He could not afford to have his boss learn of his involvement, which he felt might result in him losing his job before their network marketing business actually began generating a good income.

Richard played it safe by providing his wife with leads from among carefully selected business associates and trusted acquaintances. He had the utmost faith in his wife's ability to do this business and to professionally handle his best prospects.

The problem was that *his* associates knew *him* and trusted *his* judgment and insights about a business opportunity, and they didn't really know his wife. She spent months calling up his leads and doing presentations for them. He was even present at some of her business meetings. But because of his fear of losing his professional credibility, he never openly admitted that he believed in the business hook, line, and sinker. He never let prospects know that at some point in the future, he was planning to give this his full-time effort. He continued to portray the image that this was entirely *her* business and that he avidly supported *her* in it.

After a year, she had sponsored a few of her girlfriends, a couple of guys she knew from work, and a few of the wives of her husband's business associates. But their business never really took off as they had expected. Susan and Richard ultimately slipped from business building into merely product wholesale buying and she eventually went back to work. Both of them were disillusioned about network marketing. Rene was developing a close personal relationship with both of them and knew that, if any two people could succeed in this industry, they were Susan and Richard. They had the connections, the motivation, the innate ability, and the respect of their friends and associates. Susan obviously felt that if she could not make her MLM business work, none of her family and friends could either. But it was the fear of losing his job and professional reputation that held Richard back from participating in the business with Susan. The fear of something that may never have happened destroyed the possibility of their success.

The lesson here is that whoever knows the warm list prospect best should make the call. Prospecting the other way certainly put Susan into a funk because she didn't understand what had happened. She just assumed that she wasn't a self-starter. She, who had been one of the top women earners in corporate America, had failed in her own networking business. She was depressed and Rene had little ability to fix it, change it, or help her understand it. Rene was only two years in the industry at that time and could not pinpoint the problem. But, in hindsight, there is no doubt in Rene's mind that if she had coached Richard to put himself and his reputation on the line with this business, he and Susan would be two of the top earners in the industry today. They had phenomenal potential. They would have been great working side-by-side. This fear of lost credibility holds back countless new distributors in our industry. As leaders, we must not be afraid. Once we are absolutely convinced of their potential, we need to encourage men and women to take a stand and go for it all the way!

We don't mean to undermine the very real fear that exists in starting a new venture. It is a legitimate one. Why burn the bridge that currently supports you before you know whether the new bridge you are building will hold up through storms and outer pressures? The solution is in what we call "balanced risk-taking." If you don't let prospects know how completely and totally convinced you are about this industry and your company, you will fail. That is for sure. On the other hand, if you flaunt your new business around the office, you could lose your job and your source of income before you have replaced it. Somewhere in between is the answer. Unless you have sizeable savings, you may have to postpone sponsoring your boss if he is someone who would be truly threatened by your outside business involvement. You may even have to put off sponsoring everyone in your immediate environment. But there are plenty of other current clients, former clients, and sideline associates who would be interested and/or know other people who might be interested to hear about a business opportunity that creates personal freedom and financial security. With these people, don't hold back. Prospects need to know that you are a believer. Let them know, in no uncertain terms, the depth and breadth of your conviction about the power of this type of business to transform your life and theirs. Encourage husbands like Richard to state at each meeting their ultimate intention to do this business full-time, and soon.

Steve Sledge of Dallas, Texas, is someone who took the risk of losing his professional credibility. He and his wife, Caroline, joined this business about the same time as Susan and Richard, but they worked it as a couple, putting everything on the line. In Steve's own words, "I showed one of my former real estate colleagues the power of network marketing, the huge expanding markets in which we were positioned, the honesty of my company and the potential of the compensation plan, and he wasn't interested. He asked how I could bring myself to do something so 'unprofessional.' I was 1,000 percent convinced that I had hold of the financial opportunity of the century and answered him this way: 'Bill,' I said, 'If I'm wrong, I'll fail and you can tell everyone that Steve failed in that silly pyramid deal. On the other hand, if I'm right . . . I'm rich. What story will you tell them then?'" The operative words were "1,000 percent convinced." Steve was and Richard wasn't. But even if Richard had been convinced, he was unwilling to share that fact with his associates, and therein lies the difference. Today, Steve and Caroline enjoy being at the top of their compensation plan with many successful leaders in their organization. It's now a global organization spanning a dozen countries, but it began as a simple conviction in their hearts that was unchangeable, and succeeded because both were willing to say so.

They made it to the top by their shared willingness to do whatever it took to make their business work. During the early days, even though they were long on commitment, they were short on finances. To make ends meet, Steve actually threw a newspaper route in an exclusive subdivision near their home early each morning to earn extra money. He claimed he was so excited about his business that he couldn't sleep anyway. As Steve recalls the story, "I laugh when I remember the look on peoples' faces when, because sometimes I was a little late, they were waiting in their front yards as I flew by in my gold Mercedes and they suddenly saw a newspaper come flying out through the sunroof. Little did they know that their 'paperboy' would, within only a few years, build a worldwide business from his home that would earn him in excess of $1 million."

Fourth Warhead: Embarrassment from Prior Failure in MLM

Another more common reason people will use to justify not approaching warm market leads is embarrassment. They are mortified because they've already been in three MLM deals and they can't stand the thought of approaching their family and close friends a fourth time. It's actually a legitimate concern. It's human nature, but it's not sufficient justification. Because some people have been involved in several companies, they now have one of the best approaches possible. Here's the basic dialogue we teach our new distributors who are concerned about this problem. After a bit of small talk, they then share this information with warm market prospects:

"You and your wife know that I've been researching the field of MLM quite carefully. In fact, in an effort to become extremely knowledgeable, over the last few years I have enrolled in several different companies in order to learn from the different experts. Well, I'm happy to tell you that all the analysis finally paid off. I've been able to master enough about the industry to pick the global organization that allows people to earn $30,000 to $50,000 a month in the shortest amount of time. I've spent a lot of time, money, and energy doing my homework and now I'm so excited I seem to be losing sleep every night. I need to see you as soon as possible to find out if you would be interested in earning this kind of money."

Instead of portraying your past involvement or your new distributors' past involvement as a liability, turn it into an asset! Wouldn't you much rather purchase life insurance, or an automobile, or actually anything from someone who has had the broad experience of representing more than one company? If this is your situation, then be sure to use this strategy to approach the people in your warm market.

Fifth Warhead: Qualifying the Leads

There is a critical difference between traditional business and MLM. Traditional sales and marketing reps are taught to always qualify their prospects. For example, a Xerox rep wouldn't attempt to sell a $3.5 million laser printer to a company that didn't need it or couldn't afford it. To qualify a prospect is to determine, before an attempted sale, if indeed that prospect both needs and can afford your product or service. But we call MLM the "great equalizer" because anyone can achieve staggering levels of success. To decide in advance that one person is too important to be approached about your business, or another is too inadequate to succeed, can literally be economic suicide. Do not, under any circumstance, attempt to determine in advance who is qualified and who is not, who may be interested and who will not be, who is approachable and who is not.

> To decide in advance that one person is too important to be approached about your business, or another is too inadequate to succeed, can literally be economic suicide.

Consider one of the most successful distributor teams: Tom and Terry Hill. Terry left the corporate world as the number one Xerox salesperson in all of North America. She was an expert at qualifying her leads. Tom was a stockbroker for Merrill Lynch. During their first year in network marketing, they had to break a lot of old habits by not qualifying their leads. What finally drove it home for them was when, early in their networking career, they held an opportunity meeting in their home. During the showing of the video, both Tom and Terry left the room (a no-no in the business). When the video was over, one gentleman came down to their office and said, "Thank you, but the business is not for me. I appreciate your time." As he turned to leave, he put his head back in the office and whispered, "By the way, the other guy is asleep." Tom went in and turned the video off and the man woke up. As Tom thanked him for coming and started to hand him some information, the prospect stood up and said with the utmost enthusiasm, "This sounds incredible. I'm in!"

When the timing is right in someone's life, it is right, no matter how wrong everything seems. Even an unconscious man can evidently become excited. Today, this distributor has hundreds of distributors under him in both the United States and Australia. He is one of the strong legs in the organization built by Tom and Terry, who have now sold their MLM business and moved their family to a small town in Tennessee. After all those years in the corporate world, they both feel extremely fortunate to have left the stress behind. Now they both have the time and money to live the laid-back life they have always wanted.

Another one of our frontline distributors was a college student earning $800 a month as a student teacher. His brother David was a detective investigating hit-and-run accidents in Houston, Texas. We are, of course, referring to Dennis and David Clifton, two of the real legends in the network marketing industry. They joined the business along with Dennis's father-in-law, scholar and theologian Dr. Roy Blizzard, Jr. All three men and their wives have become multimillionaires and respected industry leaders. The brothers often tell the story that when they came into the business, no one rolled out the red carpet. The company president didn't call and welcome them into the company anticipating that they were a couple of "big hitters." They were just a graduate student and a cop. They were scared, and their wives were petrified. David's wife, Jackie, was fully aware that her husband only had to put in thirteen more years in order to have full vesting in a $17,000-a-year pension program. What intelligent wife like Jackie wants to walk away from that kind of security? Everyone starts out in network marketing as a "little hitter." Big hitters are team-made and are recognized as such by their results. The proof is in the printout.

Dennis and David are quite literally two of the most sought after speakers in the entire network distribution industry today. Yet before they entered network marketing, neither could have even gotten a job interview with Exxon or Sony because neither had a business education or former experience in management. Today, they manage an international organization of more than 100,000 distributors in twenty countries and account for over half of our MLM income.

We could go on listing other distributors who had no previous success prior to MLM, but these stories should make our point. Don't play God. Even if a man or woman has a menial job, don't assume that they are incapable of building a large dynamic organization. On the other hand, don't assume that because one of your friends is a doctor, MLM would be beneath him or her. Many doctors may be in a state of mind where they detest the practice of medicine and are looking for an alternate way to make the same amount of money. Whatever you do, don't succumb to this Warm List Warhead: Don't make the mistake of qualifying your leads.

Sixth Warhead: Conflict of Interest

Some professionals hold back in building their network marketing business because they are concerned about conflicts of interest. As a minister, Mark was afraid it would be a conflict for him to approach individuals in his congregation. Rene was a County Commissioner and afraid to approach her constituents. Since this was a large part of our world, it put a serious restriction on prospecting our warm markets. So we understand that this is a legitimate concern. It can even be a question of ethics. Whatever you do, you do not want to jeopardize your present career. *You* want to decide when you are leaving your profession. You don't want it decided for you.

We have two suggestions that may help. First, when you are on the job, never mention the name of your particular network marketing company, but prospect through "lifestyling." That is, approach people through the normal course of your life—clients; customers; store clerks; people at the health club, the bank, the grocery store—complimenting them about the personality trait that drew you to them (make it genuine). Let them know that, with that quality, they could be outstanding in your business and are exactly the kind of people with whom you are looking to partner. Tell them up front that you cannot discuss the matter there (say, for example, "This isn't the place" or "It's against company policy"), but that you would like to find a time that would be good for both of you. Then ask permission to call them. Exchange business cards, and write on the back of theirs the best time to reach them. This is the method Rene used extensively, and it was very effective for her. By handling the situation straightforwardly, few constituents ever complained about her having a conflict.

If that method doesn't work for you, you might consider Mark's approach. He never did approach his congregation, but he recruited one couple from the church who did. And they used his name for credibility.

Target Marketing

YOU may want to consider prioritizing your warm list by using target marketing, which involves focusing your prospecting efforts on selected groups of people within your inner circle of influence who have a potential interest either in (1) the business opportunity, part-time/replacement income, and/or tax deductions; or (2) your product and its specific benefits to them.

The research of Dr. Charles King offers us an example of target marketing: An aerobics instructor at a health center introduced her line of vitamin supplements to members of her aerobics class, all upper-middle income, thirty- to fifty-year-olds. Based on the shared demographics and interests in healthfulness, physical fitness, and exercise, several of the class adopted the products. Within six months, the instructor had a customer base of over sixty regular retail buyers. Some of the customers later became distributors in order to buy products at wholesale or develop their own businesses. Based on her "formula" for target marketing in health clubs, the instructor continued meeting with aerobics instructors from other area health centers. She introduced the concept, sponsored the individuals into her downline group, and trained them to develop their organizations by duplicating this process. Of course, if your goal is to build a huge international business, the key to success in target marketing is to focus on several groups with whom you have rapport, and not put all of your energy into just one.

When to Use Three-Way Calling

LET'S assume that you are convinced of the importance of calling the people on your warm list. So what happens next? How does this team approach work? Three-way calling can be a valuable tool, as long as it is used at the appropriate time.

Most prospects will hate the idea of three-way calls *prior to* a personal presentation. If they know they're going to have to suffer the indignity of making their first call to their family and closest friends with their sponsor (even if they are very close friends), they literally refuse to go any further than purchasing their starter kits. That's why in our collective twenty years, we have always avoided three-way calling as a first contact with a prospect. The new distributor is actually right to want to avoid this strategy.

Think about it intelligently. Does a professional or corporate executive really

need to gang up on his friends—that's precisely how it appears to the prospect. If a distributor can't even pick up his own telephone and get his family and friends to a meeting, or review an audio-visual presentation in the privacy of their own homes, that person probably does not have what it takes to succeed in network marketing. Period. End of story. Once trained, your new distributors should always be allowed the courtesy of talking to their closest friends and family without the presence of some hyped-up sponsor trying to overcome objections and prove how brilliant she is to her new distributor. Three-way calling, at this stage, is a very unnatural way of networking. Besides, when the business is presented properly in the initial approach, there should be no serious objections to overcome. If there are a lot, that person is not a prospect anyway. Call him or her again in six months. Don't badger them with your upline on the other extension. The only way this could be helpful is if your sponsor is listening silently on the line during your first few calls in order to offer some constructive criticism afterward.

The best time for three-way calls is *after* a prospect has seen the presentation. It is most effective *after* someone has been exposed to the concepts of network marketing, likes what he or she has heard but still has some reservations—this is the best time to bring an upline associate into the mix. Here's a sample script of what you might say to a serious prospect: "You are asking some really good questions, and as I told you, I'm new to all this. But my business associate has been at this longer than I. Let me see if I can get him on the phone with us right now." You simply press your conference button on your telephone, dial your sponsor or upline, and press the button again—and bingo, you have an instant three-way call. Or if you prefer, give out the private number of your upline to your prospect, and let him or her call when it is convenient. Serious prospects will make that call.

There are advantages to each of these strategies. The three-way conference call allows your new associate to learn by hearing how a prospect is "closed." It also reinforces your new associate's belief in the business. This is sometimes quite helpful to a new network marketer. The two-way direct call from prospect to upline offers more flexible scheduling, and sorts out a serious prospect from a lukewarm one. Just taking the initiative to call shows a certain eagerness for the business. Mark prefers the direct call. Rene is more comfortable with the three-way call. Just be sure to use them appropriately—that is, never until after a full presentation has been made to the prospect or your audio-visual business briefing has been reviewed.

Using a Follow-Up Card File

NOW, we'll share the most important tools for building and maintaining a warm list. Pay attention to this advice, follow it without deviation, and you'll likely wind up among the big-money earners. In a very short time, this method will enable you to have more prospects than you have time to call.

Purchase a twelve-inch-long card file cabinet. In addition, purchase twelve dividers, one for each month and thirty-one numbered dividers for each day of every month. Index card dividers can be purchased already labeled and numbered. Then purchase several hundred index cards and write the name of one warm market prospect at the top of each card. Next to each name, write his or her telephone number. Beneath the name on the left-hand side of the card, write the heading words "date last contacted." On the right-hand side, write "actions and results." Every time you obtain any person's name and telephone number, especially new people you've just met or prospected, create a new card. Of course, for computer buffs, there are software programs for organizing and following up on leads. What matters is that you have a system for keeping track of your prospects.

Now for the critical system: From that point forward, you are going to call every single person on your prospect cards every six months until they either sign up or die. *Never, ever* are you to throw away leads until they become distributors or you attend their funerals. As you speak with your prospects and they tell you all the reasons why this isn't a good time to get together, politely ask them if you can contact them at a later date. They'll almost always say *Yes.* Move the index card to that month in your follow-up file. The day-by-day dividers are, of course, used in the current month. Some people will need a follow-up in two days. Or if you fail to reach some people, you should put their cards in the next day's file.

The average full-time worker in any field in America, Europe, and Asia will change jobs every 3.7 years. Try to contact prospects every six months. No matter how adamantly they rejected you previously, eventually you are going to catch them during a period of job transition. If presented properly to people during those inevitable transitions, network marketing will be next to impossible to turn down. Remember what we've stressed before: Network marketing is all about timing. If prospects are in the right time in their lives for change—it doesn't matter how poorly MLM is explained—they'll probably decide to give it a shot.

Conversely, prospects who are not in the proper time of life probably won't be receptive no matter how articulately or professionally the business is presented.

Steve Sledge says he had fun using the follow-up system: "Sometimes after I explained the power of network marketing to some of my former business associates and showed them the $5 \times 5 \times 5$ illustration of logarithmic growth, they smiled. Some even laughed and said, 'Hey, Steve, give us a call when you get rich!' So I did—every last one of them!"

Starting with Warm Market Prospecting

SO now you know some of the excuses people will throw at you in an effort to put off prospecting their warm lists. But why is it so important that sponsors encourage them to do it? Warm market prospecting is much easier than the cold, cruel world of trying to persuade people you've never met to quit their jobs and join you in MLM. "Cold market" prospecting requires professionalism, enthusiasm, competence, and moxie. You are trying to convince veritable strangers that they should abandon their weekly paychecks and comfort-zone jobs or professions to follow you into an entrepreneurial pyramid. At least, that's how prospects view it. This is where the numbers play an important role. You will talk to a greater number of people in cold marketing than in warm in order to generate the same favorable responses. In those circumstances you better be confident, self-assured, and proficient at responding to the primary objections brought up at recruiting meetings. Cold market prospecting is aptly named—it's "cold."

Because your warm market is comprised of folks you know, it is much more understanding and forgiving than are total strangers. There's an old saying in our industry: "Every great multi-level marketer was a lousy multi-level marketer first." No one starts out poised and self-assured. So it just makes good sense to approach your strongest relationships, those with your family and friends, first. And you're not alone. Your sponsor should do your first two or three presentations for you in your home with your friends or support you by phone if long-distance. (We'll discuss that later in this chapter.) But now let's examine the proper way to approach warm market leads.

Success Results More from Attitude Than Ability

BECAUSE attitude rather than ability leads to real success in network marketing, your biggest asset is *enthusiasm*. But we're not talking about some fake excitement that is a learned behavior, or following some script written by your upline associate. We're talking about natural enthusiasm, that is, your excitement after realizing you could be only months away from earning $20,000 a month! Again, we remind you that if you aren't truly excited about this business opportunity, read or listen to anything that will build up your enthusiasm—it is essential to effective prospecting. Whatever strategy works to motivate you and get you in a positive frame of mind prior to calling warm market prospects, employ it. The deeper your *belief* level, the greater your chance of success.

It also helps to realize that you are first and foremost an *educator*. You are not a salesperson, nor are you a professional recruiter. Your job is to teach as many people as possible that there's a better way to live and to earn residual income. The only way you're ever going to convince people to change careers and to join you in MLM is if you can get them to agree to sit down with you for forty-five minutes to take an objective look at your business. When you call your warm market leads, your only objective is to get them to seriously consider your company. Probably nobody in the history of the network distribution industry has been so persuasive as to be able to convince prospects over the telephone

The deeper your *belief* level, the greater your chance of success.

in their very first call to change jobs and join their company. Nor do we know distributors who can consistently sell products or services over the telephone. So don't try! Network marketing is a business of education. You may want to begin by having your prospects review an audio-visual package, but eventually you need to interact face to face. It is about teaching people how to teach others to build an organization of people who use and share products and/or services.

And keep in mind, the more information you give to prospects over the telephone, the less likely they will be willing to listen to an audio or attend a business presentation. Try to raise their *curiosity* over the phone rather than satisfy it. Do not give information out during your first call or answer a lot of questions. Share your enthusiasm and set a time and place for the meeting to which you are inviting them. Make sure you are talking from your heart, inviting those with whom you truly wish to associate.

MLM is an ingenious industry in that its leaders and founders learned long ago that people usually make decisions based on certain emotions. A *desire for more money* is one of the reasons you can count

on to motivate prospects to attend meetings. Later in this book we will also show you how *fear of loss* is what motivates many folks into creating wealth. No product or service, except perhaps a lure to a better career, is exciting enough to cause people to want to change professions. But the possibility of having *total control of their time* and a monthly income of $20,000 to $30,000—maybe even $50,000!—gets the attention of most people, even the most cynical.

So here's another approach to friends and family. Begin with small talk, but purposefully cut that off as soon as possible and in an extremely enthusiastic manner, nearly out of breath with excitement, say something like the following:

"I've got to tell you the real motive for my call. In fact, I can't hold it back any longer. My wife and I are so excited about what we've blundered into, and we want to share it with you because, frankly, we can't think of anyone else we'd rather spend the rest of our lives in partnership with than the two of you. Listen, I'm going to ask the same question of you that was asked of me a couple of weeks ago. 'If you were absolutely convinced, after a full due diligence, that it was possible for you to earn—legally and ethically—up to $20,000, $30,000, even $50,000 a month, and kick back and relax in a few years, still earning that much without a major investment, would that be a business that would interest you?'"

If you take some time to study this approach, you'll notice that there is absolutely no reason for objections to surface. You have asked the prospect a question in which all the possible objections have been skillfully addressed. First, you encourage him to research the opportunity. It's moral, it's ethical, and there is minimal start-up cost. The potential earnings are substantial, they are residual, and even more important to people in this global economy, success will allow him considerable free time. If, after hearing this question, your friend argues at all, regardless of the objection, you'll know that he or she *is not* a prospect today. Don't badger your reluctant prospects. Be sure to end the conversation on a positive note, asking permission to check back with them in a few months. Simply write on the prospect's card "wasn't interested" and place it in the folder to remind you to call again in exactly six months' time. Remember, this is a business of timing—finding people who are ready for change.

No Need to Sell People on Network Marketing

ONE of the biggest mistakes most new distributors make is arguing and attempting to "sell" people on the business at the wrong time. Think about it a moment. Where's the objection to the question we've posed? There is none. So what does it accomplish for a new distributor to stay on the phone with his friend trying to overcome every objection and pestering him to death? Or worse, what if an upline associate is on the call also badgering the prospect? Even after six months that friend will not be open and receptive, even if the time is right.

Alex Marr of San Francisco, California, learned this lesson the hard way. "When I first decided to pursue a network marketing business, I was in my last year of law school. When I told my friends and fellow law students of my decision, I was completely unprepared for the onslaught of well-meaning but tremendously negative advice I received. Most friends laughed, some openly showed their disgust for the industry, and a few went so far as to print up brochures with my name on them that said things like 'snake oil' and 'fraud for sale.' None of them, however, would look at the facts about my company and the opportunity associated with it, even though those friends were both intelligent and about to embark on a career in law, where looking at facts before making judgments is one's entire profession.

"I was discouraged initially, but I knew I had a great opportunity. I set out to assemble mountains of evidence proving that network marketing in general, and my company in particular, was legitimate. That's what law school had trained me to do. After a year of assembling books, articles, newspaper clippings, along with audiotapes and videotapes, I approached some of my friends again. I was much more confident because I had the facts on hand to back me up. But nearly all my friends still refused to come to a presentation, even after having seen the facts and figures I had put together! I was completely blown away! How could they refuse to join my company, when all of my statistics clearly showed that it was in their interest to do so?

"The lesson I learned sunk in over the next few weeks. I can convince a person intellectually that joining my network marketing company is a great decision, but if that person does not believe he can succeed in my business, or if he does not believe in himself and his own abilities to learn and grow, all my facts and statistics are useless. He will not join my company, and even if he does, he won't do anything after he has joined. I wasted a year assembling information to convince people who were just not interested, when I could have been out making presentations to people who had expressed real interest. Mark Yarnell summed up this lesson well: *'A person convinced against his will is of the same opinion still.'* Now I don't waste time showing facts to anyone until I have sifted for interest first. I could have shaved a year off my learning curve if I would have followed that advice earlier."

Patrick Schumacher of Payson, Arizona, had a similar learning curve in this business. He read in *Success* magazine that the next time you are with a friend, ask him if he has ever wanted to start his own business. " 'What if I could show you a business that you could start for about $500, with the potential to pay you what a CEO of a Fortune 500 company makes, and the company with whom you partner would take care of all R&D, packaging, payroll, opening of foreign markets, and legal matters? Would you like to know about this business?' I e-mailed that same message to a friend who works for a high-tech company because he complained to me that the company he worked for had just cut his commissions. He responded that he was not interested. Rob didn't even ask me what the business was about, no interest, nothing. I couldn't believe it!

"Then two weeks later my sister-in-law visited me and used the products that we have in the shower. She loved them and wanted to know how she could get some. Once I sponsored her, she spent around $1,000 on products and was unable to stop talking about how excited she was. Within two months, she told me she was quitting because she didn't have time. She manages her husband's plastic surgery practice, so I asked her if she thought that people who spend thousands of dollars on plastic surgery would want to use these products to maintain a youthful appearance. No answer. I thought maybe it was something I did, until I remembered the SW rule: "Some will, some won't, so what, because someone else is always waiting." Once I understood the four letter word, *next*, I began to always move forward and never look back."

Patrick's approach is a solid one. And now, so is his attitude. Network marketing inevitably requires you to talk to many people within your circle of influence. By reaching out to enough people, you will eventually find those for whom the time is right. And that is when the personal relationships begin—what we call "relationship marketing."

No Need to Pressure Friends into the Business

ANOTHER mistake made by a new distributor is to pressure twenty friends to get into the business (and they do, oftentimes merely to shut the recruiter up!); then the new distributor spends the next six months trying to drag those people across the finish line. For many, many well-meaning people, network distribution is the process of selling people on our industry, then doing everything possible to make those people successful. Unfortunately, that's literally the antithesis, the exact opposite, of what our business is all about. Our job is not to do it all for them. It is to teach them how to do it for themselves. We are educators. We teach people a new way to buy and sell products and services and a new way to make a living. The more people we educate (by getting them to review an audio-visual package and then sit down in our homes and hear the whole story), the more money we all earn. And the more people we approach with extreme enthusiasm about partnering in a business that will generate big money and free time, the more people we get to our homes in the first place.

So make absolutely certain that you leave no one off your warm market list.

And when you begin calling them—on your own, remember, no three-way, gang-up calls—make certain that you are in an enthusiastic frame of mind. Share your desire to be involved in business with them and focus your prospecting question around big money, free time, and a lifetime partnership.

The philosopher Maurice Nichol, a student of Russian-born spiritual teacher Georgei Gurdjieff, used to say, "All people are asleep. And in order to awaken them from their stupor long enough to introduce them to a new idea or way of doing things, you must give them some sort of conscious shock." We agree. What we've come to recognize is that unless you use high income numbers, most people will remain asleep. The promise of $20,000, $30,000, even $50,000 a month—income levels actually achieved by the top earners—is usually enough of a conscious shock to awaken most folks to your presentation. Then, if the time is right, and if they've been thinking about changing careers or fearing being laid off, they might respond affirmatively, listen to an audio presentation, and actually come to a meeting. That's one of the keys to effective network marketing. Many people have the leadership potential to do this business, but may not reveal it to you unless the timing is right.

Making Unexpected Friends Through Warm Market Prospecting

SOMETIMES your warm market list can expand almost to the other end of the spectrum, simply by making your business and products known to those within your circle of influence. Neldia Hudman Ahlquist, like so many ex-wives, did not get along with her ex-husband's new wife, Joyce Hudman. Both are from small towns just outside of Houston, Texas. Neldia describes the situation: "The tension between us was so strong that at one time when Joyce was working at a law firm with a mutual friend, she asked the mutual friend to ask me not to come to the office while she was there. After she left that law firm, one of the partners would purchase gift packages of my products for all the secretaries, who loved them so much they told Joyce about them. Once I even asked my ex-husband to buy one for her Valentine's Day gift. He laughed at me and said, 'she wouldn't use anything that you sold,' but he bought it anyway. To my surprise, after using what he bought, she called and asked what other products we had and asked if she could come over. We did a skincare clinic and she left as my new distributor.

"We are now close friends, and work together in the business. It has made a wonderful difference for my children. We recently roomed together in Dallas for a regional conference with our company. Everyone looked puzzled when I introduced her as my 'wife-in-law.' To make things even funnier, last week I went to her house to wait for my son. There were two other ladies there—one was engaged to the other one's husband and was there to pick up her son. They too had come together through our business. It's amazing the friendships you forge when you work in this business. You make friends with people you never thought possible."

Putting the List to Its Fullest and Best Use

DON'T let any of the Warm List Warheads strike you. Reach out to everyone on your list, starting with those in your city whom you would enjoy as partners in the business. Contact your top twenty or thirty family members and friends and invite them to take a look at this exciting opportunity. If possible, your sponsor should be there with you for your first two or three home meetings. It's best to present the opportunity to small groups of three to six people at a time. Invite twice as many guests as you want to allow for the "no-shows," which are an inevitable part of this business. Focus your first ninety days on "relationship marketing"—that is, reaching out to those closest to you to extend the invitation to create a business partnership intended to enhance the quality of your lives. Over the course of your first year, devote almost all of your time to approaching the remainder of your list, setting appointments, and presenting the opportunity. Notice that we didn't say "Take them to someone else's meeting." These are *your* prospects, *your* appointments, and *your* presentations. Using your warm list, keep doing this over and over until you reach your desired goal. Of course, once you have sponsored new associates, train them to duplicate your efforts: to use and share your products and services with a small circle of friends, and then to prospect, set appointments, and assist them in doing their own meetings with those on their warm lists. Like the presentation, do this training in small groups in your home once a week— we suggest Saturday morning. Once your new associates complete their assignments—order products, set their goals in writing, and begin making their warm list—they then qualify for a one-on-one personal training session with you.

If you want to stretch your list to its fullest and best use, learn to ask for refer-

Remember to ask for referrals. If you can learn to replace every *No* with just one new prospect, your warm list will never run out.

rals. When someone on your list says *No*, that is the time to ask them for the names of one or two of their colleagues who might be interested in this opportunity. The secret to asking for referrals is to be specific. "Whom do you know there at the factory who is already thinking about leaving? Who is the most dynamic person among your friends at work . . . or the one everyone looks up to?" Remember to ask for referrals. If you can learn to replace every *No* with just one new prospect, your warm list will never run out.

SUMMARY

- A "warm list" is a group of individuals from your present and past whom you know well enough that were you to pick up the telephone and call them, they would recognize you once they heard your name.

- The direction of the twenty-first century is to build on warm market relationships as opposed to the philosophy of "throwing mud on the wall" and hoping some sticks.

- The larger you build your warm list, the more solidly you will establish your business.

- Make sure new distributors are taught how to use triggering devices in order to help them recall at least 2,000 friends and acquaintances.

- Remember not to yield to the arguments and rationalizations new distributors use in order to avoid approaching their warm markets.

- If you let your doubts stand in the way of launching your business, you are guaranteed to fail, but if you go forward and persevere, you will succeed.

- Move past your comfort zone and offer everyone on your warm list this opportunity, especially those you feel are already too successful to consider doing this business.

- Professionals have a natural tendency to refuse to openly acknowledge their participation in network marketing, but this refusal can negatively impact their business because their doubts and insecurities can be sensed by both prospects and distributors.

- If you can't let your associates at work know about your involvement in network marketing, be sure, during in-home presentations, to show that you are proud and enthusiastic about the industry and your company.

- Your reluctance to approach your warm market, because you have been in other MLMs and have already approached the same people in the past, can easily be overcome by assuring your friends and family that your research and analysis has finally led you to the right company.

- Never qualify your prospects: To decide in advance that one person is too important to be approached, or another is too inadequate to succeed, is economic suicide.

- If your professional career has a potential conflict of interest that hampers recruiting efforts, you can either:

  1 Prospect through "lifestyling," that is, by approaching people through the normal course of your life, letting them know, without mentioning your business, that you would like to get together with them when it is appropriate; or

  2 Sponsor someone who knows your business associates and can ethically approach those people.

- You may want to consider prioritizing your list by using "target marketing," wherein you share a personal background with certain groups from your warm or lukewarm market.

- Always allow your new distributors the courtesy of talking to their closest friends and family without the presence of their sponsor on the line.

- Three-way calling is most effective *after* the presentation—not before. Or you may prefer to have the prospect make a direct call to your upline associate.

- Use a card filing system to track your prospects.

- Call all the people on your prospect cards every six months until they either sign up or die.

- Beginning with the warm market is best because approaching friends and relatives is much easier than approaching strangers.

- Attitude is more important than ability in network marketing.

- During your recruiting efforts, think of yourself as an educator more than as a salesperson.

- Until the presentation, your intent is to stimulate the curiosity of your prospects, not satisfy it.

- When contacting warm market leads with the possibility of partnering in business, emphasize big money and free time rather than any specifics about the company or products.

- When prospects object to an enthusiastic, big-money/free-time partnership, don't argue with them; simply file their card and call them again in six months.

- "A person convinced against his will is of the same opinion still."

- Remember the SW rule: <u>S</u>ome <u>w</u>ill, <u>s</u>ome <u>w</u>on't, <u>s</u>o <u>w</u>hat, because <u>s</u>omeone else is always <u>w</u>aiting.

- Focus your first ninety days on "relationship marketing"—that is, reaching out to those closest to you to extend the invitation to create a business partnership intended to enhance the quality of your lives.

- During your first year, devote almost all of your time to prospecting, setting appointments, and presenting the opportunity until you reach your desired goal and teach your associates to do the same.

- When someone on your list says *No*, that is the time to ask for the names of one or two colleagues at work who might be interested in your opportunity.

- If you can learn to replace every *No* with just one new referral, your warm list will never run out.

CHAPTER 6

Fending Off the Scatter Bomb

Stay focused amidst all the distractions.

THE NEXT GREAT OBSTACLE in the battle for success probably afflicts every single distributor who ever enters our industry. We call it the Scatter Bomb. It is quite easy to fall into this booby trap because of the very changeable nature of our business. Simply put, the Scatter Bomb is a mental explosion that diffuses the focus of distributors, causing them to stop using the system they have been taught and to frantically follow any and every new network marketing system that comes along. The Scatter Bomb occurs frequently in the first year, sending new distributors in search of any new leader, company, sales aid, or system that might enable them to succeed more rapidly or more easily.

This divisive weapon is quite deceptive because it comes disguised as the ulti-mate new tool or as the perfect strategy for success. Sometimes it's a new manual or video, which many new distributors assume will be more effective than the work program currently used, merely because it's new. Other times it's a new leader who comes to town with a brand new way to do the business, and since he's making more money than you, his system must be better than yours. When your spirits are really down, it can even be a new company with a better compensation plan. Whether the Scatter Bomb takes the form of a person, system, or company, the very worst thing you can do in your first year is yield to the temptation to change direction every time a new system comes along.

This business is a process of system duplication, and therefore each time you change your system, everyone in your downline gets confused. In network marketing, the worst battles in the entire first year will be the internal ones you fight each time you're tempted to find a faster, better, easier route. Remember, if someone in your upline is earning the amount of money you strongly desire and you continue to duplicate the exact system that got him or her to wealth, you too will eventually get there . . . but not if you are always changing the system.

There are many different ways to do the network distribution business and fortunately each of them is equally lucrative. There's no one way to success. But if a network marketer becomes so scattered that he or she is constantly changing from system to system, thereby compelling downline associates to change, failure will certainly follow. In this chapter we will prepare you to fend off the inevitable Scatter Bomb by bringing to your attention the detours you and your new distributors will be tempted to take.

Always Changing the System

WE have personally lost great frontline distributors, many of whom could have become legends in this industry, because they just couldn't stop changing systems. In fact, in one case, we lost the leaders of an entire foreign market.

Just imagine the possibilities if: you started on the ground floor in a brand new country with 1,500 serious prospects who came to learn more about your business on opening day; the company you represented was a billion-dollar MLM company already successful in twenty other countries; and all the new distributors signing up were within your first five levels. Also, assume that your sponsors were extremely well known and had all the training manuals (audiotapes, videotapes, books) translated into every language on your continent and then set up a second home in your part of the world in order to spend significant time supporting you. Under these circumstances, failure seems impossible.

Believe it or not, failure *was* the end result: the key leaders quit the business within eighteen months. They failed because they changed their name from the Yarnell Organization to another unknown group, gradually eliminated every system we taught them, and consumed much of their time routinely changing their training materials—it was the ultimate Scatter Bomb. Every one of our systems had proven success, and every one of theirs rapidly failed. But they still maintain that their organization collapsed because they just didn't have a good enough compensation plan. And we provided them with many other forms of support, financial and otherwise, that we haven't even mentioned! The truth is that they and all their downline were victims of the Scatter Bomb. But frankly, as their sponsors, we have to accept a great deal of the responsibility for their failure because each time they made a system change, and it was very frequent, we protested only gently.

Unlike the typical recriminations in traditional business after such a collapse, we are still friends with this group of distributors despite the failure. This experience was an important and painful lesson for us, so we want to pass it on to you so that you might avoid our mistake. And here's the primary lesson: New distributors must literally be indoctrinated into duplicating your system. They must be taught in the beginning to follow the system of their sponsor and not deviate from it. Today we tell our newest associates in no uncertain terms that the day they deviate from our system is the day they lose our support. It's a serious matter for us. What we've learned is that even if you handpick the best recruiters and most committed people in a newly opened foreign market, set them up with all the training tools they need, help close their best prospects, sign them up during an opening day launch attended by the company's highest dignitaries—even if you do all that—if those people are unwilling to duplicate one simple system that has

proven itself elsewhere, they are destined for failure. That's the frightening reality about the Scatter Bomb.

Business Without Blinders

THE metaphor of Scatter Bomb also refers to the inability of new distributors to ignore all the inevitable distractions in the first year and maintain a clear vision of where they are going and how they are going to get there. New distributors become scattered very quickly by a veritable smorgasbord of companies, recruiting systems, videos, manuals, and numerous other sales systems available to them. New distributors must be warned to put on blinders during their first year. Consistent duplication of one simple success system is essential in order to avoid confusion in one's entire downline, which is precisely what occurs each time a leader changes systems midstream.

Even worse, some overzealous entrepreneurs jump right into recruiting without any goals or systems around which to base their business plan. Many new network marketers are like the man searching for his keys one night. A neighbor sees the man spending hours laboriously searching for something in the grass. Finally, she goes to ask if she can help. "What are you looking for?" she asks.

"I lost my keys," he replies. As she begins to crawl on the ground with him, she inquires, "You lost them in this yard?"

"No," he responds, "but the light is better here."

There are countless distributors who want to work the business in ways that are more comfortable to them, more fitting to their self-image, more in keeping with their old work habits. The "light" may be better there, but if your goal is to achieve financial security and personal freedom, you may have to get out of your comfort zone and work where the light is not so good or the ambiance is not so elegant. The good life will come soon enough if you pay the price in the first year.

Having faced many challenges in her life, Pia Dietzen of El Dorado, Arkansas, learned this lesson repeatedly before entering the world of network marketing. She left Denmark to come to America and got her real estate license within five months of her arrival; shortly thereafter, she became a full-time student while holding down a full-time job, all during a pregnancy. She went back to work within weeks after delivering her baby through C-section; throughout all of this, she managed to get her black belt. "What keeps me going on these ugly days when nothing seems to go right?" she asks. "I believe that inside all of us there is a driving force that will help us just as long as we stay focused on our goals. I teach my distributors not to give up, no matter what. I tell each distributor, 'the longer you stay and continue talking to people, the closer you will get to your goal. Never lose sight of that light at the end of the tunnel.'"

Drs. Joe Rubino and Tom Ventullo of Andover, Massachusetts, had practiced dentistry for ten years before being introduced to network marketing. Although they had built a very successful dental practice, they had lost all their enthusiasm for dentistry. The fire was gone, but dentistry was all they knew. The concept of network marketing was initially appealing to them, but both were shy and introverted. To build a successful business they would be required to break out of their comfort zones and learn how to speak with others. Of course, all of the usual concerns came up for them: What would people think? How would they look to their peers?

Because of their self-imposed limitations, they felt trapped and without a sense of direction. What could possibly turn two introverts into top network distributors in a business usually excelled at by extroverts? They had been "playing small" all their lives; their focus was on playing it safe and avoiding risks. While

As Norman Cousins wrote, "The true tragedy in life is not death, but that which dies inside us while we are still living."

---

this philosophy sheltered them from the dangers of the world, it also carried with it a tremendous price. Playing "not to lose"—instead of "to win"—was draining the partners from the inside. The adversity they had to overcome, like so many others living in quiet resignation, was to conquer a fear of the world that was slowly and steadily killing their spirits. As Norman Cousins wrote, "The true tragedy in life is not death, but that which dies inside us while we are still living."

Once Joe and Tom woke up to the reality of their resignation and what it was costing them in terms of health, happiness, relationships, and their potential contributions to the world, they made a conscious decision to play full out. They needed to find a compelling reason to do what was uncomfortable, as well as nurture a self-confidence in who they were and what they had to offer. Part of their vision was, and still is, to expose millions of people living in resignation to the limitless possibilities for change in their lives once they simply choose to become open to them. With the support of their network marketing team and after working

with some personal coaches, they decided to implement an action plan and to expect success. Nothing changed externally. The entire shift was in their mind-sets.

After just six years of effort in network marketing, Drs. Joe and Tom fully retired from dentistry with an income far greater than that from their dental practice. They speak and write internationally on how to succeed in network marketing. In December of 1995, Joe was featured on the cover of *Success* magazine, which called him a "millionaire creator" in the cover story entitled "How Network Marketing's Entrepreneurial Elite Are Building Fortunes at Breakneck Speed." His book, *Secrets of Building a Million-Dollar Network Marketing Organization*, has been highly acclaimed for its comprehensive approach to becoming financially successful by developing a life purpose. They are living testaments to the fact that all of us can harness the life-changing power of this industry to make a difference in our own lives while also contributing to the lives of countless others.

Karen Johnson, formerly a pink Cadillac winner with Mary Kay, and one of the strongest female speakers in the business, joined a new network marketing company in partnership with her husband, Bill Curtain. She looked upline to her role models—Charlie Miller, Jay Primm, and Marc Barrett—all of whom had achieved the top level of their company in record time. She believed that if they could do it, so could she. So she quit her job, Bill sold their business, and they joined up. They achieved the level of executive in the minimum time in January of 1991, the same month the Persian Gulf War erupted. Unfortunately, their four qualifying executives watched the news instead of working the business, and within sixty days all four had lost their vision and quit.

As Karen explains, "Seven months later, Bill and I climbed our way back to having four new qualifying executives, only to have Barbara Walters appear on *Nightline* featuring our company with the infamous question: 'Is it a *dream* or a *scheme*?' This television broadcast launched the most intense media and regulatory scrutiny ever encountered by any network marketing company. Over the next ten months, as our company was ruthlessly attacked by the media, all four of our qualifying executives lost hope. Even though our company was exonerated after the investigation, we lost three more qualifying executives. Defending our company in the media and to the regulators

exacted a heavy toll. After all that work, we had lost a total of eleven executives. Our families were begging us to go back to corporate America. We just couldn't. We had a dream.

"In June of 1992, we were thrown another curve. Our company diversified, and suddenly we had to go from our comfort zone of being knowledgeable about cosmetics and personal care products to learning about antioxidants, chelated minerals, and metabolic conditioning. But we did it, and by August of 1993, our first full-fledged executive emerged in our organization. It took three more years of hard work, but finally, in September of 1996, we reached the top level of our company." Karen remembers back to her days with Mary Kay, where she was often told "The greater the individual's potential for success, the greater the adversity that individual will have to face. Gold is tempered through fire—how can we aspire to the greatness of leadership if our commitment is never challenged?" Karen and Bill, who successfully met the challenge, now live in Redondo Beach, California, freed from the shackles of corporate America and of owning a traditional business. When asked why she was able to hang in when everyone around her fell out, Karen said that it is essential to have your destination clearly in sight, even before the journey ever begins.

Achieving your goal is a process of getting accustomed to a new and better reality—one in which you can actually see yourself.

It is clear that success for Drs. Joe and Tom, Pia, or Karen and Bill was tied directly to their undaunted sense of purpose. Each was successful at building their networking business because of an ability to shut out every distraction around them, whether internal or external, and stay the course with clear vision of where they were going and how they were going to get there. Achieving your goal is a process of getting accustomed to a new and better reality—one in which you can actually see yourself. Keep focused on the end result while (1) preserving your belief that it is possible, (2) blocking negative influences, and (3) not worrying about *how* it will come to pass.

Changing the System Midstream

MORE than likely, one of the first manifestations of the Scatter Bomb will be the temptation to change, even just slightly, the system of recruiting you were taught. For example, your sponsor might tell you the critical importance of approaching your warm list by expressing your desire to have a business relationship with each of them and sharing your excitement about the potential of big money and free time because of the universal appeal of both. And while you are nodding your head in agreement, what you are really thinking is, "I can't approach my friends and family with an idea as outrageous as earning such extraordinary income." So you begin changing the approach: you avoid your best prospects or mention a smaller income figure or none at all in favor of promoting your products. Never mind that your sponsor insisted that you need to use the big-money, free-time approach, you know in your heart that your friends and family members simply cannot relate to that kind of money.

You don't argue with your sponsor because you've already promised to use his system, but you think you know what's best. And guess what? If you think that way, so will all your recruits. We don't know what there is about our industry that makes it seem so easy, but all who sign up immediately begin to believe that they know more than their sponsor or, for that matter, more than anyone who's ever been in this industry. The greater their innate leadership skills, the more likely they will want to reinvent the wheel.

The way to prevent new distributors from changing the approach is to anticipate their notions during training. New distributors may not understand the importance of starting their business with relationship marketing or quoting large income figures in order to create a conscious shock. So teach them how easy it is to get sidetracked. Tell them right up front, "Now you are going to be tempted to postpone reaching out to your most viable contacts or change the numbers because you're concerned about discussing so much money with your friends. Do it anyway. It is important that you use the exact approach we teach you."

Make sure new distributors understand that network marketing begins with relationships and requires numerous contacts and tenacious follow-through. Another part of the approach they will feel compelled to change is to lower any numbers you give them in training. If you suggest they need to personally sponsor at least 100 people over time, they often decide that 50 frontline recruits are enough. If you advise that full-time distributors may need to approach at least 100 prospects a week once they move into cold

marketing, they often decide that 30 or 40 is plenty. If you suggest targeting 2,000 people on their warm list, they will, usually without telling you so, think you are out of your mind. Such changes to your system, which new distributors are convinced will not block their success, is the first element of the Scatter Bomb. Remember, each time you teach a module of your system to new recruits, make absolutely certain that you stress to them that *any* deviation from your system could result in failure.

The mere act of warning your recruits about first-year challenges during a fun, relaxed training session will help you later when you need to constructively criticize them after they become rebellious or unfocused. Of course, if you don't want to waste time talking about all these things and you have no system created by an upline associate who is earning big money, just hand this book to all new distributors when they sign up. (How's that for a shameless endorsement?) But, remember, the best advice will come from upline leaders, because they have already proven themselves in your specific company.

The Lure of Other Deals

SOME changes will come from outside your sphere of influence and seem beyond your control. We want you to be prepared for any and all diversions and challenges that threaten your downline. The amazing truth about MLM is that once you have established yourself with a company, you can literally waltz through decades without anyone trying to lure you away. Yet in the first year you become a distributor, the competition will come out of the woodwork and beg you to switch companies. Success and perseverance will earn you respect, whereas your newness makes you vulnerable.

Mark tells the story of his very first exposure to a successful upline distributor. "There I was, excited about finally putting a face with the name of a guy I already respected by virtue of his income and lifestyle. He was living in another city, so when he called to see if he could help me in any way, I asked if he would consider driving the 150 miles to my city sometime to visit with my top distributors and coach them about the business. I was astounded by the speed with which he accepted my invitation. He told me to get everybody ready for advanced training and that he'd be there in a week. I was elated. Back then our leaders were not yet caught up in the hotel-presentation mania, so I didn't set up a citywide meeting. I simply invited twenty-five of my best distributors to my home for an advanced training session with our upline

hero. Although my real mentor was Richard Kall, this leader lived closer and was only three levels above me in the company. He was allegedly earning over $15,000 a month, so I figured my people would be in good hands.

"I remember it like yesterday. We had a real Texas cookout—great barbecued ribs and all the wonderful trimmings. While the others were eating, I was delighted that my great upline hero wanted me to take him to a quiet room in the house to discuss the meeting that was about to start. I took him upstairs to my office and we sat down in a couple of chairs facing each other. Before I could say a word, my wayward upline said, 'Mark, get ready to lose sleep tonight. I have found the ultimate payout and recruiting video in this company called USA Vitamins. If you think our company has a good comp plan, listen to this. . . .'

"I was shell-shocked. The first major Scatter Bomb of my first year in MLM had just exploded. And this one was sure to get everyone off course, because he was getting ready to address my top twenty-five distributors. I had to think fast because I didn't want to make a scene and I only had half an hour to prepare a strategy. As he talked, I sat there racking my brain trying to figure out what I could do. Finally, I thought of a comeback: 'Look, Doug, you've hit me cold on this and we cannot let my wife know that you've presented this to me without her or she'll be extremely offended.'

"Doug said, 'I understand, my wife's the . . . ,' I stopped him with my last comment.

"'Look . . . just pretend you haven't said anything. I want my wife to see this great deal, and the last thing we want is for you to say anything to any of these distributors. My wife and I need to be on your team when you pitch them; you know what I mean?'

"Doug nodded in agreement and became extremely cordial. He was sure he was going to recruit us. He promised not to say one word until the three of us were alone later that evening. The meeting went smoothly and nobody had any idea that our great mentor was already in another deal. Of course, once everyone was gone, I really let him have it with both barrels, specifically pointing out what a fool he was to jump ship in the first year. We parted as enemies because that's the way he wanted it. But he still calls from time to time to share his latest MLM venture and explain why I should join him. I think he's been in half a dozen companies since then. Imagine what he must be thinking when he realizes, had he stayed and continued to work, he would be earning in excess of $100,000 a month for the rest of his life, off of our efforts alone."

We have a saying that we share with every new distributor: "The grass is always greener, 'til it's time to mow." We can guarantee you, just as certain as the sun will rise in the east tomorrow, that your new recruits will be courted by other MLM companies in their first years as distributors. It's a certainty and must be addressed in the training process of all new distributors. A good thing for distributors to always keep in mind is that the trickle-down theory works better in our business than in economics. Teach your leaders anything and if it works, everyone in your organization will learn it rapidly. Those of us who have been in this industry for many years have learned a very real success principle: *perseverance*. Distributors who have stayed with one company for many years, and built new legs in each of those years, are now very wealthy. Those who think the grass is greener soon learn

---

Distributors who have stayed with one company for many years, and built new legs in each of those years, are now very wealthy.

that true, lasting wealth can only be achieved through long-term participation in one company.

We've heard all the arguments of those distributors who honestly believe that, to succeed in MLM, one must belong to two or more companies. But the proof is in the printout. We've never met one person who has successfully built more than one downline at the same time. And we've met hundreds of people over the years who swear by the two-company system. But listen closely: IT DOESN'T WORK! It takes every bit of focus and effort you've got to reach the top payout of one solid network marketing company. Have no doubt, several of your distributors will become tempted by other programs and some will actually attempt to prove us wrong. Until that's done, we've got to keep stressing the facts. No one has successfully done it yet!

Some people will participate in what we call "positioning for the pop." That means that they will jump from company to company, knowing full well that each company will not remain in business long-term. But they'll jump from the gold deal to the offshore deal, hoping to pick up some front-end, quick money in the process. Never mind that these are pyramid schemes and only a few people will win. Never mind that the company is likely to fold any minute. All that matters

is that they pick up a little easy money along the way. Watch out for those scoundrels—they are the folks who give our industry a bad name.

In the world of traditional, corporate pyramids, entire companies are created to search for executives to fill their clients' needs or specialties. If you are a physician who is tired of private practice and you're looking for a partnership of specialists or some directorship at a hospital, all you need to do is find the number of an employment agency that specializes in the medical field. There are dozens of them. If IBM needs a specialist in some technical engineering position, they not only advertise but will also frequently call an employment agency specializing in engineering.

Here's our point. In a free society, people will always seek to better themselves. Corporate executives aren't particularly hurt when some head-hunting agency hires away their upper managers. It happens—it's a fact of life. Yet if one of our leaders begins sniffing around other network marketing companies, or worse, actually goes to a presentation, my God you'd think the sky was falling. Rumors begin flying around at fiber-optic speeds. Upline associates are immediately notified and an entire search-and-rescue program is launched by every money earner within six or seven levels in an effort to keep that poor fool from defecting. They all think that if the company loses *that* leader, they're ruined, that it's liable to destroy the enthusiasm and momentum of the entire organization. Bull!

The truth is, all new distributors will probably be tempted, several times in their careers, to change companies. Remember the SW rule: "Some will, some won't, so what, because someone else is always waiting." We're all adults, and we certainly don't want to retain those who are plodding along in our company, who are making no progress and draining our time, when they might be happier in a different company. We say, "Godspeed and good luck." But long before they are ever exposed to a new, competitive company, we make certain that they've been prepared for that eventuality, and that they realize that every time they start over, they are hurting their reputation just a little bit more and distancing themselves from wealth one more time. Unless you pick a real dud of an MLM company, it's possible to do well in any number of them.

The key to success is to stop jumping ship and stick with one. Peter Hirsch has given a name to the frantic search that people take as they go from company to company looking for that $10,000 first-month fix: the "cocaine mentality." In contrast, he recommends the surer, safer approach: the "carrot juice mentality," which recognizes that it is only from the steady building of a healthy organization that long-term residual benefits are derived. In MLM as in life, as we sow, so shall we reap.

Diffusion by Other Leaders

THE temptation to follow the teachings of "expert" journalists or to become involved in other MLM companies would seem to be a natural part of business, but what about Scatter Bombs that are dropped by leaders within one's own company? How dangerous are those diversions? Extremely. In fact this problem causes distributors, especially in their first year, to become scattered and ineffective, and is the most difficult to combat. Unless leaders explain this very carefully, they could quite easily become the targets of scorn and ridicule from leaders within their own company.

More often than not, the Scatter Bomb is perpetrated by pseudo-leaders who may have never before succeeded in building a successful downline, but by virtue of former experience, believe they know what they're doing. There's a significant difference between ten years' experience and one year's experience ten times. That's why we always encourage our distributors to primarily recruit individuals with no former experience in MLM because they are so much easier to train. Those who are basically MLM junkies, jumping from company to company, are often the very "know-it-alls" who can cause your new distributors so many problems.

Let's take a look at the confusion potentially caused when leaders set off the Scatter Bomb. Let's pretend that you are in your first year of MLM and you've done an exceptional job of building your organization. You have 850 people total and are earning a reasonable $3,000 a month. Your groups are growing exponentially and all of them are following your training format. Then your people start excitedly discussing the fact that one of the company's leaders from a completely different upline group is coming to town to train his people and, since it's an open meeting, everyone in town is invited. Obviously you can't stem the tide of enthusiasm if you've failed to discuss this threat beforehand with your people, and you certainly don't want to seem jealous or overprotective.

Of course this is just your sixth month in the business and none of your strongest leaders have been in the business long enough to make any real money yet. So they are extremely vulnerable at this stage of their careers to any new concept that would seem to propel them to wealth a little faster or easier. The meeting occurs

and you sit there and cringe as the speaker introduces a brand new prospecting system that has supposedly proven very effective. You notice your people are taking copious notes. This is the same system your upline associates taught you is not as effective as their own. In fact, they tried it years ago and found that it wasn't a system that was easily duplicated. Be prepared in this situation: Usually about half your leaders will go charging out and implement this exciting new system, only to fizzle in six months, but, in the meantime, it will sidetrack your leaders just enough to ruin their momentum. How in the world do you stop this kind of "internal" Scatter Bomb?

A psychiatrist we greatly admire once said, "Ninety percent of the solution to any problem consists in awareness of that problem." Again, if you train your people effectively in the earliest stages, you'll have already dealt with, if not eliminated, this problem. Here's how to do it. During your training session with new distributors, you should state the following:

"We consider it our job as your mentors to assist you in earning millions of dollars and regaining total control of your time as quickly as possible. And we can assure you of two things: (1) we will never keep information from you about systems that work, and (2) we will never allow you to make the mistakes that, experience has taught us, can cause failure. Can you all understand our motives? We want to see that you succeed. As your mentors, we insist that you agree to one very important stipulation, because if you won't agree to this, we can't help you. Fair enough? (Get their consent!) You must be willing to promise us right now that you will never, under any circumstances, change to new systems because a leader in town has promoted them, or recommend books and materials to your downline until you check with us. That is, until we get you to an income of $15,000 a month. After that, you can do whatever you want. Is that a fair deal? (Again, get their verbal consent at this point.) We cannot afford to have you scattered and unfocused, or teaching new concepts to your downline, or doing anything else counterproductive! In fact, we suggest you check with us before you attend any big meeting in your first year. Fair enough?"

By calling the attention of new distributors to this inevitable booby trap, you are doing a great deal toward preempting it. More importantly, you are requesting their permission, in advance, to repeat this admonition each time a new leader comes to town peddling sales aids. And when you do bring it up on your voice mail to your entire downline the week before the leader hits town, they will not consider your warning as stepping out of line or expressing jealousy. If you don't breach the subject at training and teach all your people to do the same with all their frontline, every time a new leader comes into town, your people can be set back months in their efforts. You see, it's not necessarily that the new system doesn't work. The problem is that each time you introduce a new system to your entire downline, everyone starts all over again at ground zero. And we all know that it takes months of effort to become proficient at any new marketing strategy.

The Parasite Mentor

THE next factor that will cause new distributors to become scattered is what we call the "parasite mentor"—someone who has never built a legitimate organization, yet has written a book or recorded an audiotape to teach others how to do so, and claims to be a mentor. Let's say that one day a new second-level distributor calls you to introduce herself and innocently lets slip that her sponsor (your frontline associate) is engaged in some new recruiting activity with which you are completely unfamiliar. So you call your frontline associate and gently mention your conversation with his new recruit and, after a bit of small talk, you quiz him about this new direct mailing system. He becomes embarrassed, but then explains to you that he just read a great book by a well-known author (whom you know has never actually built his own organization). Regardless of the fact that mass mailings have never worked effectively for anyone in your group, he is using it and teaching it to others.

Folks, we recognize and respect the fact that we are all independent distributors who have the right to do this business any way we desire. But as the head of our own organization, each of us has the right to decide whom, among our people, we wish to actively support. Make certain in training new distributors that they understand that you are going to support only those that follow your system. And those who change your system without your approval will lose your support. Why are we so adamant about this? Because we want you to succeed and we know our system works. But we don't know about others.

Another problem can stem from a successful network marketer who has a burning desire to become an author. But beware of these books—they can be quite "inventive." We have seen lots of materials churned out by successful network

marketers that contain systems and strategies that have *never* been utilized, by them or anyone else. But motivated by a fiery zeal to get a book or tape released, the concepts seem logical at first glance. The problem is most new distributors who read materials written by leaders accept them as gospel. We've often pondered how many poor souls must have failed at network marketing by emulating these unproven recruiting and training techniques, presented by successful distributors who never actually used them. It's sad but true.

If you're a new distributor, we encourage you to track upline until you find a highly successful distributor and follow the exact systems he or she has used. If you enjoy absorbing knowledge about the industry, at least call a veteran in your company to get suggestions on truly useful books by authors who have successfully built huge organizations. Don't lose your vision by following systems of "parasite mentors" or new authors describing unproven systems. Some who have written bestsellers in our field have never built anything. Other authors have been in twenty different companies and will, in fact, join yours if you order 10,000 books. But they are often disseminating strategies that do not work or have not been tested, and if your new distributor reads and implements them, it will cause months of wasted time.

Scatter Bomb Fever

THE next diversion is often inadvertently created by your own company, when new products or services are introduced. Often, it's what we call a "sizzle product"—a new, exciting technology or specialized niche item that causes distributors to lose all decorum and sense of propriety, and start jumping around like Old Festus Bean on a train trip to the Yukon during the great Gold Rush. Irrational comments and erratic behavior on the part of new distributors generally accompany the announcement of these new products. Especially when a major field leader joins in the fever, the "sizzle product" Scatter Bomb can be quite devastating. Let's take a look at one example.

This type of Scatter Bomb fever began in one company with something as innocent as simple math when a distributor calculated that he would earn an extra $30,000 the next month if everybody in his group ordered just one of the newly released product. It progressed to the point where frenzied medical doctors rented warehouse space and taught medical assistants how to operate fork lifts in order to warehouse the supply which would re-

sult in $20 million of profits next year. What made this situation all the more frightening was that this frenzy occurred when no one had yet seen or even used the product, and no studies about the product had been released. All this activity stemmed from rumors that the new product was really great and that everyone in America would be in lines a mile long to purchase it. Company leaders dropped the hint that the supply was limited and could become back-ordered, thereby keeping the fever at a high pitch as distributors bought more than they needed to be sure they didn't run out. We saw thousands of victims of this misdirected activity and, even a year later, some distributors were still distracted from building their business. Some were threatening to sue everyone in the known world, and others were still angry over the $20 million they lost.

So how in the world do we protect ourselves and our distributors against this type of Scatter Bomb when it's a new product from our own company? How do we maintain rationality in the face of a screaming frenzy initiated by our upline leaders? Well, to be honest, we're not certain there is any protection, given the truth about greed and human nature. When a good solid company releases a new exciting service or product, nothing can really keep people from becoming excited. But at least you can remain balanced. Tell your leaders to try the new products and to recommend that everyone in their groups try them, but not mortgage their homes in order to buy them. Wait until the new product has fully proven itself before getting too excited. And above all else, "please don't rent that warehouse space just yet!"

What we've learned is that the real money is made a few months after the new products have proven themselves, not during the initial hype. If distributors jump the gun at the launch of a new foreign market or a new product, they typically last only a short time in this business. About halfway through the second month, at a time when we truly don't know yet about the long-term nature of the commodity, it may actually still be on back order. Around the third or fourth month, if the product or service is truly what it's been portrayed to be and the company has produced enough to supply the demand, thus enabling us to purchase all we want, then the real volume, based on usage instead of hype, begins. That's when we truly notify all our friends and family and begin developing a new addition to our recruiting speech.

Perhaps the biggest danger of all is that the launch of a new product or service, which has real sizzle, can scatter distributors enough to shift their focus from selling financial security and time freedom to just selling the new product. That's a real hazard—you don't want your best recruiters redirecting their approach from the MLM dream to a single service or product. Remember, prospects will never be as excited as we are about a new toothpaste or CD-ROM. In the midst of their selling a new service or product, distributors should continue to focus their prospecting approach on how to earn $20,000, $30,000, even $50,000 a month and achieve total financial independence. Tantalize your prospects, if you like, with your excitement about the new items coming or new foreign markets opening up, but keep it in perspective. Most of all, maintain a balanced outlook with every new product. Don't go overboard and build your presentation around any one product or service before it is a proven success. Frenzies never yield stable growth.

Lack of Structure

MANY distributors suffer from lack of structure in network marketing—particularly those who were accustomed to the world of traditional business. After all, they got used to the Monday morning rahrah meetings, production quotas, and supervisors breathing down their necks demanding more and more. In network marketing, you are your own boss, revving up your own engines, and setting your own pace. The systems in traditional sales are the antithesis to those utilized in networking. Some corporate salespeople—such as Terry Hill, after she left the Xerox Corporation as their number one salesperson—feel disoriented and displaced at first without the traditional structure.

Many people need a detailed plan of action and a timetable, complete with daily quotas. This keeps them from becoming scattered and creates a strong sense of direction. Once you have set specific goals, use a day planner, or a scheduler, or anything else that will assist you in keeping yourself on track.

For others, time itself is a problem. Such people may feel overwhelmed by their already busy lives. How can they possibly fit one more thing into it—especially something as time-consuming as a network marketing business. Or perhaps, having jumped in without a plan, they use their time inefficiently, running around town, hither and yon, fighting traffic, doing one-on-one meetings, presentations, and training. They feel completely at loose ends and are unsure about what really constitutes productive activity.

Pam Delahanty of Francestown, New Hampshire, found the solution by turning to her upline associates for coaching. She describes how dissipated she felt trying to keep up with her life and her business: "The biggest challenge I had was time. After all, I already worked full-time as a dental hygienist; on top of that, I was a mom to two very active toddlers; and then there was my husband, with whom I wanted to spend time. I felt stretched, torn, and at times guilty as I tried to spread myself in all directions. I felt out of balance, out of control, and out of integrity. I saw myself wearing too many hats, as mother, wife, friend, employee, and now as a networker. Though I felt a strong belief for this industry and the possibilities it could provide, it was difficult for me to find the time and energy to share it with other people given my already full and hectic schedule.

"I turned to my upline associates, Dr. Jay Clark and Linda Young, for help, and at their suggestion I began exploring my core values. What I found to be most important to me are relationships, fun, spontaneity, and the peace of mind financial freedom brings. Once I determined this, I took a look at how I could work these into my life and my business. What if I could share the benefits of the products and the business when I was going about my daily life, without putting on a separate hat! What if it was spontaneous and even fun? Since having incorporated these elements into my business, I am more energetic because I'm not wasting time worrying about what I am going to say, or how I am going to look, or even what the response will be. I used to think energy was dependent on how much sleep I had or what I ate. I now believe I will have all the energy I need just by getting myself into worthwhile action. Action creates energy.

"I'll never forget one of my first outrageous, impromptu conversations after discovering my new enthusiasm. A policeman stopped me on my way to my first sponsoring interview because I had rolled through a stop sign. I explained with much enthusiasm how nervous I was with this new business venture, and he let me go with just a warning, a smile, and a good luck wish. As a thank-you, I gave the officer a sample of our toothpaste. A week later, I was stopped again by the same officer, this time to purchase product, and years later, he is still a loyal customer."

When a longtime family friend first introduced Sunie Nelson of Fresno, California, to network marketing, she was working from sixty to eighty hours a week and holding down two jobs. Sunie immediately informed her friend that she couldn't take on network marketing because she absolutely had "no extra time, period!" But the more she thought about her predicament—a relentless work schedule and $40,000 of debt hanging over her head—the more she decided she had nothing to lose. She gave up television and some sleep, deciding that television would never get her where she wanted to go and that she could catch up on missed sleep later. Sunie began sharing the opportunity and products with everyone she knew. She created a work plan, stayed with it, and within two months she earned the distinction of being the first in her company to become an executive director in such a short time, a record that lasted five years. After two more years, she reached the top level in her company, and now has earned the freedom to enjoy her real love: competitive slalom waterskiing.

One of the primary excuses people give for not joining our industry is that they don't have the time. However, both Pam and Sunie found a solution to this problem. They avoided the Scatter Bomb and focused on doing the work necessary to build their groups. Not so surprisingly, once they realized what the business could mean to them, they both found the time.

If you are having difficulty organizing your time, harnessing your energy, or keeping your attention focused on your business, seek the help of a mentor. Ask someone, preferably in your upline, or someone else you want to emulate, to coach you. It can be done once a week in as little as a ten- or fifteen-minute telephone conversation. Rene has been a mentor to Karen McGeehan of West Linn, Oregon, for some time. Each Monday, Karen reports her business activities to Rene, summarizing the number of people she prospected that week, the number of appointments she set, and the number of people to whom she made a presentation—her real measure of progress. Her goal is to do ten presentations a week, which results in her sponsoring between five to eight people a month. When she is off her target, Karen and Rene will talk about what got in the way of her meeting her goals that week, and then perhaps Rene will assist her in redesigning her mind-set to block any negative thoughts. When we are out of the country, Karen faxes or e-mails her report to Rene; even if they don't talk, they share some communication in writing. Over time, Rene and Karen have built a close relationship. You may find that a mentor can help structure your activities, making all the difference between success and failure.

Going It Alone in a Team Sport

IT is the role of the new distributor to plant the seeds, which the various upline associates need to water. It is easy to get scattered if distributors try to go it alone in this business. But the fact is we are all part of a team. New distributors must learn to utilize upline support until they, like their role models, achieve wealth and independence.

John Prange of Kutztown, Pennsylvania, was a veterinarian in his fifties who had been successful at everything he'd ever tried, until he tried network marketing. According to John, "It took two years for me to realize that something was wrong, that I was not succeeding as I normally had in my other endeavors. I was able to recruit lots of benchwarmers into the business, but none who wanted to play on the team." John was really bothered by his apparent failure and turned to his network marketing team for help.

It was suggested that John look into taking a personal development course to find out what might be missing in his life—something that perhaps he didn't even know was missing. One program led to another and he made a discovery: "I realized that I had never honored anyone by listening to them but had always listened with my own agenda. I began to look at the fact that my life had been designed by me, many years earlier, to play out exactly as it was playing out, and I currently had no control over the play unless I was willing to make some major changes in myself. I was fascinated by the joy of writing a new script wherein I could develop a game bigger than life with no particular ties to the outcome. But the most important part of this plan came when I began surrounding myself with a community of individuals who would support me in my decisions and commitments and who would always be there for me.

"Then I learned that it was a two-way street. I had to be able to give positive, directional feedback to my players to help them win the game based on their own expectations. I had always wanted to be the good guy to my friends, wearing the white hat. But now I could see the value of letting other members of my team know when they were getting off track with their businesses. As the one soliciting support, I needed to make strong, clear requests. As the one giving support, I came to understand that my associates could not read my mind. They joined me in this business believing that I would lead the way. So I began making requests of them that honored their individual visions and supported them to stay on their own chosen paths to success."

What John discovered was that being part of a truly supportive team is the key to success. It comes down to a few simple steps: (1) Consider the unlimited possibilities and shape your vision around the vast choices; (2) Develop a game plan, delineating specific daily steps toward building your business that will include identifying those characteristics in your life that you believe could be improved; (3) Get into action. Don't procrastinate— Just do it!; (4) Make clear requests from a coach or upline mentor for your own personal growth and give honest feedback to your downline, being mindful of their personal objectives. Then watch your business grow beyond your wildest expectations.

Because of the multi-level structure of our industry, we are all part of a team— sometimes coaching and other times being coached. When it all works according to plan, the multi-level compensation program is absolutely warranted and justified. To try to go it alone in this business is to swim upstream. It is a team business in which, in the course of every day, there should be some giving and receiving along

Because of the multi-level structure of our industry, we are all part of a team— sometimes coaching and other times being coached.

the way. If you want to avoid being scattered and keep total clarity of vision, you need to reevaluate how to better serve and be served by your team.

Distractions Caused by Personal Crises

NONE of us works in a vacuum. The success of our business is commensurate with our enthusiasm, and our enthusiasm is affected by our personal lives. Dr. Dennis Pezzilesi of Middletown, Connecticut, found comfort by focusing his complete concentration on his business while going through the greatest tragedy of his life. Dennis's story puts many other crises in perspective.

"On February 28, 1992, at approximately 10:30 P.M., I was involved in a car accident that changed my life forever. Before this tragedy, I was a successful person, or so I thought. I excelled in everything I ever did in life. I was a perfectionist who was able to do many things and do them all well. But the problem was deep down, I was unhappy. I wasn't passionate about anything in my life. This instability led to my divorce, a drinking problem, and finally the accident that was the turning point in my life.

"I had been drinking that night, like I had on numerous other occasions in my life. That's how I disconnected from reality. On this particular night, I ran a red light and broadsided a car with two passengers. The passenger was not hurt, but the driver, Renford Gilling, was killed.

"From that moment on, my life activities consisted of being sued, appearing in court, going bankrupt, trying to run my medical practice with my name in the headlines, facing a possible ten years in jail, and trying to sustain a marriage to my new wife, Bonnie, the most supportive person in the world. On the inside, I felt guilt, shame, sorrow, fear, and despair, all mixed together. I wished I had been the one who died. This was a tragedy of immeasurable proportions and it was buried inside of me, eating me up.

"I was convicted of misconduct with a motor vehicle and sentenced to four years, suspended after thirty days, with three years probation. I was put on random urine tests for two years, alcohol counseling, and AA meetings. My license was put on probation for two years. I went bankrupt and had to close my office. I did 3,000 hours of community service. But nothing, I felt, could make up for the life I had taken.

"In August of this same year, I discovered network marketing. My company president believes strongly that network marketing is an opportunity for personal growth, which will then lead to financial growth. With the help of my new networking family, I learned how to stop hiding my tragedy and, instead, turn it into a positive force for gift-giving. I have told my story to hundreds of people, who in turn have affected thousands of others— Don't drink and drive. Instead of wallowing in the shame of it all, I now honor Renford Gilling by saving lives in his name as I tell others his story and mine. If it weren't for the philosophy put forth by our incredible industry, I know I would still be drinking and living in guilt and despair. Instead, I have a beautiful relationship with my wife, a wonderful three-year-old son, a thriving medical practice, a network organization that is growing geometrically, and most of all, I am living my passion—which is to powerfully affect the lives of millions."

Dennis was fortunate to have found a supportive wife and an understanding team in his network marketing company. He could easily have allowed his tragedy to diffuse his energy for the rest of his life. Instead of yielding to chronic alcoholism and utter despair, he has turned his attention toward concentrating on the lives he can still save. The exponential growth that is so strongly promulgated by our industry is far from being just about money. As it is exemplified in Dennis's personal life, the concept is a force for change in hundreds of thousands of lives. Dennis has overcome his reluctance to hide his story. By his openness, he has made a significant impact on others.

Each time we sit down with new prospects, we must realize we have the opportunity to make a difference in their lives. But for that to happen, we must find a way to get through their resistance. When prospects see a business opportunity that seems too good to be true, one that doesn't fit their self-image, they will either pass on the opportunity or get in and then quickly get out. It is only when people can

We can't avoid crises, but we can prevent them from completely diverting our attention from our work by accepting each one as a stepping-stone to both personal and business excellence.

visualize the end result that they will consider joining you in this business.

Network marketing is a business of storytelling. Don't be afraid to show your vulnerability. If your story has a human quality, it has a much greater chance of touching people and breaking down their barriers during your presentation. We can't avoid crises, but we can prevent them from completely diverting our attention from our work by accepting each one as a stepping-stone to both personal and business excellence.

SUMMARY

- The Scatter Bomb is a mental explosion that diffuses the focus of distributors, causing them to stop using the system they have been taught and to frantically follow any and every new network marketing system or leader that comes along.

- Effective network marketing is a process of duplicating systems; each time you change the system, everyone in your downline gets confused.

- New marketers can be handed everything on a silver platter and still fail if they refuse to duplicate a simple system that has already been tried and tested.

- Novice distributors must be taught to follow the teachings of their sponsors and not deviate from them.

- Distributors must be warned to put on blinders their first year because of the veritable smorgasbord of competing companies, recruiting systems, videos, manuals, and numerous other sales systems available to them.

- Successful networkers build their businesses on their ability to shut out every negative influence around them, whether internal or external, and stay the course with clear vision, focusing intently on their goal and plan of action.

- One of the first manifestations of the Scatter Bomb will be the temptation to change, just slightly, the recruiting system you've learned, by either softening the approach or lowering the income or recruiting numbers.

- The way to prevent your new distributors from attempting to "reinvent the wheel" is to anticipate it early, and warn them during training of the importance of following a proven system.

- Counter the threat that first-year networkers will be offered other deals by:

    1 Warning them of this fact.

    2 Teaching them that perseverance with one company is the key to success.

    3 Explaining to them that trying to build two downlines in separate companies will lead to failure.

- Most new distributors will be tempted several times to change companies, but, remember, no single person in your organization is absolutely indispensable.

- As you continue to build your group, new leaders will emerge under those who choose to leave.

- Keep your group from jumping from one system to another by preparing them ahead of time to glean new facts from a new speaker while never changing to a new recruiting or training system.

- The key to building a successful business is to stick with one system long enough to allow it to work.

- Ask a trusted upline associate for recommended reading, and don't lose your vision by following authors not recommended by your mentor.

- Scatter Bomb fever can be caused by an announcement, often from highly respected leaders within your company, about a soon-to-be-released product or service that they say is so unbelievable that everyone will soon be clamoring for it. Be skeptical of their claims until you have used it yourself.

- When you or your associates occasionally fall victim to Scatter Bomb fever, don't change your plan of action, simply continue on your steady course, while including a mention of the exciting new addition in your presentations.

- Many distributors suffer from a lack of structure—particularly those who were accustomed to the structure of traditional business.

- If you have a problem organizing your time, use a planner or scheduler to help you stay on track.

- Make clear requests for your own business and personal growth from a coach or upline mentor and, in return, give honest feedback to your downline associates, being mindful of their objectives.

- If you want to avoid being scattered and keep total clarity of vision, reevaluate how to better serve and be served by your team.

- The success of our business is commensurate with our enthusiasm, which in turn is affected by our personal lives.

- It is only when people can visualize the end result that they will consider joining you in this business.

- When you experience a personal crisis, don't be afraid to include it in "your story" to help break down the barriers during your presentation.

- You can't avoid crises, but you can prevent them from completely diverting your attention away from your intended objectives by using each one as a stepping-stone to propel you to success.

CHAPTER 7

Eluding the Meeting Mines

Avoid the pitfalls of counterproductive meetings.

EVERYONE WHO HAS COME OUT of corporate America recalls different highlights of the experience, but without exception, all of them recall the endless meetings. Many managers, who still have some desire to be productive, get extremely frustrated with the meeting syndrome; they are absolutely convinced nothing of value ever happens in meetings. The greater the attendance at the meeting, the less productive it seems to be. Meetings can be great obstacles for workers who are results-oriented.

There has been a deluge of displaced executives flocking into the network distribution industry. They bring with them some valuable resources, most notably their wide base of professional contacts and high-level management experience. But they also bring some disastrous

habits, many of which may have caused the downsizing of corporate America in the first place. (We will discuss this in more detail in chapter nine.) That same executive who was paid a fairly high salary to go from meeting to meeting in his former career has a strong inclination to carry that habit into our industry.

In the very first year of network marketing, probably even the first month, new distributors may find themselves exposed to one of the prime causes of failure in our profession: lethargy. Because this is brought on by the very people whom they regard as successful, it will be difficult to resist. Lethargy results from what we call Meeting Mines. In the battle for success, these mines seldom cause "death" (outright failure), but they often lead to the maiming and disfigurement of a networking career, that is, they keep some new associates from rising to their full potential. Once they step on these well-camouflaged explosives, new distributors may end up disabled and limping through the rest of their careers. If new distributors are lucky, they will be able to avoid these particularly destructive explosives until after they have achieved a reasonable income. Those unfortunate enough to be led through this minefield by their sponsors in their first month may indeed be among the earliest of our "dearly departed" associates. Although Meeting Mines usually just maim, they *can* be fatal.

Take some time to consider how our industry works: Income is paid when products or services are ordered. The larger our organization, the more orders are placed. CEOs in our industry pay people to do "word-of-mouth" advertising, instead of building overpriced retail stores and hiring expensive public relation agencies. The more people we personally recruit and train, the larger our organization, and the larger our income. There-fore, effective recruiting and training meetings are the foundation of our business. In network marketing, no one pays you to waste time sitting around in strategy meetings. Unless you are talking to people about our business, you are not really working the business. New distributors will never be as enthusiastic about personal sponsoring as they are in the first year. It is the most critical time in the career of a network marketer. In this chapter we intend to describe Meeting Mines carefully and provide you with an effective defense against each of them.

First Mine: Hotel Meetings

JUST about the time a new distributor has learned how to become a leader and has his group on track, some out-of-town leader inevitably blasts into the community and holds a citywide hotel meeting. Although lavish and appealing to new people, it can often result in teaching your group bad habits. Or it may be a regularly

Unless you are talking to people about our business, you are not really working the business.

scheduled hotel recruiting meeting at which one or two of the local leaders speak and to which you are encouraged to bring new recruits. Such meetings are going on at all hours of the day at every major hotel in the world. Occasionally the speaker is reasonably good and lots of distributors are encouraged to attend—as many as a thousand people can be present. But of all the ways to build a dynamic network marketing organization, a large hotel meeting, as the first and primary contact with your prospects, is perhaps the very worst.

In spite of the fact that Mark's mentor, Richard Kall, said, "Don't do a hotel meeting when I make my first trip to Austin," Mark set one up anyway. He packed 300 people in a ballroom, convinced that, given his communications skills, Richard's success, and a ground-floor networking offer, they'd sign up half the audience. Mark sat up all night putting his identification number on more than 100 distributor agreements. Out of the 300 prospects, only 3 signed up and all of those had quit in sixty days. Mark had just stepped on his first Meeting Mine and resolved to never do it again.

Hotel meetings were first developed by network marketing companies that sold durable goods as a means of quickly sifting through large numbers of people in order to find one or two people with big money to invest. A former president of one such company told us jokingly that their best "closers" used this method to "sniff out overly eager prospects with at least $30,000 to invest." The problem is, when these companies were run out of business or prevented from front-end loading distributors with garages full of products, their hotel meeting system remained popular.

But hotel meetings are among the least effective recruiting systems. Network marketing has always been a "people business." When prospects are subjected to a large, impersonal meeting room, the intimacy of our business is completely lost. Long before fax machines, computers, VCRs, and hotel meetings, Mary Kay created more female millionaires than any other corporation in history. Amway built a billion-dollar empire in America using private, in-home meetings and is today still four times larger than their nearest competitors. For some strange reason, during the last half of the '80s, when MLM really began to blossom, most companies opted for hotel meetings rather than in-home meetings. Hotel meetings can only be of value if they are used occasionally as a supplement to regularly scheduled in-home presentations. Let's analyze why.

Hotel Meetings Can Not Be Duplicated

First, the setting of a hotel meeting is all wrong for network marketing. The number one fear in business is public speaking. New prospects, whose first introduction to our business is via the hotel meeting, will be immediately fearful of success. They walk into the Hyatt, see a well-dressed couple addressing hundreds of attendees with a microphone and think, "I can't do that!" Most people fear public speaking. We sometimes wonder how many millions of would-be successful MLM distributors have walked out of hotel meetings and chosen never to participate because they thought they might be required to stand up and deliver a public speech. The thought can be quite intimidating. No one need ever deliver a speech to become a millionaire in our profession. Yet that's not the understanding of many who quit before they ever begin, believing that public speaking is a large part of network marketing.

In addition, there's the money issue. It costs a reasonable sum for leaders to rent a ballroom or meeting space at a hotel. So, at the meeting, either the leaders lose money, which most can't afford, or they make a profit, which encourages others to emulate them. But what about the message that is sent to prospects and other members of the group as they glance around the room and discover, with simple mathematics, that the leader is making money off them.

There will be some resentment at the thought of a leader profiting from the meeting. Moreover, some entrepreneurial leaders will get the idea that the way to make money in network marketing is to conduct these large meetings. Other leaders even go further by selling books and tapes to participants. It can become so profitable that one leader, formerly with one of the biggest MLM companies, confided in us he can gross over a half million dollars in a weekend by charging for hotel rooms, food, books, tapes, CD-ROMs, etc; however, he has the advantage of being a professional convention planner, with plenty of money to invest. Not every leader has the resources to duplicate that approach nor should he or she really need to have them. The nature of our business is to earn money from the sale of products and services—not peripheral materials.

Hotel Meetings Create Dependency

Network marketing is successful when leaders are recruited who, in turn, recruit other leaders. It is meant to create independence. Many companies insist on the use of the term "independent distributor." Yet hotel meetings have just the opposite effect. For those who do join and buy into the concept, they think, "Great! I don't have to work to be successful; all I've got to do is send my friends, family, and associates to the Hyatt each Thursday night and these great speakers will do it all for me." Of course that never works because ultimately the only people who make real money in MLM, with very few exceptions, are those who conduct their own meetings. Effective recruiting meetings need not be large and no one needs to deliver formal speeches.

Attending meetings at hotels should not be confused with real work in this business. Too many new distributors find that it's much easier to become professional meeting attendees than it is to face the rejection of frontline recruiting. At the outset of your MLM career, it is important to understand that sole dependence on hotel meetings for recruiting and building a large organization is based on an erroneous principle: "This is easy. I don't have to work. I'll just send people to meetings!" Absolutely not true!

A Low Turn-Out Causes Embarrassment

If you think no-shows are hard to take when the meeting is held in your home, think about how you might feel when this happens at a hotel meeting. There is no worse experience in this business than to rent a hotel room and have a handful of people show up. Ask any leader in the business. Almost everyone has been there and done that at least once. Dave Johnson recalls one such moment in his first year of the business . . . nearly ten years ago: "Early in my career, I felt it necessary to grab at any chance I had to talk to people in hopes that they may join somewhere in my line. One of my second-level distributors, Dr. Hung-Tai Wang, invited me to conduct a training meeting in Bethesda, Maryland, at the Hyatt Regency. He promised me that there would be 175 people in attendance. So I maxed out my credit card, cashed in my last free miles on United, and went to support my downline.

"On the target Saturday, I arrived at the ballroom at 8:30 A.M., one hour before the 9:30 start time. Nobody was there. At 9:00, Dr. Wang arrived. At 9:15, it was still just the two of us. At 9:25, there were five guests. By 9:30, Dr. Wang was pacing up and down the hallway looking for lost distributors. At 9:45, he was quite distraught wondering where the other 170 guests were.

"We did conduct the all-day seminar for the five attendees and three of them are still in the business today. However, Dr. Wang admitted later that he wished the overhanging chandelier would have fallen on him and ended it all right there. The moral for me was the realization that you never know when you'll meet your next top leaders. Just think of what could have happened to those three leaders if we had discounted their attendance and cancelled the seminar because of lack of expected attendance."

The fact is that the meeting could have been held in Dr. Wang's home and spared him the embarrassment of all the no-shows. They were extremely lucky they didn't come away with nothing to show for their efforts. Of the countless stories we've heard over the years, no one else in this entire industry has described a similar hotel experience with such a positive outcome. Today, Dr. Hung-Tai Wang has one of the largest organizations in Asia and is one of the highest paid distributors in the business. Dave Johnson and his wife, Coni, live in Reno, Nevada, the same town in which we live. Rene worked closely with them during those pioneering days and we have all become close friends. As upline to Dr. Wang, the Johnsons are the leaders of one of the largest Asian organizations and among the highest paid distributors in our company. They travel extensively and live a life that others can only dream about.

Paula Cook Ehrlich tells a similar story of her early days in the business when she accompanied her husband on a business trip to Texas. "While there, I decided to hold an opportunity meeting for a few people we knew. I was planning to use our hotel suite for the meeting and had taken a few key products with me to show everyone.

"I happened to mention this to my upline and he said that he had a very large organization in Texas and that he would put out a voice mail about the meeting. He said that I should get a meeting room at the hotel, which I did, for about fifty people. I called him when I'd done this and he said that he didn't think the room would be large enough, that I should get one that would accommodate about 100 people. That was two days before the meeting, and, at that point, the only room the hotel had available was one for about 200 people. So we decided to rent it, setting up water stations at the back and a large product display at the front to take up any extra space. Of course, then I had to have more products and display materials than I had brought with me, so I had the company send, via overnight courier, a complete product package and then scurried about town to find what I needed for the display.

"When I reported back to my upline, he said he'd put the message out a couple of times on voice mail and that we should have a good crowd. He added that this would be great training for me. He was right—I just had no idea how costly the lesson would be.

"Well, the evening of the big event came and we had the most beautiful product display and professional handouts on each chair summarizing the business opportunity and products. Two of my associates had come early to handle the registration desk. But only fifteen minutes before we were scheduled to start, *no one had shown up!* At that point, we said to each other, 'Wouldn't it be funny if no one came? Ha, ha!' Well, guess what? By our scheduled start time of 7:30 P.M., there were four people in the room and they were four of the original ten I had invited . . . in a room that would hold 200. We did sponsor those four guests, so it wasn't a total loss—just a very expensive evening. They must have gotten a clear picture that the market wasn't saturated yet. My husband jokingly said that if there was any scam in this business, it was that my upline had a downline in Houston! We had a good laugh over it.

"When I got back to my room, there was a message from my upline asking me to call him and let him know how the meeting went. When I told him, he was horrified! And I will never forget his first question to me: 'Are you going to quit?' To tell you the truth, it never even entered my mind to quit. When I told him, 'No, of course not,' he said that I 'had real char-acter. If I wasn't planning to quit, then I would definitely make it in the business.' As it turned out, there was a glitch in the voice mail system, preventing anyone from hearing the announcements. My upline offered to pay for the room, which I declined, but we've had many laughs over it since.

"In the years that followed, I thought of that comment often when I really did feel like quitting—it kept me going!" Today, seven years later, Paula and her husband, Mort, are living on Miami Beach, having reached the very pinnacle of their company, drawing an income from an organization that stretches across more than twenty countries. They are living the lifestyle of which they've always dreamed, and still believe that anyone can do this business if they are willing to overcome the temporary setbacks along the way.

A handful of people showing up in a home or hotel suite would have been a normal MLM gathering. But a handful in a hotel ballroom is not a good feeling if you are the host. It's also quite costly. Most networkers can only afford to make this mistake once.

Hotel Meetings Are Not Private

Hotel meetings, by their very nature, systematically screen out 25 percent of the population. Just use a little common sense. Many doctors and accountants cannot afford to be seen by patients or clients at a hotel recruiting meeting for Multi-Level Marketing. Many corporate leaders and company owners won't risk being seen in these meetings by their subordinates or customers. Teachers fear bumping into parents of their students or, even worse, their principal! We once recruited a pediatric cardiologist who sat in our living room and said, "You know, my own sister tried to get me to attend one of her meetings when some great out-of-town leader was speaking in Austin, but I declined. How confident would the parents of a five-year-old be if they bumped into their physician at an MLM recruiting meeting the night before he was to perform open heart surgery on their child? The only reason I am here now is because it's a private meeting!" Remember, the first time a new prospect sees our business, the best possible setting is your living room, be it ever so humble.

Hotel Meetings Do Not Exemplify Freedom

We are always insisting to new prospects that "freedom" is our greatest reward. So imagine a guy on Thursday night at 7:30, loosening his tie and walking into a meeting of a hundred people. He's thinking about the fact that he's already put in forty-two hours this week at his company. How is he going to explain to his wife and children why he now needs to go out to meetings at night, too? Nobody wants to spend what precious little time they've got at night searching for a parking space at the Hilton. Large, weekly hotel meetings destroy the concept of freedom by forcing people to add to their already overloaded schedule after their regular work hours.

Hotel Meetings Create an Illusion of Saturation

It's impossible to saturate any area with too many distributors—yet the perception of saturation can discourage new distributors. A presentation is naturally more appealing when it is given in one's living room with a few friends discussing the tremendous ground-floor opportunity in network marketing. We all know that, relative to the entire population of most cities, a gathering of 300 people is a drop in the bucket. Yet, to new distributors, it may seem as if everyone in their immediate area already knows about this deal. A new distributor may think, "My gosh, in this room alone, 299 people are ahead of me in this business!" The impression of joining a company at an early stage is destroyed by the initial perception of hundreds streaming into a large hotel recruiting meeting.

Hotel Meetings Do Not Promote Personal Development

Personal growth and development have always been the true assets of our industry. But only a very few people experience personal growth by standing up in front of an audience with a microphone. For most people, leadership skills are better developed in small in-home meetings to recruit new frontline distributors, coupled with weekend training sessions in which networkers are taught to lead their own small groups. We believe the most positive outcome of success in our industry is not financial independence or time freedom, but rather personal development.

We have proudly watched many of our personal recruits, some of them the most unlikely to become success stories, develop into remarkable leaders by sheer force of will. Rather than conducting their recruiting meetings for them, we encouraged them to take charge on their own. And while some successful leaders are proud of the former doctors, lawyers, and corporate CEOs they've sponsored, we are exceptionally proud of our humble frontline recruits: a housekeeper, a student, and a police officer, all of whom have be-

come millionaire legends in our industry. Along the way, we managed to recruit a few dynamic professionals like Terry and Tom Hill, but for the most part our highest percentage of successful frontline leaders were formerly ordinary, wage-earning people.

The message we want to convey at every meeting with every single prospect and distributor is a simple one: "We are in a low-investment, low-overhead distribution business in which average people can achieve wealth and independence through hard work and the legitimate movement of products and services." Here's the message we *don't* want to convey: "We are in a pyramid system in which those with public speaking skills, who get in early, can lead profitable weekly, monthly, and annual meetings by selling books and tapes and hosting motivation rallies." The latter message is the one being projected by those who insist on regular hotel meetings. Thus, the first Meeting Mine a new distributor is likely to encounter in the early battle for success is the frequent hotel extravaganza. Hotel meetings are not an effective tool in building a legitimate network and they are not easily duplicated by the masses. Hotel meetings are a great way to bring your group together periodically on special occasions, like when upline leaders in your group come to town, or for a formal presentation of awards or special recognition, or just for bonding. But most of your time should be spent in face-to-face prospecting or at home making calls and doing your own presentations.

Second Mine: The Part-Time Adult Day Care Center

THE second Meeting Mine actually occurs most often in the home. We call it the part-time adult day care center. Generally it's created by well-intentioned upline leaders who open their homes to any and all downline associates whenever they are not at work. New people and old feel they can drop by any time to pick up products or just have a cup of coffee and visit their upline. It's a bit of an ego boost for those who have never had many friends, and it's a wonderful way to improve one's social life. It's also much easier to coach existing distributors who respect you than it is to endure the rejection of recruiting meetings with new prospects. The problem is, if your goal is to build a large organization, this method won't help you. It's like having a 24-hour drop-in center for the homeless and is about as profitable. This socializing may be fun, but don't deceive yourself into believing that your daily or weekly drop-ins are productive or helping grow your business. They aren't.

Third Mine: The Church Service

ANOTHER less effective get-together is what we call the "church service." Generally, it's a weekly recruiting meeting in which frontline distributors bring guests to the leader's home for a presentation. If these meetings really worked, they would render themselves obsolete in a matter of days. Here's why. If in the first week five people come to a recruiting meeting and everyone duplicates the process, by week three there should be 155 prospects—the original 5, their 25, and their 125 altogether. Most homes won't comfortably seat that many. And even if they do, by week four they certainly can't handle 780 folks.

Obviously, the reason some leaders can continue to do weekly in-home meetings for their downline for years is that the group doesn't grow exponentially. If your goal is to build a close circle of friends for the purpose of weekly personal support, or if you merely wish to have a small group of individuals who look up to you, there's no better way than the weekly MLM support group. It's great for folks who don't have a church affiliation but need weekly, two-hour bonding sessions with a group of like-minded people, but it's no way to build an international network marketing organization.

If you wish to earn a great deal of money and achieve total control of your time and destiny, you must become a leader and conduct your own meetings while teaching your front line to do the same.

If the exponential growth were to work as it should, besides having a totally unmanageable number of people, leaders would soon find that they had created a destructive codependency. If you wish to earn a great deal of money and achieve total control of your time and destiny, you must become a leader and conduct your own meetings while teaching your front line to do the same.

Rene shares her own personal experience from before we were married with this type of gathering in Reno: "As a former nun, I earned the right to conduct weekly church services. It was in my nature to enjoy conducting them, and I believed at the time that I was doing a great service for my downline. I am a teacher at heart and I loved presenting the business opportunity to our new prospects. I was going to be holding them anyway for my own prospects . . . why not do them for my distributors as well? Many of the more self-sufficient in my group did branch out with their own home meetings, but once a week, on Tuesday evenings, I had thirty to forty people gathered together—both distributors and their prospects. As long as I continued leading them, many good things came from those meetings: New people joined us in the business, but it was the closeness and friendships that we built that I really treasured.

"At the end of 1991, Mark and I married. My life changed dramatically, including considerable travel with my husband to support his, now our, downline across the country. I gave up my weekly meetings and, almost overnight, my Reno group disintegrated. Partly it was due to the fact that our company was experiencing the most severe media scrutiny in the history of network marketing. But mostly it was because I had made most everyone in the group dependent on me. When I closed the 'church' doors, it shut down business for many of my associates. It was a hard, but important, lesson for me. If you are holding your own 'church service' by choice, at the very least, continue to encourage the independence of every single person in your group along the way. It is important for their own personal growth and for the growth of everyone's business."

Fourth Mine: The Deception Meeting

THE next Meeting Mine is called a lot of different names by a lot of different marketers. Some call it the "dinner meeting" because it usually involves friends who have been invited to a dinner party. Others call it the "curiosity meeting" because the approach used to get friends and associates to the house does not explain why they're invited, so the friends attend because they are curious to see what their hosts are "up to." Actually, we call it the "deception meeting" because those of us who were ever invited to one still remember how angry we were at our friends for leading us on. In fact, many of us avoided network marketing for years because our only exposure to the industry involved this kind of trickery. Before you use this kind of meeting to snare recruits, be forewarned that it is not only ineffective, but it can lead to real resentment among friends.

The "deception meeting" is based on a very serious misconception. Some distributors with companies that have been in business for over a decade are afraid to tell their friends the name of their company out of fear that a well-known name will lead them to believe that the market is already saturated with distributors, and therefore won't be inclined to come to a presentation. This fear is erroneous for two reasons. First, the name of the company generally should not be mentioned when you are inviting people to a meeting anyway. Second, no business is ever saturated in any community. The fact that your friends may have already heard of your particular corporation doesn't mean they won't be interested. What is objectionable is being invited to a social event or an intimate dinner with friends that is really a recruitment meeting.

Deception or curiosity meetings are in-home business presentations in which the prospects are led to believe that they are merely going to dinner at a friend's home. When guests arrive, they are usually introduced to others in attendance, who are sponsors of the host, and perhaps another two or three couples who are prospects. Once the dinner is over, a formal presentation is given to illustrate the logarithmic growth of MLM. That's when the guests realize they've been "had."

This kind of meeting is a fraud right from the start. Most people with any integrity will refuse to recruit their friends using such deception, and those who are persuaded to do so usually fail. Throughout our travels in America, Asia, and Europe, we have met countless individuals who have refused for many years to consider any involvement in our industry because their initial exposure was based on a deception meeting.

Fifth Mine: The Office Meeting

ANOTHER kind of Meeting Mine is the office meeting. Even though he was warned by his upline mentor, Richard Kall, to never get involved in the office process, Mark ignored him and yielded to the temptation in his fifth month. By then, he was earning enough money to be able to afford the office. Mark often tells the following story to MLM groups.

"I had become a 'Big Biness' man. I actually pronounce it 'biness' because it's such a joke. 'Big Biness Men' are important guys. We usually drive a Mercedes, wear $2,000 designer sport coats, flash a Rolex on our wrist, and carry a platinum American Express card. Above all else, we need a fancy office and high overhead expenses to prove our worth. In all seriousness, the very things we attempt to escape by entering network marketing are frequently the things our egos dictate we

must have once we're successful. When I started earning over $15,000 a month I decided, against my mentor's protests, that I needed to move my network marketing business to an office location. After all, with that kind of income, I felt it was time to begin conducting meetings in an environment where I had my own desk, secretary, fax machine, and conference room. So I found a beautiful space in the nicest office complex in Austin, Texas, and signed a six-month lease. Then I hired a part-time secretary to take all my important calls and, poof, I was a 'Big Biness Man'!

"Guess what happened? First, my closing ratio declined by almost 50 percent. Not only that, but I had a significant increase in no-shows to my presentations. What telephone calls I did take were people complaining about the attitude problems and general incompetence of my secretary. So I had to spend time teaching her the fundamentals of telephone behavior. By the second month, no one I interviewed signed up, and the few I recruited in the first month were clamoring to hold their meetings in my office and refusing to do their own in-home meetings. By the third month, I had moved my office back home. Here's what I learned: Office meetings don't work nearly as effectively in our business as do in-home presentations. When I went home, my closing ratios jumped right back into the 20-percent range, and my downline distributors were much happier doing their own in-homes when I was again doing so."

We realize that advising against offices will be unpopular with many of you who already have offices and approach business in this manner. But our objective isn't to have you love us. Our goal is to get you to the same kind of income we are earning without unnecessary, costly overhead. However, if you choose to keep an office, at least do so knowing all the facts. First, renting an office can not be duplicated by most people because of cost. Second, an office creates unnecessary overhead. Third, office meetings do not exemplify the freedom that you should enjoy as a network marketer.

Office Meetings Can Not Be Duplicated

Most people have jobs rather than private offices and, therefore, do not have the slightest idea how to manage them. This causes havoc and unnecessary stress, which can impede one's productivity. Most people are too busy just learning the basics of MLM to have time to deal with running an office. In addition, not many people can afford an office. Neither of us could have afforded an office in our first few months in business and, therefore, would have never signed up had we been recruited in an office setting. Office space, even if you share it with other business-people, is expensive anywhere in the world. Remember, we are in a business of duplication. If we can't afford to do business in an office, on a boat, or anywhere else, it probably will also be impossible for, or inaccessible to, the masses.

Offices Create Unnecessary Overhead

Perhaps one of the biggest strengths of network marketing is the lack of overhead. In our business, you can reap the benefits of being an entrepreneur without the expense of a franchise or a small business owner's operating costs. The beauty of this business is that you can do it from your living room—there's no need to invest thousands of dollars on employees and office space. So why waste money on totally unnecessary overhead when an office is not going to increase your productivity?

Offices Do Not Exemplify Freedom

There are two major attractions to our industry: big money and free time. Prospects who come to an office interview will feel that, by joining your MLM organization, they will be tying themselves to an office. Hence, where is the freedom? If they duplicate your system, soon they will not only be fighting traffic during their commute but will feel compelled to spend much of their time there. What's worse, their leaders will imitate the process. They will feel that their presentations, too, should be held in such a professional setting. By leasing an office, you will be implementing a trend in your downline that contradicts the essence of this industry: giving ordinary people the chance to enjoy freedom outside of the traditional business site.

We have people in our downline who have succeeded through both hotel and office meetings, but none of them are earning half as much as we are. Regardless of how much you make, we encourage you, as we encourage them, to make your decisions based on what you want out of your business. Some distributors, and some foreign cultures, simply prefer the group office environment for motivational and social support. We understand these preferences and accept the fact that network marketers are their own bosses. But nothing is going to prevent us from advocating to every distributor in every country the systems that made us millions. Our intent is to give you all the facts so that

you can make intelligent decisions for yourself while establishing your network marketing business.

Sixth Mine: The Bar or Restaurant Meeting

ANOTHER hazardous situation can be found in the bar or restaurant meeting. Recruiters can't expect to be successful by conducting their meetings in public places where there's no access to a VCR, no blackboard or dry-erase whiteboard, and lots of distractions. You know, "little" distractions like a gang of drunken office workers singing songs or a sporting event blaring over multiple television sets. One of the most popular network marketing books, written a couple of decades ago during our industry's infancy, asserted that anyone could become wealthy by doing presentations on a bar napkin. But that's a lot of bunk—trust us! There's nothing at all effective or professional about doing business in a restaurant or a bar—unless the bar has a bulletin-board-sized napkin, a VCR for your personal use, and doesn't play music, sell alcohol, or entertain customers.

The secret of network marketing is to introduce as many new people as possible to our business opportunity. The method you use to sponsor your prospects should be one that can be easily duplicated and, in turn, used effectively with their prospects. It takes a lot of focus to do this right. Given the choice, your best chance for success is by hosting a small group meeting in your own home, where you have total control of the environment.

Seventh Mine: The "Other Guy's Place"

ANOTHER serious hazard is conducting your first recruiting meeting at the "other guy's place." If possible, try to avoid recruiting at any prospect's home or office. It is ineffective in the same way a bar or restaurant is ineffective: distractions. What's worse, you have zero control of the interview. A friend of your prospect happens to drop by or the phone rings and, poof, you've lost the continuity of your presentation. The child of the prospect runs into the living room crying with a scraped knee and you've temporarily lost your prospect's attention. Some people looking at our business have even been known to create distractions on purpose once they know we're coming to their home. One prospect we attempted to recruit in his own home actually invited two friends over who had failed at other MLM ventures, in order to distract us and give him good reasons to ignore the ideas we conveyed in our meeting.

It is time-consuming to drive across town to someone else's home or office. Also, why bother with a one-on-one meeting when you could be doing a small group interview, perhaps accomplishing four to eight times the results. But sometimes, if prospects cannot be approached in any other way, meeting at their place is better than not showing them your business opportunity at all. Mark showed the business to Dennis Clifton at his home, and that was definitely a trip worth making. But whenever possible, strive to get the prospect into your own home presentations, which allows you to have the control necessary to have an effective meeting. And if won over, the prospect is much more likely to duplicate the process correctly.

Eighth Mine: Technology

EVEN though new technological methods will become available in the future, those distributors who remain faithful to a simple recruiting system will prosper dramatically. Remember, if everyone can't easily duplicate your system, it won't lead to success. We know networkers who are using the Internet and e-mail to recruit and train new distributors. But more than 75 percent of all Baby Boomers are not yet online, so why limit your market to less than 25 percent of the Boomer population? Others have attempted to work with phone drops, automatic dialers, fax-on-demand systems, and other new technologies. Used in conjunction with telephone and face-to-face approaches, this "shotgun" recruiting can be effective. Using only one technology to follow-up on leads is very limiting and, by itself, will not work. While you personally may experiment with a new technology as part of your shotgun approach, you don't want to make the mistake of conveying to your organization that this new addition is your primary system. Your people will feel they can only succeed if they purchase the same equipment that you use, but some won't be able to afford it.

Above all else, remember this: We are in the distribution industry—we are paid directly as a result of the amount of products or number of services sold and used by our network. Doesn't it just make sense to distribute items and teach systems in a manner that is most easily learned by the general public and most

easily duplicated by them? Stick with this rule and you will go far in your business.

The Key to Successful Meetings Is Duplication

WE want you to understand why in-homes are so effective as well as how best to use your time during the presentation and training meetings. Remember, this is a book about how to avoid the circumstances that could cause you to quit in your first year of network marketing. We've conducted every type of meeting we just discussed and found each is substantially less effective than in-home, VCR/whiteboard presentations. Never do we tell students in our network marketing college course that the in-home meeting method is the only way to succeed. We are not absolutists; however, if you truly wish to survive your first year, we think you need to understand all the various meeting styles from the most effective to the least effective. In fact, we don't just want you to survive. We want you dramatically wealthy with all the time in the world to do what you want when you want to do it.

Having said that, now we want to share with you what we believe is the best and most easily duplicated process in network marketing today. The real key to successful meetings always revolves around the fundamental MLM principle of duplication. Any type of meeting that cannot be copied and taught by the least articulate and successful person in your group is ultimately doomed to failure and should be abandoned.

Mark had been in the business for nearly four years when he experienced a graphic example of this principle. As he explains, "I received a call from a very enthusiastic fellow named Barney, who called me from Fort Lauderdale, Florida, to inform me that he had personally sponsored more than 200 high-quality distributors, yet none of them had become successful. I asked him to describe a normal work week in his life so that I could try to figure out what he was doing wrong. His prospecting techniques were excellent and his ability to get prospects to meetings was unparalleled. He had a much lower ratio of no-shows than I did. It was when Barney began describing his meetings that I figured out the problem. I'll present his explanation for you exactly as he described it to me:

"'Mark, my wife and I have a Rolodex full of prominent people in the south Florida area. We were very successful in two businesses and recently sold them for several million dollars. After two years of fishing, we got bored and realized that we needed to be doing something productive. So we signed up in network marketing and began inviting our warm market, ten at a time, to two weekly meetings. We conducted our meetings on our 100-foot yacht. Our daughter is in one of the best sororities at the University of Florida, so we hired her this summer, along with three of her friends, to serve cocktails and hors d'oeuvres at each of our meetings. They last about two hours, during which time we cruise the harbor, play the company video, and then do the same whiteboard illustrations you teach. When we're done, we dock our boat and invite them to Saturday training.'

"Barney went on to explain that sign-ups were not a problem. All or most of his family and friends were signing up and many actually ordered more products than the initial start-up kit. Yet, only one of dozens of his frontline associates had ever signed up any other distributors. After listening carefully to Barney's story, I asked him one question: 'How many of your frontline distributors and prospects own a yacht?' He laughed and said, 'none.' He got the point. No one could duplicate the type of meeting he was conducting. He immediately moved his meetings into his guest house, quit serving cocktails and hors d'oeuvres, and eventually succeeded in sponsoring other successful distributors."

Sometimes, when we are teaching our distributors a system for recruiting or training, we will unwittingly suggest some new technique, one we've heard about but haven't actually put into practice. That's when we seriously lead new recruits astray. Here's our rule of thumb: If you personally practice a new recruiting or training procedure and actually see it work to increase volumes for a full six months, then implement it and teach it to your downline. If you've merely heard a rumor that some new system has worked elsewhere, don't give it serious consideration, or even repeat it to others, until you've actually tried it. You want to keep the in-home meetings of your downline so consistent that any prospect could attend any meeting in any city and walk away with the same knowledge and information. That's how the leaders in the top companies have done it, and it's hard to argue with billions of dollars of success.

Recruiting Meetings

THERE are many ways to prospect people, and we certainly subscribe to the shotgun approach. Use ads, fishbowls, and contests; use walking and talking, lifestyling, and the telephone; use the mail as well as the computer; use flyers and bulletin boards in every available public area. Give handouts and attend trade shows and franchise seminars. In fact, use every method available to meet prospects—but then adopt one specific meeting style in which to make your presentation. And don't change systems, especially during your first two years. The best meeting is the one in which every single detail, from location to closing comments, is easy to teach and emulate.

You want to keep the in-home meetings of your downline so consistent that any prospect could attend any meeting in any city and walk away with the same knowledge and information.

Steve Sledge recalls doing presentations in his den with a room full of people, and how his family handled his need for privacy. "I asked my wife and kids not to interrupt my meetings. The problem was that, when they were away from our home and returned to find me in the middle of a presentation, there was no way they could come in without passing through our den. So they became creative, removing the large screen in the master bathroom and climbing through the window. Time and again, I saw my family laughing, smiling, and waving to me as they made their way into our home. All the while the prospects were oblivious to what was taking place behind them." Those are the fun moments on which we all look back, remembering how we built global international businesses right out of our homes.

Begin Recruiting in Your Own City

Ken Pontius, one of America's MLM legends and a dear friend, explains the importance of starting to build your business at home in your own city during your first year. The money, skills, and knowledge it takes to sponsor long-distance distributors can be debilitating for novices. "Sometimes when I remember the comedy of errors that comprised my first year in MLM, it's hard to fathom that through perseverance, my wife, Shirley, and I now earn millions each year. I sponsored people who had no business being in our profession nor did they even want to be involved. I just pushed and pushed with the tenacity of a bulldog, never considering for a moment that people need self-motivation to succeed in life. I sponsored people who lived in other states before I had the money or the knowledge to support them. For some reason, doing business at home, in my own city, just didn't occur to me initially.

"I drove miles to do meetings only to be stood up. In one case I drove 221 miles to conduct a presentation for a minister in Missouri who promised that he had a hotel meeting already booked and filled to capacity. One sweet, little lady showed up

Network marketing is the only industry that allows common people to earn millions with a minimal investment and zero overhead, coupled with total time freedom and the joy of global travel.

thinking it was a square dance. She 'do-si-doed' right on out. I could fill ten pages with all the reasons why I should have quit in my first year, but it only takes one sentence to tell you why you shouldn't. Network marketing is the only industry that allows common people to earn millions with a minimal investment and zero overhead, coupled with total time freedom and the joy of global travel. There are three magic words that worked for all of us who have made it to the pinnacle and they'll work for you: 'Just don't quit.' "

Meeting Times and Locations

Because virtually everyone has a home, it is obviously the most logical place to conduct recruiting meetings. People frequently say to us: "Sure, Mark and Rene, that's easy for you to say because you live in a proverbial mansion." Yes, but remember, we began in humble environments. Regardless of whether you live in an apartment, trailer, or house, always use your largest room for meetings. You must have three items: a television, a VCR, and a whiteboard or flip chart. Most everyone has two of the three already, but if you don't, borrow or buy them. As part of creating a simple, easily duplicated system, we suggest that you show a video and do your presentations using a dry-erase whiteboard.

During his first year, Mark signed up people from different ends of the spectrum, sponsoring a bank president who had recently been terminated, at the same time he sponsored the wife of a painter. The former banker lived in a million-dollar home in the finest subdivision in Austin, Texas; the painter and his wife lived in a trailer. The banker quit in three months; the painter's wife today earns $6,000 a month and most likely will do so for the rest of her life. The quality of your home environment is not nearly as significant as your own enthusiasm. (Read the previous sentence one more time—it is the essence of success in MLM.)

Don't serve any food at your meetings, but if you feel the need to provide something, make it a beverage: water, coffee, or iced tea. Ideally, you should conduct meetings on any weekday during regular work hours for one hour either side of noon. These hours are best because it allows your prospects to take an early or extended lunch. The next best meeting times are evenings; the least preferable times are during weekends. You want to create the impression that our industry is a truly legitimate business that is conducted during normal business hours. The ideal number of prospects per meeting is four to eight; try to avoid doing one-on-one meetings—they are an ineffective use of your time. Of course, there is

The quality of your home environment is not nearly as significant as your own enthusiasm.

always the rare professional whom you might determine needs a private meeting, but, as a rule, small group meetings are best. For information on "The Opening Interview and Presentation," we refer you to a comprehensive step-by-step chapter on the subject in our book *Power Multi-Level Marketing*. This provides more specific information on the points to cover while doing a business opportunity meeting by whatever name you call it: business presentation, business briefing, business interview, or private business reception.

No-Shows Are Normal

Always schedule twice as many prospects as you would like to attend your recruiting meetings. For example, if you want five, invite ten. It is normal to have 50 percent no-shows at these meetings. People will offer the wildest excuses for not showing up at your business presentation. Jerry and Debbie Campisi of Boca Raton, Florida, recalling their early days of building their business, claim to have heard every excuse in the book. Here are just of few of the standouts:

"You won't believe it! My house caught on fire and burned to the ground. I lost everything I own, including your information. I feel really bad about missing your meeting."

"I had an accident on the way to our appointment. I can't believe I'm still alive. I had to go to the hospital, but I'm okay now. I want to wait a few weeks to get everything back to normal before we meet."

And their favorite: "I couldn't show up for our appointment because someone broke into my car and stole everything I had, including your starter package. It had your telephone number, so I couldn't even call you. I'm really glad you're calling me now."

How about this one: "I was so excited to meet with you until my husband came home. He told me that this was one of those pyramid schemes where they don't care about selling anything. It's just a front-end network deal, and all they want is your money. He wondered why in the world I would even be looking at something like this." (Two weeks later he signed up in another deal that truly fit his description. Everything he was telling his wife not to do, he did.)

Don't be surprised if you get outlandish excuses. In a follow-up phone conversation, a prospect's girlfriend offered this defense: "Oh, I'm sorry, my boyfriend must have forgotten. It's his pet snake's birthday. He can't come to the phone right now because he's having a birthday party." Jerry said he tried to get a visual on that one—picturing the snake wearing his birthday hat and diving into the cake. The Campisis advise that, whatever you do, don't buy into all the explanations that people offer. Successful entrepreneurs know that excuses are the nails that build houses of failure. After more than a decade with one company, Jerry and Debbie Campisi have the experience to know the truth of that statement. They have reached the top. Like us, they met and married in this business and are our close friends and travel companions throughout the United States, Europe, and Asia. We all enjoy working the business together and playing on the beaches of the world.

We have seen many successful marriages between distributors in our industry. Network marketing is a haven for finding people of like minds, hearts . . . and bank accounts. There is a rumor floating around our industry that a case is now pending before the Supreme Court that stipulates that network marketers can no longer merely marry but must also agree to a legal merger of their downlines, without the possibility of prenuptial restrictions. Of course, that is only a rumor.

Training Meetings

ANOTHER meeting that is critical for success is the training meeting. We have created a 180-minute video called *Power Training* that demonstrates exactly what we do, step-by-step, emphasizing what we consider the most important elements of successful training. However there are a few philosophical issues we need to address related specifically to training.

According to some studies, an individual with above average intelligence retains approximately 15 percent of new material taught in the first hour of a meeting, approximately 10 percent in the second hour, and beyond that, less than 3 percent. We are convinced that providing a laundry list of facts and ideas in the first training session, or for that matter in any training session, is not only unnecessary but a foolish waste of time. Why attempt to teach people important material when it has been scientifically proven that many of those folks are going to forget most of what you will present?

Our entire training system is designed in such a way as to change subject matter every fifty minutes. That's based on the solid fact that the human attention span can not remain focused on one subject matter for more than an hour without becoming saturated. Then the mind must rest before devouring a new subject. We've met distributors who conduct weekend marathon training sessions. Some leaders actually have bragged about the fact that their training is so intense and comprehensive that it takes as long as eight hours to complete. Sorry folks, that's insane.

The Subject Matter of Training Meetings

As the first step in training, we teach people to create two separate training modules of fifty minutes each on a Saturday morning from 10:00 A.M. until noon. We suggest that the first hour be a demonstration of how to complete, and how to teach others to complete, any application forms, distributor agreements, product orders, and other paperwork. This is the time to show them the products included in your starter package, how to use them, and how to build a base of ten customers. Introduce corporate literature as well as any brochures or magazine reprints that you want your downline to use. That process usually takes up the first module.

The second half of the meeting should cover goal setting with a brief explanation of the compensation plan, how to build their 2,000-person warm list and how to focus on the importance of the relationship when approaching family and friends about this incredible opportunity.

At the end of the two hours, make four assignments to your new associates: (1) go home and use the products in the starter package; (2) find ten solid customers among your close circle of family and friends; (3) set your goals in writing using the material provided; and, (4) using the memory-jogger provided, begin to create your warm list. Remember, those who are serious about their 2,000-person warm list and get their ten customers are usually the ones who succeed.

During their training, remind your new associates that even though today they are the students, next week they will be the teachers. This system is so simple to duplicate that they should feel at ease training their own new distributors the following week, doing nothing more than what you have just done with them. Stress the importance of using your system without deviation. Unless you can reduce your training system to one page, it's too complicated. That may seem like a preposterous notion, but it works! We use a one-page training format to get our new associates started, a twenty-five-page "getting started" manual at training, and a comprehensive *Encyclopedia of Network Marketing* for serious business builders. But guess which one we fax first to out-of-town distributors who want to learn our system? The one-page training format! And when we do, the unspoken objection we have to overcome in the minds of most prospects is: "This is too simple. It sounds too good to be true." We tell everyone that the system is simple, but the work is not easy.

Ours is the most wonderful profession in the world because it makes the most sense. People shouldn't have to spend countless hours in a classroom learning complicated business models from an academic who usually doesn't even practice in the business world. People learn the most while in a participatory role—making errors, yet learning from each one. With new distributors, our objective should always be to quickly cut the umbilical cord and demand of them leadership and hard work . . . at whatever pace they choose to do the business. The sooner new distributors become self-reliant and follow a simple success formula, the better. And we must constantly be reprogramming our prospects for success by pointing out how simple and easily duplicated our system truly is. Because if we don't, most people will walk away thinking: "Nobody can earn this kind of money sitting in their living room, showing a video." But we did, and so did Mark's housekeeper. And with a simple, proven, easily duplicated strategy, so can everyone else who has a home, a television, and VCR. Keep training meetings simple and limit them to two hours, tops.

Now, what about the trainees who go home, try the products, write out their goals, start putting together a warm list of several hundred people, find ten customers, and call you back ready to go? Those are the individuals—the ones you've been praying to meet—whom you bring in for a personal, one-on-one, strategy session. This is the moment when our profession changes from sifting through the numbers to forging strong business relationships. In this personal training session, you help lay out an action plan suited for each new associate, discuss how to select and approach those with whom they would like to create lifetime business partnerships, and schedule a specific day for you to help with their first presentations. This second training meeting should take one to two hours and include specific techniques for contacting their top twenty-five people, sharing an audiovisual package that introduces them to our business, and setting appointments to meet with those interested, since that is what they are going to be doing next with their warm list.

Product Training Is Not Necessary

You might notice that there's something conspicuously absent from our discussion of the training meetings. Those of you who represent a company with specific products probably are wondering why we've left out detailed product training. Our reason is this: It is totally unnecessary. Those individuals who feel a burning desire to learn about the ingredients in their personal care products, vitamins, pet food, or other consumable items should do so on their own time both by usage and personal study. But be forewarned: Distributors who are product experts seldom become the successful builders of huge international organizations! One of the significant facts, which surfaced as we interviewed America's best distributors during the research for our last book, was that not one placed their emphasis on teaching intricate details about products or services. Not one!

We are perfectly aware of the fact that some people reading this book pride themselves in knowing the function of every single ingredient in every single product they distribute. Such folks probably are upset with us for this unfair stereotype. Hey, lighten up! We have consistently poked fun at ourselves and revealed numerous ridiculous mistakes of our own. The truth is this: In our profession, those who truly wish to recruit dozens of frontline leaders over the years and build a really powerful international organization must focus on educating the multitudes about how to achieve wealth and independence. These have always been and will continue to be the most exciting "products" of our industry.

At one point, both of us still building our own individual organizations, decided to become experts on one of our hair products so we could dazzle people with our wisdom. It didn't take long to memorize the process that scientists used to fractionate the mucopolysacharides to the precise molecular size so that they would stimulate the papilla of the hair follicles in order to vasodilate the capillaries to just the right blood flow in order to improve hair fitness. And when we proudly talked about that in meetings, some of the doctors even rolled their eyes in confusion. That knowledge never allowed either of us to obtain one customer nor sign up one distributor . . . so we quit mentioning it. We replaced all that with an enthusiastic "It worked for me and maybe it will for you too. Why don't you try it?"

Don't discuss products in training other than to provide a general understanding of the primary products or services; then encourage the distributors to use them all and learn from personal consumption. Network marketing is about sharing products and services with family and friends based on your own personal excitement with the results; it is *not* an industry based on your wisdom of the intricate details of how the products work. Remember the example of telling your

What other professionals can . . . earn $20,000, $30,000, even $50,000 a month and more in less than half a decade, while enjoying total personal freedom? No one can but those of us in network marketing.

friends about a recent movie you've seen or restaurant you've discovered. The products you distribute through MLM are no different.

The eight Meeting Mines presented here are the obstacles to avoid in year one. There are certainly others, but these are the most damaging. Numerous would-be successful distributors have unwittingly failed as a direct result of hotel, office, and other public presentations.

Remember, you are a professional in a major global enterprise. There is no greater favor you can do for your new partners than to expose them to a legitimate prospecting package and recruiting meeting for your company. So, above all else, keep control of the situation. Meetings, whether for recruiting or training purposes, should be kept short, simple, and easily duplicated. Do them in a private setting, preferably in your home, and attend larger gatherings only periodically as you and your group feel the need for bonding, acknowledgment, or re-

motivation. You dictate the time and place of the meeting. You control everything about the first business presentation, and even more important, you control how your newest associates are trained. If you've been through training once, and it was done right, you can teach it too.

Maintain the attitude that you are offering your prospects an appointment with destiny. What other professionals can look a man or woman in the eye and tell them truthfully that it is possible to earn $20,000, $30,000, even $50,000 a month and more in less than half a decade, while enjoying total personal freedom? No one can but those of us in network marketing. New distributors should avoid all the Meeting Mines like the plague and utilize only those group meetings that offer an occasional means of bonding with other distributors and positive reinforcement to the system your group is using. Be proud of the industry you represent and don't be afraid to conduct your own meetings.

SUMMARY

- Attending unnecessary meetings can become the stumbling blocks that lead to your demise in our industry.

- Large hotel meetings don't work, unless used periodically as a supplement to regularly scheduled in-home presentations.

- Weekly hotel meetings are ineffective and not easily duplicated because they are expensive, create codependency, can be embarrassing because of no-shows, are not private, do not exemplify freedom, often create the illusion of saturation, and do not encourage personal development.

- Occasional hotel meetings are best used to bring the group together to hear an upline leader, provide awards, offer recognition, and create bonding.

- Most of your time should be invested in face-to-face prospecting, telephone calls, and in-home presentations.

- The "church service," a regularly scheduled recruiting meeting in which frontline distributors are taught to bring guests to the leader's home where he or she then does presentations for everyone, can lead to disaster, if continued long-term, by creating codependency.

- A "deception meeting" is a dinner party to which friends are invited believing it to be a social gathering, only to find out that they are there for a briefing about network marketing.

- It's proper to create curiosity about network marketing when inviting people to your home for a business presentation, but it's never proper to deceive them about your intentions.

- It is not wise to use an office outside the home because:

    1 It cannot be duplicated for most people.

    2 It creates unnecessary overhead.

3 It does not exemplify the freedom that you should enjoy as a network marketer.

- No one can expect to be successful by conducting recruiting meetings in any public place, such as a bar or restaurant, where there's no access to a VCR, no whiteboard, and a great many distractions.

- When possible, avoid conducting meetings at your prospect's home or office because you have no control over the circumstances.

- High-tech recruiting methods—such as using the Internet, e-mail, phone drops, automatic dialers, and fax-on-demand—can be effective when used with other approaches, but using only one technology is a very limiting system that cannot be easily duplicated.

- Successful meetings revolve around the fundamental MLM principle of duplication.

- Any meeting that can not be replicated by the least articulate and successful person in your downline is ultimately doomed to failure.

- When beginning your business, start by recruiting in your own city.

- When doing a recruiting meeting, the quality of your environment is a fraction as significant as your enthusiasm.

- Convey the impression that network marketing is a truly legitimate business conducted during normal business hours.

- Expect about 50 percent of the people you invite to meetings will not attend, even after promising to do so.

- As the first step in training, we recommend that you set aside two hours each week on Saturday mornings to teach a small group of your newest distributors the basics of how to do our business.

- Following the first-step training, set up a one-on-one personal strategy session with any frontline associate who completes your assignments.

- Product details should not be a significant part of your training because networking is a business of sharing of products with family and friends based on personal excitement and results, not based on a technical knowledge of ingredients or services.

- Meetings, whether for recruiting or training purposes, should be kept short, simple, and easily duplicated.

CHAPTER 8

Unloading the Plug-In Pistol

Recruit and train your own people instead of depending on others.

THERE'S A DEVASTATING WEApon which can misfire, injuring potential leaders in our industry. This little weapon can also backfire on new distributors, crippling and sometimes destroying their ability to recruit and train long-distance prospects. Both of us fired this weapon in our first year as new network marketers and it is discharged daily by new people in MLM organizations all over the world. We call it the Plug-in Pistol. Here's how it works.

The phone rings. It's one of your distributors, who tells you, very enthusiastically, that she has a major, well-connected prospect in another state who is so credible that he will make billions of dollars for everyone in her upline. Once those remarks are uttered, the pistol is fired: "So, I need to plug him in to someone in that

city. Do you have a leader there whom you can recommend?" Even more complex is the foreign prospect due to the language barrier: "We just signed up a distributor in Tokyo and he's so excited. What kind of training meetings do we have going on in that part of the world? We want to get him plugged in right away." The problem with trying to plug-in people in this way is quite simple: It seldom works and more often backfires, negatively affecting your new distributors, and often creating a permanent obstacle to their success. Success in network marketing is tied to our ability to prospect, recruit, and train—and teach others to do the same. No distributors have ever become successful through a "welfare mentality" of having others do everything for them. There are many examples from which to draw and, in this chapter, we'll prepare you for each of the situations you are likely to face.

Plugging into a Long-Distance Training Meeting

IN long-distance sponsoring, network marketers commonly sign up new distributors and send them to whatever training session is going on in that particular locale. Let us say this right up front before we say anything else: Most network marketers use this technique. Why? Because, frankly, they don't know what else to do . . . and it's the easiest way to handle the situation. It generally has a certain ambiance of professionalism and it *can* get people started. So, if you get "shot" by one of the long-distance sponsoring "bullets," you may be only mildly hurt. But beware, you may also be seriously wounded and not even know it yourself, and it can be fatal to your MLM career.

Here's the situation. Training is a very personal and critical step in getting your new associate started in the business. As we have written repeatedly, there are many ways to do this business, but consistency is essential to success. Changing systems frequently can be deadly for the unseasoned, and even the seasoned, network marketer. If you intend to be a re-

sponsible, supportive upline associate to your new distributor, then you want to have a strong hand in teaching that person how to get started. This creates a mentality of self-sufficiency that you want to spread throughout your organization. If you leave it to chance, or worse, plug your new protégé into whatever training is close by, then you are taking a serious risk—you may be setting up your new distributor for a welfare mentality.

Confusion often sets in about which system to use. You have mentioned to your new associate the importance of doing in-home meetings, but the local trainers you've plugged him or her into suggest that prospects be brought to their weekly hotel meeting. Even though you have stressed the importance of personal interaction with your potential business partners, at the local training meeting your new associate hears about a great new recruiting video that can be sent out to prospects, thereby avoiding any personal rejection. The worst thing you can do to new associates is plug them into a myriad of diverse systems that will leave them floundering.

So if you are convinced that systems do, in fact, matter, then please heed this advice: Be careful when you select a leader or group for your new frontline associates. Be as picky about their training as you would be about day care for your own child. In our business, how your new recruits are trained is crucial to their success. But just as the best of all possible solutions, if the choice is available to you, is to stay at home and raise your own child, the very best method for taking your valued frontline associates from childhood to adulthood in the network distribution industry is to do it yourself. And remember, duplication is the name of the game. If you send your new recruits to other meetings, so will they. If you personally train your recruits, so will they.

Recently, our own company has chosen to produce its own training materials and conduct its own leadership training conferences because of intense regulatory pressure. We are in the minority in strongly objecting to this policy change. In our opinion, it is akin to socialized child care. If you have children, imagine how you would feel if the government decided that all parents are mandated to send their children to public day-care centers of the government's choosing. All children might be raised by the philosophy of those in power. It is the antithesis to American democracy and of freedom of choice.

We are firmly against any company-imposed training of our valued, new associates in business, unless that training was created and approved by field leaders. If MLM corporate executives knew how to succeed in this business, they'd be at home with their families earning ten times their salaries, not in meetings creating sales tools they've never used themselves. Having them design our training program gives meaning to that old saying "Those who can, do, and those who can't, teach."

But at the same time we understand why the company has taken this position. The Federal Trade Commission is taking a very hard line with certain well-established MLM companies. (If you are with a newer company—less than five years old—brace yourself. If you hit the big time in this industry, your turn will come.) The FTC is poring over every little detail in the corporate brochures, catalogs, and field-produced training manuals. And this government bureaucracy is holding the company ultimately responsible for the content of these publications. In response, MLM companies have decided to take the easy way out—they are reclaiming the right to produce training materials so that they can maintain control over all content to avoid lawsuits. And that leads them to also exert authority over all training procedures.

While we understand the reason for their knee-jerk reaction to federal scrutiny, that still doesn't make it right, in our opinion. We don't believe in company-imposed training systems any more than we support mandatory day care. And we don't accept the erroneous notion that just any citywide training will do for our new distributors, especially during their formative first year in the business. The potential problems are as threatening as the inherent challenges in not being selective about the care of your own children. There are thousands of horror stories about sending a new recruit to a local training meeting held in another city.

Mark recalls a personal story of his own. In 1986, he plugged his cousin, Steve, from his hometown into a local meeting because a distributor who was quite successful was moderating it. What follows is Steve's humorous account of that particular evening. "I was turned on about the business because I was tired of practicing medicine and figured my career was taking me nowhere. When Mark sent me a newspaper clipping of him jumping over his tennis net after a game in his backyard, and I knew he had been broke just six months earlier, I got very excited. He sent me the information. I filled out an agreement and then called him back for training. He said that since a local doctor was conducting a Saturday training session, I should attend his meeting. I'll admit the fact that another M.D. was involved helped me shake my professional pride issue. After all, why should a thirty-five-year-old, successful doctor be signing up in MLM? Yet, I rationalized that this was no different than an AA meeting in that it might be embarrassing at first but, after all, everyone was there for the same reason.

"During the drive to the meeting, I began to think about all the interesting entrepreneurs and business experts I would undoubtedly meet. When I first walked in the door, my suspicions were confirmed—my negative suspicions, that is. A patient for whom I had recently performed a medical procedure that very week approached me and jokingly said, loud enough for everyone to hear, 'Good God, Doc, after what you charge for minor surgery, surely you don't need a part-time job in a pyramid deal!'

"I was mortified and turned ten shades of red as I noticed a good ten or fifteen people had heard the remark and were now staring at me. I laughed off the comment, shook his hand, then moved away, quickly isolating myself from him and that group by selecting an empty chair on the other side of the room.

"The lady I sat next to was quite well dressed and looked like a solid citizen. So, I introduced myself and made a little small talk. She confided in me that she, too, had just signed up under another couple out of town and was here at a training meeting for the first time. Then, she began telling me that her former massage therapist had actually sent her to the meeting. What excited her the most was that she had been doing what she called a treasure map for wealth, which, she explained to me, was cutting pictures of material objects out of magazines and pasting them on a canvas. Twice a day, she told me (as I loosened my collar and glanced around hoping no one was listening to this conversation), she sat down by her pictures, chanted the word *hu*, then envisioned unexpected income falling into her lap. It wasn't until she told me that, in a channeling session, her archangel Michael informed her, in ancient Aramaic, that she should attend this meeting that I walked out—never again to attend an MLM meeting."

We've heard tales much worse than this one. So listen to us carefully: When distributors in your organization call and ask if you have any leaders in Michigan, or Florida, or Texas, whom they can "plug a new person into" for training and support, tell them *NO!* This isn't a business in which you merely "sign 'em up and plug 'em in." Associates should be supported long distance until they are experienced and self-sufficient by utilizing proven training materials. Only after they are solidly established can they go to other leaders' meetings for additional support and company bonding. But it will take some time before they're established.

Always remember the Yarnells' 81st law: "Whenever you send a credible person to an out-of-town meeting, he or she will invariably pick a seat next to someone whom God planted on this earth to demonstrate that not all the squirrels are in the trees." On that fact you may depend. If you choose to send a new associate to another leader's meeting, do so by checking it out thoroughly and asking for referrals about the quality and content of the training. Don't just blindly send someone there, taking the path of least resistance. You can't expect someone with no vested interest in your downline to give your associates the same kind of attention that you would provide them. Each leader's primary responsibility is to train and support those on whom he is paid in his own line. Even the most extraordinary leaders may not mind including your associates in their meetings, but they are not likely to go the extra mile for them. Most are stretched to the limit just trying to build their own lines and support their own associates—yours will certainly go by the wayside. By simply plugging prospects into an existing meeting, you are offering them mediocre support, at best, during the critical time of getting started in our business.

Do Your Own Training

SO what should you do if you are the type of parent who, given the choice, would be inclined to stay at home, or run a business from home, so that you could raise your own children? You will probably have the same instincts about supporting the "children in your downline."

Let's assume that you agree with us that training should be a simple, easily duplicated system that can actually be reduced to a one-page training outline. Let's also assume that you have a new person who just signed up on your front line in another state. Begin by faxing him or her a copy of your one-page system. Ask your new associate to look it over carefully and offer to answer any questions in the next day or two. At the appointed time, make the call so you can answer any questions. Let him or her know the source and credibility of your system. Because you need to get it out of the way right up front, ask if he or she has any objections to the system. Conclude the discussion by letting the new associate know how avidly you believe in this system and that, if he or she wants your support in business, any deviation from this system is *not* allowed. Get your new associate to fully commit to your system.

The next step is to have your long-distance associates purchase their introductory kit and product starter package directly from the company (as opposed to buying their products from us, as we generally do locally). At that time, if the option is open to you, have them purchase a short manual (less than forty pages), put together by a leader whose system you are using, that teaches a simple, "no-brainer" way to do this business. Such a manual should be easily duplicated, able to be reduced to a one-page outline that explains a system that anyone from any walk of life can learn, implement, and teach. After your long-distance associates have started using the products and have read their short manual, arrange another telephone discussion, this time to target those issues that are the most critical in your system. Sometimes your new distributors will quit after the purchase of their first product package and before they complete their assignments. A certain amount of quick in-and-out attrition is normal in our business. But for those who continue on with you, recommend one or two of your most powerful motivational tools to help them build their business. These are the people with whom you will forge a close personal bond and create a lifetime business partnership. For these serious business builders, we then suggest that they purchase a complete training manual. We have invested years researching and writing *The Encyclopedia of Network Marketing* to guide serious network marketers to success. (Feel free to use it if your own upline mentors have not already written something similar.)

We also suggest a weekly coaching session over the phone between you and all serious long-distance frontline members of your group. Insist that they initiate the session, using the magic words "You call me." When and if they do, give them your unwavering support. (If they don't call, move on to the next person.) Be sure that their style of aproach and their numbers are reviewed during this weekly telephone meeting. Discuss how many prospects they approached that week, how many audio-visual packages they gave out, how many appointments they set, how many people to whom they actually made a presentation, and finally, how many they sponsored. Encourage them whenever their style of approach and their numbers are inordinately low. Be a mentor and lead by example. Help them "close" their serious prospects. Give constructive criticism about how your new associates might develop on more personal levels.

When coaching downline distributors, don't make the mistake of telling them what they did wrong—doing this only reinforces the mistake and puts them into a downward spiral. Have you ever figured out how to do a "don't"? When you want to assist associates in changing, suggest what you want them to "do right." Quite often the obstacles to overcome are *within* a person. If your associate is struggling with lack of confidence, suggest that she ask herself, "But what if I could . . . ?" Possibility thinking expands consciousness, increases self-esteem, and furthers the chances for success. The best coaches are those who remind people of their inherent ability. Just trying harder seldom produces results.

In short, train your people as leaders and teach them to do the same with their people. Give everyone the opportunity to emerge as a leader. And you know the SW rule: Some will, some won't, so what, because someone else is always waiting. Those who don't become leaders will gravitate toward codependency at the citywide meeting, if it exists in their locale. That's your backup plan. Maybe, just maybe, the Archangel will show up and lead them back home!

When coaching downline distributors, don't make the mistake of telling them what they did wrong . . . suggest what you want them to "do right."

The Value of a Simple Training System

TEACHING a simple system is a good start toward taking charge of the leadership of your own organization. If you begin your leaders on the right track and prove it can create success for them, you have a good chance that they, in turn, will stick with the same program and pass it on. The following is an example of our one-page training. If you like it, adapt it for your own personal use.

A good training system flows in such a way that it can be duplicated by the least experienced in your organization. As you can see from the MLM Flow Chart following the Yarnell Success Training System, it comes full circle, taking your new associates through the process and then teaching them to do the same.

THE YARNELL SUCCESS TRAINING SYSTEM

"Simplicity is evidence of the most advanced teachings."
—DR. EMILE CADY

THE GUIDELINES

1 Commit to this proven training system for one year or until you reach your financial goal. Because it is essential that you stay on one proven track, we encourage you not to expose yourself to events that teach or promote other systems.

2 Begin by carefully selecting and approaching those with whom you would most enjoy creating a lifetime business partnership, and teach those people who join you to do the same.

3 As you gradually move into the cold market, place more emphasis on the number of people that you approach. Focus on the width of your front line, rather than the depth. However, support everyone who *asks* for your help as though they were frontline.

4 Following in-home presentations or long-distance sign-ups, encourage serious people to phone an upline leader.

5 In order to stay focused, we discourage you from creating your own training materials. Rely exclusively on this proven system for the first year or until you reach your financial goal.

6 Build a customer base among your family and neighbors prior to creating a downline.

7 Focus all of your efforts on building one powerful organization and *never* try to build two or more lines in different companies.

8 Success depends on believing and investing in yourself. Therefore, never loan money or products to new distributors.

9 Be loyal to your business. Use your own products or services in lieu of other inferior brands.

10 Stay focused on the end result and take pride in your accomplishments along the way. Do not allow rejections, drop-outs, dream stealers, and discouragements to deter you from your vision. You are 100 percent in control of your own mind-set and, therefore, your own future.

THE SYSTEM

1 Attend First-Step Training with your sponsor, held once a week as a group meeting.

2 Fill out an application form. Set up a temporary account and place a product order.

3 "Just Get Ten" personal customers as soon as possible. Having received a Product Starter Package, share your enthusiasm based on personal use and results.

4 Establish written goals and visualize them as already accomplished. Stay focused on the end result and realize that your business plan will be the means to this end.

5 Begin making your warm market list of 2,000 names, prioritizing your top twenty-five preferred business partners. Set up a card file system, by which prospects can be re-approached every six months.

6 Get back to your sponsor for a personal strategy session and create a specific plan of action based on your goals.

7 Approach people with the financial security and time freedom possible in our business. Call on your top twenty-five people, telling them how much you would enjoy being business partners. Remember, it is your enthusiasm that will attract people to your organization. Meet your prospecting goals every day.

8 Provide your prospects with an audio-visual package, introducing them to the timing, trends, advantages, and excitement of our industry.

9 Next conduct in-home presentations with four to eight prospects at each meeting, all invited from your warm market list, or referrals that come from them. (Your upline will be in attendance at your first two or three meetings.)

a. Hand out articles, reprints, etc., to establish the credibility of the industry.

b. Tell your story (in five minutes' time) and the story of one of your upline associates who is already successful.

c. Explain the positioning and strength of your company. Explain why you chose this one over others.

d. Give personal testimonials about the products along with catalog and/or samples for those interested.

e. Play a recruiting video that includes company and product info and a simplified compensation plan explanation. Follow it with the board illustrations.
   - Explain challenges most workers face today—40-year plan/linear income.
   - Explain $5 \times 5 \times 5$ exponential growth allowing for 75 percent attrition.
   - Explain roll-up factor when people quit.

f. Answer any questions. Give serious prospects the phone numbers of key upline associates and encourage them to call or arrange a three-way call if they have questions.

g. Hand out Business Overview and close with three reasons to join: (1) wholesale buyer, (2) business tax advantages and travel write-offs, (3) creation of a lifestyle with wealth and independence.

h. Invite prospects to next Saturday's training session.

10 Ask for a Commitment: sign up as a business builder, a retailing distributor, or a wholesale buyer. Alternatively, they may choose to become a customer or, at the very least, give you a referral.

11 Name the product package and list the exact training materials you wish new associates to purchase. List phone numbers showing where to order.

12 Conduct First-Step Training once a week for new distributors. Set up a Personal Strategy session for distributors who have completed the assignments: purchased products, set goals in writing, started developing their list and building their customer base.

THE RESULTS

Dramatic income, absolute time freedom, and the satisfaction of knowing you have helped others to create the same.

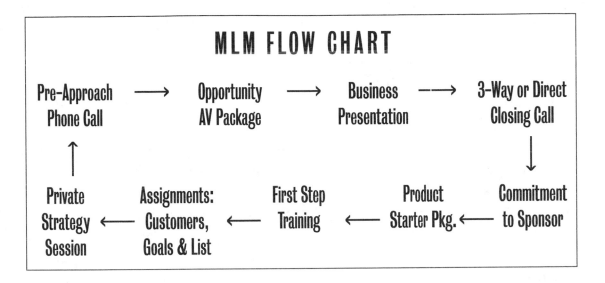

MLM FLOW CHART

Pre-Approach Phone Call → Opportunity AV Package → Business Presentation → 3-Way or Direct Closing Call

Private Strategy Session ← Assignments: Customers, Goals & List ← First Step Training ← Product Starter Pkg. ← Commitment to Sponsor

Plugging into a Long-Distance Recruiting Meeting

IF sending someone to a long-distance training session is questionable, entrusting a valuable prospect to someone else's recruiting meeting without your presence is pure lunacy. It makes about as much sense to us as sending your secretary to an adoption agency to pick out a child for you and your spouse. We wouldn't even send someone else to pick out a pet dog or cat. Why would anyone leave a highly regarded business associate in the care of a total stranger at some randomly selected meeting? When it comes to introducing a prospect to our business, we have one fundamental and unwavering belief: Net-

work marketing should be presented in a small group in a private setting. To do otherwise is to defy the very nature of networking. It is, after all, a business of friends telling friends—not a formal production with lights, cameras, slide shows, and action.

If you are introducing your network marketing company to a long-distance prospect, we suggest that you begin with as much personal involvement as is humanly possible . . . from a distance. Go into this knowing that long-distance recruiting is more expensive than local recruiting. It involves packages, long-distance telephone calls, postage, and more calls. Don't even begin unless you can afford the cost. In your pre-approach phone call, having carefully selected those you wish to contact, share your excitement about the business and the prospect of working together. Send your prospect an audiotape, videotape, or multimedia package that explains, in the simplest way possible, your excitement about the network marketing industry, your company, your product line, and your organization. Look over your package and its presentation, imagining how you would feel all over again if you were the one receiving it. Does it really answer all the questions you had then?

Send out these materials only to those who indicate a genuine interest in learning more about network marketing. And don't mail out a greater quantity than you can follow up and support. In all, it's going to take at least two one-hour, long-distance calls. Use your first phone conversation to tell them the story of how and why you became involved. Get a commitment, in advance, of a time you can call to discuss the business after they have received the package and had time to look at it. Getting someone to look at your videotape, or listen to your audiotape, can be a real challenge. That is why we use this method *only* for select long-distance prospects, or an occasional local prospect whom you are unable to get to your presentation any other way. Your closing ratios with long-distance prospecting will be less than face-to-face presentations.

Your follow-up phone call becomes a mini-presentation—be sure to highlight the critical aspects of the business, the money to be made, the simplicity of your system for building this type of business, and how you will work closely with them to teach them, step-by-step, exactly how to succeed. Answer their questions and listen carefully for objections. Use upline support to close your serious prospects—ask your prospects to call one of your business associates who has more experience and success than you. This can be done either by a direct or three-way call. Usually more than one phone call is required to progress to the closing point.

Now, having made a long-distance presentation (through your package and calls) on a personal basis with upline support, you are ready to sign them up. Once you have done so, you *may* choose to have them attend a local recruiting meeting where a respected leader in your company is speaking. As suggested earlier, you need to carefully select the group and its speaker(s) before encouraging your prospect to attend. Under no circumstances should you allow your prospect to attend the training meeting that follows the recruiting meeting, unless the training leader is a well-regarded member of your upline or a mentor whose system you are following.

If your prospect is still holding back from a commitment because of some ob-

> The inherent ethics of network marketing comes from allegiance to the person who thought enough of you to first introduce you to the business.

jection, you have a serious decision to make. Dispatching your prospect to an opportunity meeting in another city is akin to sending your children to New York City unaccompanied. However, if you are unable to close your prospect in any other way, it may be worth the risk at this point. It is a decision you should make carefully. If you choose to follow this plan, do so if, and only if, the loyalty is securely established between the two of you. The inherent ethics of network marketing comes from allegiance to the person who thought enough of you to first introduce you to the business. Send your prospect to the meeting with the caution that it is merely a supplemental support to the system you will be using. Call your prospects the moment they arrive home, or at the latest, the very next morning, to get a pulse reading on their reaction to the meeting, the speaker, the guests, and the presentation. Don't assume that all is well once you have discharged the Plug-in Pistol, that is, once you have sent your potential business associate to a local meeting. You should feel reasonably con-

cerned. You can breathe a little easier once you have followed up with your prospect and received a commitment to follow your system, which occurs about 20 percent of the time.

Plugging into a Local Recruiting Meeting

EVEN though we don't believe it is effective, we understand why networkers send new associates to recruiting or training meetings in other cities before having personally worked with them. But why on earth would anyone send their valued prospects to another leader's meeting within their *own* city, for their very first exposure to network marketing? It doesn't make sense when, with a simple system, you are perfectly capable of getting them started on the right track yourself. To succeed, you need to share your knowledge with your new associates and teach each of them to do the same. Hotel meetings should be treated only as a backup, a reinforcement, the second part of a one-two punch. But no new prospects should have their very first exposure to network distribution in a large, formal setting.

Peter Hirsch, author of *Living with Passion*, recalls his introduction to our industry: "My MLM nightmare started during my first business briefing. A friend picked me up to take me to a hotel meeting, which is now, after almost eight years in the business, something I am very much against. The immediate impression that hit me smack in the face was, 'If I join this company, I'm no longer entitled to wear natural fibers.' I guess the people running the meeting were trying to give people the feeling that 'if we can do it, you can too!' But that's not the feeling I got. What I sensed was, 'nobody in this room knows how to speak or dress and they probably can't read. I don't want to be with these people. I don't want to be like these people . . . HELP!!!!! GET ME OUT OF HERE!' I stayed because I didn't have my own car. (By the way, that's not a justification for taking guests in your car. The answer is to not have hotel meetings, and whenever you have a business presentation, make it good! Make it so that your guests will want to stay without being held hostage.) When my friend dropped me off at my house, he gave me a product to try. I was tired of arguing, so I

just took it. It was a water filter that looked like a thermos.

"The evening was so awful that I couldn't fathom why anyone would join the company. I imagined someone sitting at the kitchen table with a water filter on his right side and a gun on his left, saying to himself, 'Before I go for the gun, I may as well try this water filter thing.' One week later, I joined the company. Why? Two reasons. First, the product was very good. I liked it and I saw a need for it. Second, desperation. I hated what I was doing for a living—I was a practicing attorney—and saw MLM as a way out.

"In my first month, my organization moved close to $100,000 in wholesale products. Life looked grand. You see, I knew plenty of other attorneys who were also miserable. I was on my way to a lifestyle of the rich and famous. Then the real nightmare began. My second check was lower than my first. My third check was lower than my second. What was happening? They never said at the meeting that this could occur! The trend continued and soon I had nothing left. The crash was devastating. Then it hit me. I had to actually *learn* this business. I had to learn MLM. In my first week with that company I was taught the ancient MLM art of front-end loading. I now realize that there is nothing worse in network marketing, from both a legal and ethical perspective, than suggesting that people purchase thousands of dollars of product that they obviously don't need and likely won't sell."

Peter eventually left that company and learned to do the business, like us, in small group settings, personally making his own presentations and doing his own training meetings. What he learned in the process was not to worry about the first order. From hard experience, he shares the belief with us that real volume, as opposed to promotional volume, is the way to build a solid organization. "If you build your business or customers on smaller orders, you will always have a business. If you build your business based on front-end loading, it won't last. Instead, you'll end up in the NFL—No Friends Left." Peter Hirsch is one of the rare people who "walks the talk." He not only wrote the book, but everything he does is about "living with passion." How much passion does it take to walk away from your company, when you are the top distributor earning several times more than you've ever earned in your life, because you don't agree with its practices? Peter knows because he did. He has become a close friend whom we greatly admire as one of the most ethical and conscientious young men in network marketing.

Issues of Integrity

OF course, there are many more practical reasons for avoiding plugging quality prospects into meetings, whether in your own city or others, if you cannot participate. Some time ago we were speakers at a meeting where a couple set up a table in the front reception area in order to register all the attendees. When the meeting began, they simply walked off with the list and the registration money. Later, they began calling those people who were on the registration list. What we discovered was unbelievable. They were actually leaders in a totally different company who used this same deception on more than one occasion to steal prospects from other distributors. That's how insane things can become at large meetings!

But let's talk about a much more insidious form of theft—namely, prospects being stolen by leaders from one's *own* company. Not only does this happen, but all too frequently it's perpetrated by those leaders who are at the very top of companies. Sometimes it happens with the full knowledge and blessing of corporate owners and staff, though they never dare admit it.

Peter Hirsch called us not too many months ago in a despondent mood and asked if we could get together and spend the weekend. Because we're great friends, of course we invited him over. This young star was a top earner in his company, responsible for recruiting and training a very large organization. We found out that weekend that the corporate leaders allowed another leader, who was given preferential treatment by the company, to steal an entire downline from him. He came to tell us that he had quit and walked away from an income of $30,000 a month. That takes courage—more than most of us have.

Fortunately, this is not a common occurrence among company leaders, but it does happen. We have seen company owners themselves face many ethical dilemmas in network marketing. Some companies finally reach the big money only after sacrificing some or all of their reputation in the process. Other companies have insisted on high ethical standards, but have not been able to pull in the big money. Some try to make money from the sale of required, ongoing support materials—audiotapes, videotapes, and printed manuals—instead of from the sale of actual products. We have seen companies charge many times the actual value of a so-called training program and try to pay the downline from these revenues—something that, when investigated, we believe would never pass FTC standards.

Like so many of you, we are extremely idealistic in our expectations concerning the network marketing industry. When we first became involved, the industry had a rather poor public image. But we knew the truth. This was a clean, solid industry having as its preeminent purpose the sale of massive quantities of quality products and services by word-of-mouth, while paying network distributors what they are truly worth. That's what enables us all to lead quality lives. With the ongoing development of the industry, some of that idealism has been compromised. As we look at various companies emerging today, we see no network marketing company who has made it to the big money— that is, to a half a billion dollars in annual sales or more—and not compromised something in the process. No company is in a position to cast the first stone at any other company.

However, the ethical lapses in network marketing pale in comparison to traditional business. Last year, for example, the biggest bank in Japan was caught cheating and forced to pay $2 million in fines to Americans. In 1995, seven CEOs of the largest tobacco companies stood in front of a Senate investigative committee with their right hand in the air and swore that "Tobacco is no more addictive than marshmallows and contains no 'booster' additives." Two years later those same corporate heads settled all future lawsuits for $2 billion with the proviso that they will never again advertise their products. Recently we saw a Winston billboard at one of the main intersections in our town stating "We've gone naked, and taken out all the additives. No bull." How proud would you be to be involved in that industry?

This is our message to MLM newcomers: Take pride in our industry and select your company based on realistic expectations. Select the one that has the very best record based on your values. But we don't believe any company in existence today would receive a check mark in every column: top money earners, complete harmony among field distributors, respected corporate leaders, level playing field, high ethical standards, perfectly balanced front-end and back-end compensation plan, quality products that are in-demand and competitively priced, the potential for longevity, a globally seamless marketing plan, and no more than average attrition. Perhaps one day a company will come along that can uphold the highest ethical standards and break all sales records as well. But even if that never happens, network marketing companies still ethically outpace the majority of traditional corporations worldwide—there is really no comparison.

With the maturation of network marketing comes the loss of innocence. Those companies that last more than five years have a generally favorable record for high standards. Unfortunately, even in those companies there is a growing number of distributors who are quite unscrupulous. Given the nature of our industry, unethical behavior can only be controlled by the individual distributors themselves—we can set standards on whom we invite to join our organizations—or by corporate leaders who have the courage to terminate those who clearly violate company policies. If this problem is not dealt with in the early stages, and the wayward networker is allowed to continue operating unethically, there comes a point of no return. Eventually, an unethical distributor will become too big and too powerful to eliminate without bringing harm to the company and, for that matter, to the entire industry.

We can preserve the integrity of our industry by only affiliating with those companies that demonstrate the will to strictly enforce policies devoid of favoritism or selfish greed, as well as by screening new associates in our recruiting selection and training process. Simply put: Select a company that isn't afraid to terminate a big hitter who breaks the rules, invite principled people whom you trust into your organization, and train them to do the business ethically.

Fear of Loss

GET ready for a scary fact. Whenever you suggest that anyone in your organization attend a meeting in another town with no supervision, you must be prepared, and maybe even expect, to lose that distributor to another leader. Here's an example of how it might happen. Bob has never been involved in network marketing and doesn't understand the simplicity of our industry. His friend, Steve, has heard about a meeting in Bob's town that is conducted weekly by a local leader. So, before Bob is ever enrolled, he is "plugged into" the local meeting. Of course, when he arrives on his own and explains he's not yet signed up, some local leaders will be all too pleased to help out. Often they will first befriend Bob and then, during the course of the evening, attempt to persuade him that he should set aside his allegiance to the distributor who first introduced him to this business and sign up with them instead. They eventually lure him with promises of having special ties to their company or suggestions that he cannot be successful without local support. Why sign up under an acquaintance 500 miles away when he can sign up here at home under a sponsor who can more adequately support him?

Though it's a lie, Bob doesn't recognize it. Nor does Bob yet understand the structural integrity of our industry. The need for local support is a myth; were that not so, Bob would be limited in the development of his business to just his own area with no potential for expansion. On the contrary, the secret to building a successful business is to become the leader of your own organization—never dependent on others for extended local support. The exponential growth of a network marketing organization lies in the distributor's

---

The exponential growth of a network marketing organization lies in the distributor's ability to teach others an easily duplicated system for sponsoring and being sponsored, anywhere in the world.

ability to teach others an easily duplicated system for sponsoring and being sponsored, anywhere in the world.

So Bob shouldn't try to bypass Steve, the person who introduced him to the business. Although Steve may be inexperienced and distant, somewhere above him is a person in his upline with the necessary power, income, and experience to work with him and teach him proven techniques for succeeding in this business. But not realizing that, Bob very innocently signs up under the local group and decides to call Steve in a couple of weeks and break the news to him gently.

There's no telling how many thousands of distributors have quit our business after plugging-in leads to meetings in other cities only to have their prospects stolen by an unscrupulous leader. Of course, this could never happen if new distributors were taught not to entrust prospects in other cities to meetings until they've been signed up and trained. Even then, it isn't necessary. In our opinion, the entire notion of local support and weekly hand-holding meetings is not the way to build a successful organization. Both of us were sponsored by out-of-town leaders, and then trained and supported by telephone. In fact, Mark didn't meet his mentor, Richard Kall, until Mark was earning over $15,000 a month. The first time he called Richard, he was given a system over the telephone and he went out and followed it. Even though it was Mark's first participation in networking, he learned enough in that phone conversation to earn serious money after just four months in our company.

International Recruiting

THERE'S a real risk of collapse of the structural integrity intrinsic to network marketing in foreign markets. Breach of loyalty between you and your group, however promising in a newly launched market, is often a direct result of the Plug-in Pistol. It can even happen without entrusting someone to another leader's meeting. Success in a foreign market is dependent on several things: (1) the loyalty and communication between the sponsor and new distributor, (2) well-translated training materials offering a simple, proven system, and (3) the self-reliance and proactive nature of the start-up group in that country. Success does not result from merely finding one good person and "plugging" him or her into whatever training session happens to be offered locally. However, failure is quite probable!

If done properly and taught truthfully, *anyone* can succeed at, and teach others to succeed at, the business of network marketing. Success doesn't require a

Success in a foreign market is dependent on loyalty and communication, well-translated training materials, and the self-reliance of the start-up group in that country.

myriad of formal meetings, training centers, product seminars, and other hoopla. But here's the problem: As unscrupulous networkers, of whom we spoke earlier, grow logarithmically, they can cause you big problems. Perhaps one of them meets your distributor at a corporate gathering, or at an open meeting, or at a training center, and finds out he or she is sponsored by someone thousands of miles away in another country. With no respect for the structural integrity of this business, the unscrupulous networker will suggest that your distributor would be better off sponsored under a local leader. Why? Because by so doing, he or she can share an office, or use the training center, or receive close support from someone who knows and understands the local culture.

Does a network marketer really need those things to succeed? No, but your distributors could easily be led to believe that he does. A really unethical leader may even offer your distributors "kickback money" to buy their loyalty away from their original foreign sponsor. Then your recruits—the shining lights of your hopes and dreams for building an inter-

national organization—are taught how to stop ordering under their current ID number, which links them to you. Instead, they are taught to sign up under a new number—and the theft is complete. Then your former distributors are taught how to duplicate this process with all of their recruits. This practice has been the single greatest heartbreak for many decent network marketers. And it doesn't just happen to new, first-year marketers. Ten-year-old veterans are also its victims. And when it occurs in significant numbers, it becomes virtually impossible for a company to trace, find, and return all the lines to their rightful places in the original order.

We have a message to corporate leaders who may be reading this chapter: This practice can be stopped, but it must be nipped in the bud. They must come down hard, at the very first occurrence, on those who make use of such practices. One strike, *warning*; two strikes, *fine*; and three strikes, *they're out*. The company's punishment should make a statement loud and clear: We will not tolerate unethical behavior in our distributor force. Period. End of story. If a company fails to terminate a networker who shows a pattern of unethical behavior, then the precedent is set. The activity will be duplicated and multiplied by the very nature of the business. Once the monster is created, there is no controlling it.

The situation we are describing has been experienced firsthand by us and many others, and we can tell you unequivocally that it has caused more heartache than all the other challenges in this business put together. If your company is still young and you have yet to expand internationally, do everything in your power to insist on strictly enforced international policies—including the termination of highly productive distributors, if necessary. Once the company shows how serious it is about international policy enforcement, the word will spread. Those who might consider such a practice will think twice, not wanting to risk their termination. But if a company waits too long before sending out this message to its worldwide distributor force, it may be like trying to put the evils back into Pandora's box.

Network marketing is a colossal business and it becomes even bigger when you enter the international scene. Some legends of the business have confided to us that they've lost millions because of prelaunch, illegal activities. All that money went directly into the pockets of those who advanced into the country with products and paperwork before its official opening. But what breaks our hearts is that many honest leaders in our industry had their one lead, and chance for wealth, stolen by such brazen crooks, without any company intervention.

International recruiting can be difficult even if you have the financial means to avoid the Plug-in Pistol altogether and can personally supervise the new market, taking up temporary residence there. If, for any reason, something feels wrong about a prospect or meeting, follow your instincts and say *Next*. Rob Hayman of Pompano Beach, Florida, had been with his network marketing company about six months when the corporate leaders made their first expansion into the Pacific Rim. Rob decided to go for it. Why not? The answer to that question becomes clear as Rob explains: "I spent five months in Hong Kong and then went to Taipei. One day I was riding in a taxi and found that the driver spoke English quite well. I invited 'Eagle' back to my apartment to show him our business. My upline associate always taught me that if someone was within three feet of you and breathing, try to recruit him.

"Eagle became very excited and said he knew just the man who could build a huge downline. The only catch was that we had to meet him early that morning at 2:00 A.M. My instincts screamed *No*, but I wanted to build a huge downline. If this guy was so powerful, then I'd go there. Eagle picked me up at 1:30. I wore my best suit. This was a heavy hitter and I needed to impress him. We drove through several side streets and then down a dark alley. Eagle parked the taxi and we walked for another block until we came to what looked like a garage with a side door. Eagle knocked three times. Someone opened the door just a crack, and the man and Eagle spoke in Mandarin Chinese. My knowledge of the language at that time consisted of 'Please bring me the check,' 'Where is the bathroom?' and 'Are you ambitious?' We were led down a long hallway that resembled the tunnel to a dungeon. Finally, we entered a room that was 'tastefully' decorated with two chairs, a beat up sofa, one desk, and nothing else. A man finally entered the room after about fifteen minutes. Eagle and the man spoke to each other for about thirty minutes. The only thing I picked up on was that the man's mood went from serious to angry to extremely hostile. I kept asking Eagle, 'So, is he interested?' Eagle kept saying that we'd talk later.

"When we finally left and were walking down the alley to the taxi, I noticed Eagle kept turning around every few yards and looking back. After we got in and started driving, I demanded to know what the heck had happened. Eagle confessed that a friend of his had borrowed a large sum of money from this man, in an attempt to get a major crime boss from the United States to leave him alone. At this point, I told him to stop the cab. I got out and told him to find another sponsor.

"The second thing my sponsor told me is to 'do whatever it takes.' I now believe this phrase does have its limitations." Cold recruiting in a foreign market can be extremely difficult, especially for a first-year networker. Since that time, Bob has gone on to build an organization of thousands of people in more than twenty countries and is currently at the top of the compensation plan in his company. Think what he could have lost had he let that unpleasant experience get the best of him. He should have followed his instincts that told him a 2:00 A.M. meeting is bizarre.

Each company has a variety of ways of dealing with the international market. Some go into a foreign country and find a local partner without opening it to their distributors at all. Others allow only those who have achieved a certain level of success to work in the foreign market. Still others require their marketers to meet qualifications all over again in each individual country in which they choose to build. Others have one seamless global plan, which is open to every level of networker within the company. Familiarize yourself with the international expansion policies within your company. Seek the advice of your upline associates about your entrance into the foreign market in your first year. Depending on your situation and the company you've chosen, it could be the best or worst option of your networking career.

As a general rule, we discourage newcomers to the industry from dabbling in the foreign market unless the country is their birthplace, or they have close family there, or their best friend in the whole world lives there. The foreign market is extremely difficult even for an old-timer. It takes a self-starter with absolute loyalty and a proactive approach. And it takes money to keep the lines of communication open. However, if you are new and are determined to enter the international market, then immediately consult with your sponsor, or a successful mentor in your upline, and begin to brainstorm exactly how you are going to capture your share of this special market. One thing is certain: If you are able to create a solid leg of your organization in a foreign market, it

can be one of the most lucrative undertakings in your networking career. But your success will depend on your personal contact and leadership, not on "plugging in" your key distributors to some local training center.

If you thought long-distance recruiting and training was difficult and expensive, international recruiting is more so. Just as you should do with your out-of-state recruits, you must be willing to take charge of your own group. If you can't make a trip to the foreign market to personally supervise your distributors (always the most effective way), then show them everything you can about the business utilizing phone, fax, e-mail, and mail. If English is understood, then the process is simplified somewhat. There are many industry recruiting tools that you can borrow. Our Web page, for example, has some basic information about our industry and how to select the right company. It is accessible to anyone in the industry who wants to use it at two addresses—*http://www.yarnell.com* or *http://www.powermlm.com*. Most major companies, and many MLM leaders, have their

---

If you are able to create a solid leg of your organization in a foreign market, it can be one of the most lucrative undertakings in your networking career.

own company Web site, fax-on-demand, and other similar technology set up for recruiting and training purposes. Turn to those technologies used in your own company to pull together the best support materials at hand. While building a foreign market is not easy, with the help of modern technology it is more possible to succeed than ever before.

Through the various mediums at your disposal, make as full and complete a presentation to your foreign prospects as if they were sitting in your living room. It's important to recruit proactive distributors in another country. Make sure your foreign prospects understand the importance of assuming a strong leadership position. The right person will be invigorated by this challenge. The wrong person will feel a desperate need to "plug in" to someone. As always, present all the information available—especially your story, as well as details on the company and product line, timing and trends of the MLM industry in their country, how money is made through leveraged income in your compensation plan. Once you have answered any questions, have a strong player from your upline team follow up with that prospect on your behalf. Unless you have a trusted upline associate or mentor visiting that market, never, ever, send your prospects to another leader's business briefing. Under these circumstances, with

your being thousands of miles away and not part of the same culture, the risk of losing your recruit is simply too great.

Let's assume that a prospect in a foreign market has decided to sign up under you and really go for it. Now the hard work begins. You must train this prospect based on the system you know works and teach him or her to do the same. We suggest that you begin by first sending a simple, one-page training outline. Your new associate can easily adapt and translate it for that particular market. If a leader in the industry or in your company has a book, manual, or audiotape/videotape training package available and already translated for that market, and it fits with your system, then by all means direct your new group to purchase and utilize that material. But if you have nothing more than the one-page outline, you can still train very effectively. We have also found teleconference calls to be a solid way to build a foreign market. Given the fact that telephone systems are not as advanced in other countries as they are in the United States, this is not always an easy undertaking. But no one said this business would be easy. If you have a leader in that country willing to go to the trouble to set up weekly teleconference calls, take full advantage of it—these weekly calls are a tremendous support mechanism. If language is a barrier, and an English-speaking leader is needed on these first calls, use simultaneous translation by someone who is bilingual.

But whatever you do, keep control of your new group. Start them out right, keeping the system simple and easily duplicated. Impress on them the importance of using your system if they are to be on your team and supported by you and your upline. Reassure them that you will notify them when upline leaders visit their country, and that eventually all materials will be translated for them. But the value of getting set up early is self-evident.

Our message is a simple one: If you unload the Plug-in Pistol and take back control of training your own recruits, you will elude countless problems that are of growing concern in our industry. Losing distributors to other leaders simply won't happen to you if you avoid the welfare mentality and choose a self-sufficiency mind-set. By protecting yourself and your downline from conflicting systems, you can avoid misfires which cripple new distributors. Take charge of your own organization and teach your people a simple system, which they in turn can duplicate with their recruits. Use your upline for support but don't expect anyone to recruit and train your people for you.

SUMMARY

- The Plug-in Pistol fires each time a network marketer signs up a new distributor long distance and then "plugs in" that recruit to any local training meeting that is available in that particular city.

- Select the long-distance leader or group to whom you entrust your new frontline associate with the same scrutiny that you would use to choose the daycare provider for your own child.

- Just as the best of all possible solutions is to raise your own child, so, too, is it best to train your valued frontline yourself.

- Plugging in your new distributors to just any citywide training, especially during their formative first year in the business, can create confusion and cause irreparable damage to their careers.

- Conduct your own training with your long-distance distributors by:

    1 Faxing them a one-page outline of your system.

    2 Answering all their questions over the phone.

    3 Getting a commitment that they are willing to follow your system exclusively.

- As your new associates move through the process, continue their training by:

    1 Requesting that they purchase a short manual that expands on the one-page outline.

    2 Reviewing the short manual with them over the phone.

    3 Recommending to them one or two motivational tools.

    4 Offering to coach them once a week.

    5 Conducting individual personal strategy training sessions over the phone.

    6 Recommending that they order a complete training manual once they prove to be serious business builders.

    7 Closing prospects for them and being available and supportive whenever they call.

- When coaching downline associates, suggest what you want them to "do right" rather than reminding them of what they're doing wrong.

- Only after you have your new distributors solidly on track should you agree to their attendance at citywide meetings in their locale.

- The first time your family and friends are introduced to network marketing, they should see the presentation in a private setting.

- When recruiting long-distance, stay personally involved with your new prospects:

    1 Do a mini-presentation by phone, fax, e-mail, or mail.

    2 Send your prospects multimedia information and follow it up with a phone conversation.

    3 Use the support of your upline associates for closing.

- If closing your new long-distance prospect is impossible, check out the kind of meetings being held in that area and encourage your prospect to attend only the business presentation portion of the best meeting.

- The preeminent purpose of network marketing has always been to consume and distribute quality products by word-of-mouth, while paying network distributors what they are worth, thus enabling them to live quality lives.

- You can preserve the integrity of our industry by (1) affiliating only with those companies that will terminate even a "big hitter" who breaks the rules, (2) by inviting honest people into your organization, and (3) by training your new distributors to respect the structural integrity of our industry.

- Some unscrupulous marketers attempt to destroy the structural integrity of our industry by unethically inducing other distributors' prospects, who attend meetings unaccompanied, to join their own downline by implying that they cannot be successful without local support . . . which, of course, is a myth.

- The myth of local support implies that distributors are limited to recruiting in their own city with no potential for global expansion, which is totally contrary to the nature of MLM.

- The exponential growth of a network marketing organization lies in the distributor's ability to teach others how to become leaders who in turn can teach others an easily duplicated system for recruiting anywhere in the world.

- Success in a foreign market is dependent on:

  1 The loyalty and communication between sponsors and new distributors.

  2 Well-translated training materials that offer a simple, proven system that is easily duplicated.

  3 The self-reliance of the new start-up group in that country.

- Success does not result from merely finding one good person and then "plugging in" that recruit to whatever training happens to be offered locally.

- New recruits in foreign markets are often tempted to switch their allegiance from their original sponsors to local downlines who erroneously claim that training centers, signing bonuses, cultural ties, and other hoopla are critical for success.

- It is vital that corporate leaders crack down on policy violations before they get out of hand.

- As a new networker, don't dabble in foreign markets unless the country is your birthplace, you have close family there, or your best friends in the whole world live in that country . . . or you have a downline who meets these requirements.

- With the advancement of technology, building an organization in a foreign market is more possible than ever before.

- The Plug-in Pistol won't backfire and hurt you if you take charge of your own organization and teach your recruits a simple system that they in turn can teach to their recruits.

CHAPTER 9

Deflecting the Executive Explosion

Recognize the upside and downside of corporate executives joining MLM.

WHILE CONDUCTING A RE-cent MLM college class in South Korea, we were asked a loaded question. In a most sincere manner, a gentleman inquired, "What have all those corporate managers in America, who are being laid off by the thousands, been doing for all those years when they were *on* the job? If the American corporate strategy for increasing profits is to simply get rid of executives and managers, how could those people have been productive in the first place?"

Before either of us could give an answer, another South Korean gentleman offered this explanation. "American corporations," he said, "are just like a handful of our Asian businesses. Executives go to meetings all day to plan future meetings, and write memos promising to send another one soon." Of course, everyone laughed enthusiastically. On the surface it would seem that a large gathering of MLM professionals would just naturally be biased against corporations. Yet there was profound truth set forth in that response. In this group were several former corporate executives who had turned to network marketing, and they knew firsthand that men and women in traditional corporate management positions are not being productive. "Memos and meetings do not profits make"—the Yarnells' 39th law.

We have friends who, after struggling to earn their MBA degrees, joined marketing divisions of Fortune 500 companies and then worked hard for as long as a decade before being promoted into management. Once promoted, they began attending meetings and writing memos. We certainly realize that there are corporate managers who assume tremendous responsibilities and work long hours. But many don't. That's why it's possible to lay off thousands and yet increase profits. Theoretically, if we were to go into a company and terminate 20 percent of the management, the bottom line would be negatively impacted. But in most cases, the profits are enhanced—that's why downsizing has become the darling of Wall Street. Investors love to see the companies in which they have invested begin to lay off their employees because it generally results in an increase in stock values.

Never before have so many high-powered executives been downsized out of their professions. In the last decade, many of them have been attracted to the financial independence and flexible lifestyle offered by the MLM industry. First-year distributors will undoubtedly find themselves engaged in a battle brought on by this change in global economics. We call it the Executive Explosion because of the monumental convergence of such a huge new pool of displaced corporate executives into network marketing. Generally, these are men and women who made a great living in corporate America, graduated from the finest MBA programs, weathered the first two decades of man-

agement cuts, but ultimately found themselves fired from the very position for which they slaved for years. Not only are they competent, well-trained, and polished professionals, but they are also quite effective at playing the corporate politics so prevalent in traditional business.

We recognize that corporate executives, business owners, and men and women in specialized fields come to our industry with one invaluable asset—respect. Most people have a high regard for the education, experience, and expertise of management executives and, because of their credentials, distributors will be inclined to listen to what they have to say. But as the Executive Explosion continues to gain momentum, traditional business men and women will also create problems as they attempt to carry many of their former practices into the network distribution industry—practices that simply won't work in our business. In this chapter, we will point out the advantages to our industry as former executives continue to join, but also recommend solutions to the challenges they bring to the industry, which inevitably will have an impact on every distributor's effectiveness. And these challenges will extend not only to the entire downline, but often to the upline as well.

Advantages Gained by Corporate Executives Joining MLM

BEGINNING in the late '70s and continuing right into the greedy '80s, thousands of corporate managers turned to the network marketing industry for entrepreneurial jobs. But never has there been a greater influx than in the last decade. No longer regarded as "the little lady's part-time, home party plans," network marketing has gained increasing momentum and grown into a respected industry in the '90s. Meanwhile, prices for franchises have soared amidst overkill legal fees and inevitable government interference. Both the low downside and high upside potentials of MLM are being discovered by an increasing number of white-collar professionals: college graduates, college professors, successful corporate managers, Chief Executive Officers (CEOs), physicians, dentists, health care specialists, CPAs, attorneys. The credibility of the industry is building under the influence of this sophisticated new generation of professional networkers.

As more professionals join network marketing, the trade press is reporting on our industry and individual companies in a much more positive light. Network marketing is being discussed in such leading publications as *The Wall Street Journal, Forbes, Success, Working at Home, Chicago Tribune*, and by the Associated Press, as well as in a wide range of regional newspapers and special interest publications. This credibility is also extending into the university sector. Over the past decade, there has been an ongoing debate as to whether or not Harvard University teaches network marketing. We think it's an issue of semantic gymnastics. Maybe Harvard doesn't teach network marketing, but, in April of 1997, Harvard Ph.D. Dr. Charles King gave a lecture about network marketing at Harvard to the Harvard Law School Office of Student Life Counseling, the Harvard Association of Law and Business, and the Harvard Business School Marketing Club.

Challenges Posed by Corporate Executives Joining MLM

FACED with no substantial savings or transitional income, many downsized corporate executives turn to MLM in a desperate attempt to recapture their former lifestyles. These are good men and women who frankly don't know the first thing about our profession and don't understand that they don't. When they see a group of former blue-collar workers and non-corporate types whom they feel have somehow blundered into $30,000 to $50,000 a month without a degree or any sophisticated knowledge of business, it captures their attention. They figure that if people with less education and experience can achieve that kind of wealth, then there is no limit to what they can do, especially with their credentials. These men and women are faced with two challenges as they enter into the field of network distribution: first, an unmistakable desperation stemming from their loss of prestige and sudden withdrawal of benefits, company cars, and income; second, a misguided conviction that they can transfer their corporate management style into network marketing. Because so many corporate managers have recently entered our profession, it's only natural that corporate practices would begin to infiltrate network marketing. But they've brought into our industry the very practices that led to low productivity and unjustifiably high incomes in their former traditional corporate management positions.

On the other side of the coin, there are two obvious challenges that displaced corporate executives pose to our industry. First, because they are typically very high achievers with great egos and impressive credentials, former executives can often intimidate new distributors who sponsor them. Second, these former executives are inclined to employ many of the tools they used in traditional business: systems which are simply not effective in network marketing. Once intimidated, sponsors no longer command the respect necessary to coach such executives. So the executives take immediate control and begin implementing their own high-tech systems and attempt to manage everyone. Don't make the mistake of assuming that someone you sponsor who has special credentials and comes from a strong corporate background knows more about our business than you do. As Aaron Lynch points out in his wonderful book *Thought Contagion*, "Less credentialed people can recognize the restrictive effects of credential systems well enough that they don't even try to impart beliefs to someone with impressive credentials." If you have been in the business longer and have been trained properly, it is critical that you exert your power and train your corporate executives as you would instruct anyone else you sponsor. If you take control from the very start, you will earn respect.

Robert Holloway of Dallas, Texas, represents the corporate dissident as well as anyone we know—but one who did it right by duplicating exactly what his mentors taught. His career progressed from his early days as a scientific programmer and engineer, through the real estate development stage with his business partner Roger Staubach, to his current network marketing empire. Almost no corporate executives join network marketing because they're at the height of their success. Most join this business hoping against hope to put the pieces of their lives back together. Robert was no different. He describes his own situation, "The beginning of my career in MLM was not one of the highlights in my life. My real estate business had slacked off considerably, with very little potential for positive change in the near future. I had watched an exciting and profitable real estate career go sour. The markets had completely evaporated.

"One year prior to my introduction to network marketing, a former real estate developer had come to me with this great idea about water filters and said if I would just get in his business 'I could make him a lot of money.' I asked, 'What about me?' and his reply was 'Oh . . . well, you can make a lot of money, too.' That did not sit well with me although I was impressed with the proposed earnings potential.

"About one year later, I was invited to a business presentation on a new growth opportunity. It sounded like a real estate deal. Little did I know until I arrived that I was being invited to an MLM presentation. I had a lot of overhead and the last thing I was interested in was network marketing . . . especially selling skin care products and shampoo. My background was in engineering and development and my pride said this was the last thing on earth I wanted to do. I had just lost millions of dollars in real estate downturns and now I was going to call friends to tell them of my new MLM career and ask them to join me? At first glance, I could not see why any of my friends would want to do that. Now, after building a multimillion-dollar business and developing a quality lifestyle, I can't think of one reason why everyone wouldn't want to join me. But I had learned from working at IBM, and especially after struggling in the commercial real estate market, that if success was going to happen, it was up to me."

The Mind-Set of a Corporate Executive

ROBERT Holloway shares some of his insights into understanding the mind-set of corporate executives and businesspeople: "I began to contact my closest friends and found that most wanted to improve the quality of their lives and make money. But I wasn't prepared for the second part: Most were unwilling to do anything about it. I found that most people had come to accept their fate in life—layoffs, downsizing, corporate mergers; they had very little hope and no dreams to follow. They were not happy where they were, but the fear of doing something that might further erode their situation was greater than the anticipation of the positive results from taking charge of their lives.

"Many corporate people today can't envision themselves being successful in a new venture because they see themselves, in many cases, totally unhappy in their chosen fields. How could MLM improve their status? The answer, of course, is that their personal future is yet to be written. Why not direct the future in a way that brings 'continued, expansive growth' as opposed to stagnation and 'confused regrouping.' The challenge is to understand that our job is not to find people and change them. Our task is to find the ones who have already come to the conclusion that they need to change and then get them the information they need to satisfy their research. Those who develop positive outlooks and apply our concepts with commitment and consistency are able to build dynamic, successful businesses. This is one of the most rewarding opportunities available today. In the next few years, thousands of lives will be dynamically changed for the better through network marketing.

"This business is all about timing, catching people at the right time in their lives when they are open to new areas of opportunity. If you can give corporate executives good information relative to their specific concerns, then you have reasonably good odds that they will move to the next level of investigation. Once they use the products, see the potential of expanding multibillion-dollar markets, and sense the rewards of the marketing plan, they will be ready to be involved in the training system and the business-building process.

"I have discovered two essential facts about dealing with the corporate person or business professional: (1) They want information that documents that the business is legitimate; (2) They respond better if you are yourself committed and building a business, because they understand that you can show them how to duplicate your success. If you are a new distributor, you may need to use your upline to close corporate people. Mark Yarnell had to go a full six levels upline until he found someone with experience—Richard Kall. None of the distributors between Richard and Mark were seasoned leaders. The process is still the same. Prospects need proof and direction. The faster you provide these resources, the faster they can do their research, make a decision, and move to the next stage. Either they are ready to get started, the time is not right, or this business is not for them." The first two are positive decisions, but many inexperienced networkers will not recognize the second stage as positive. And if you will use the follow-up card-filing system, which we recommended in an earlier chapter, with those for whom the time isn't right, you will eventually sponsor some of those people, too. If the business is not for them, ask for referrals.

As Robert explains, "Most people completely misunderstand when a corporate person says *No*. It's not that they don't want to make more money and have free time, it's just not the right time for them to pursue it. Six months can change everything. Most people don't understand this and see it as personal rejection. A person new to MLM often doesn't realize that being turned down just means that the timing simply wasn't right. Don't take it any more personally than that. I am convinced, more than ever before, that the timing today could not be better to launch a career track in network marketing, one that can change a person's life for the better."

Robert's forthcoming book, entitled *From IBM to MLM*, explains in detail the steps necessary to take control of your life, develop a vision, become energized, and put your plan into action. He and his wife, Karen, live in Dallas, Texas, and work the business together. With all of their success, they now have the time to pursue their real passion—sailing and exploring faraway islands, stopping in each little port along the way. Last summer, we had the joy of being introduced to the sport with them while yachting our way around the Sir Francis Drake Channel in the Caribbean. Greece is next.

Corporate executives can become among the greatest distributors in your organization or they can blow everything and ruin your entire downline. We have seen both happen. The way to prevent the latter from happening is to exert your strength from the very beginning and let them know how very different MLM is from traditional business. We have been very fortunate to learn a great deal from Terry and Tom Hill. They are the only truly high-powered sales professionals we've ever sponsored: Terry was the number one Xerox sales rep, and her husband, Tom, was a Merrill Lynch stockbroker. They have been invaluable teachers to us with respect to the Executive Explosion. They taught us about the executive mindset and the necessity for structure. More importantly, Terry shared with us many of the sales strategies employed in corporate business and, specifically, why they don't work in our field. We want to begin by examining a few of those strategies to see why they are ineffective.

Networking Strategies: The Antithesis to Traditional Business

NETWORKING strategies are often the very antithesis to traditional business and conventional marketing systems. Corporate executives often erroneously believe that strategies that brought them success in traditional business will work in MLM. Sadly, most don't. But because of their egos and previous leadership habits, they instinctively seek to "reinvent the wheel." As these respected executives bring in new systems and create new sales tools based on traditional business, they unwittingly lead other distributors astray. Because of their credibility, they can sway their up-line as well as their downline. Of course, many new distributors just naturally assume that these formerly successful exec-utives know what they are doing and adopt their traditional strategies as a means of succeeding in MLM. We're going to say it once more: Take control, be deci-sive, and lead yourself.

Give Up Meetings and Memos

It isn't easy for a corporate person to give up meetings and memos. They are ingrained in executives. So first and fore-most, teach your new frontline distributors coming from the business world that MLM is a work program and that success comes to no one during the time that they are at-tending meetings and typing memos. One of our frontline leaders sponsored a former manager of a large division of Phillips Pe-troleum. Within the first week we started getting lengthy memos—either faxed or e-mailed to our home—detailing the amount of work he was preparing to do. One day we called him and thanked him for the memos, but explained that it wasn't a valuable use of his time. He was crestfallen by our comment. To him, memos were life. He quit after two weeks. He didn't under-stand that memos mean nothing in our business. Action is the only thing that counts. New distributors, especially from corporate America, must be taught from day one that product usage, prospecting, and recruiting are what lead to success. Memos and meetings are time-wasters.

Replace High-Tech Systems with Personal Storytelling

The most common mistake by corporate professionals is the overuse of high-tech systems in building a network marketing business. While current high-tech communications seem very advanced, they can also be a rather cold, sterile way to relate to others, and simply don't prove effective in our business. Many corporate professionals who join the simple, home-based business of network marketing will try to structure it to look like the business world from which they came. They want to create slide shows, use projector overheads, and give computer-generated PowerPoint presentations. They will try to assemble formalized presenters and printed charts, rewrite manuals, and generally mimic the activities that were relevant in their former position. Some will even set up offices (see chapter seven).

For a former corporate executive, the most difficult aspect of our business to grasp is that MLM is designed to be something that all folks can do. If you try to turn it into an exclusive country club or corporation, you defeat the very essence of network marketing, which is about having significant numbers of people in your organization, prospecting, recruiting, along with using and sharing the products and services. Make certain that every step you take can be duplicated by the very least skilled in your organization. If done properly, ours is a business that sends prospects home thinking

to themselves, "I can do that! I have a living room, and a VCR, and friends who need more money and time with their families. I really believe I can do this business."

This is a business of storytelling and sharing personal ups and downs. Traditional business instructs you to emphasize your strengths and past successes. To break down the walls of resistance, network marketing teaches you to share your vulnerabilities—the circumstances leading to your hitting bottom—as well as your successes. It is generally the down times that open the door to network marketing for many people; but more importantly, it is hearing a very personal story that makes other people relate to you as a "real" person. It is very difficult for typical corporate executives to share their weaknesses with others. They have rarely, if ever, been encouraged to do so. But it is the emotional, passionate, personal side of this business that creates its deeply human appeal. Systems such as slide shows, e-mail recruiting, high-tech computer Web sites, hotel meetings, mass mailings, and a host of other traditional, impersonal marketing strategies do not work nearly as effectively in the simplified, easily duplicated field of good old-fashioned, work-at-home network marketing.

Lead by Example Instead of by Delegating

Once in network marketing, traditional business executives must leave behind their habit of delegating responsibilities and begin to lead by example. Executives are forced into the trenches in MLM; for many, letting go of their former image is unbearable. Most managers, administrators, and supervisors have spent their lives telling others what to do and overseeing their activities. That same behavior in network marketing can lead to the rapid death of your entire organization. Do you know why? Because ours is a business of duplication. Whatever you do, your people will duplicate. If each one is managing his group and no one is prospecting, recruiting, and presenting the business opportunity, then that organization will stagnate. The healthy organization begins with action at the top. The leader should be in the trenches—prospecting, setting appointments, frontline recruiting, and using and sharing products and services with a small customer base. The leader should not be supervising anyone, but rather showing them what to do by example. If you duplicate that throughout your organization, then you will certainly have a living, breathing, thriving business.

Never Qualify Your Prospects

Because of the Executive Explosion, new distributors will recruit people who were formerly quite successful marketing reps with major corporations. One of the very first rules of thumb followed by professional salespeople, and brought with them into MLM, is the importance of "qualifying a prospect." For example, a typical marketing rep selling $3 million laser printers usually tries to make certain that a company both needs and can afford that specific printer—that is, qualifies the prospect—before making an approach. But when executives and marketing reps use that principle in MLM, it doesn't work. Here's why.

Those who succeed in building huge organizations in our industry are fre-

The healthy organization begins with action at the top. The leader should be in the trenches—prospecting, setting appointments, frontline recruiting, and using and sharing products and services with a small customer base.

quently people who have no business background, no former sales experience, no college education, and for all practical purposes appear to be those who would not succeed. Our best description of the type of person you are trying to recruit is one whose back is against the wall financially; who is driven by a cause; who is coachable and willing to follow your system without changing it; who comes across enthusiastically; and, finally, who enjoys working with people and seeing them become successful. But when executive types come on board, they unfortunately tend to qualify their prospects and exclude many who would ultimately make them a fortune, all because they don't appear qualified. The best advice we can give to corporate executives who have just entered our industry is this: "Wake up each morning and resign as General Manager of the Universe." Don't play God. Anyone can do this business. Whether they will put forth the effort is entirely up to them . . . not you.

It is also important to keep in mind that a farsighted networker will make room for all kinds of people in his or her organization: wholesale buyers, retailing distributors, part-time organization builders, as well as people who pull out all the stops and take this opportunity to the moon. You don't want anyone to feel out of place in your network. As long as your people are taking steps to achieve the goals they have set for themselves, they should feel a sense of belonging in your group. A typical and successful organization will consist of a balance of all types of people with all kinds of objectives. It will be made up largely of wholesale buyers who are faithfully ordering and reordering products and/or services month after month. A good organization will also have a share of retailing distributors intent on selling products or services as their primary means of earning an income. Next there will be part-time networkers who are working toward building an organization of distributors for the purpose of replacing their income. And, finally, the smallest group will be those who are full-time maniacs going crazy with this business, setting records in MLM history. Always look for the serious business builders with whom you can partner, but make a place for everyone in your organization. Truly, the more diverse the merrier. There is no value in qualifying your prospects.

Organization Building Versus Retailing Products

WITH this influx of executives into the network distribution industry, there is a far greater understanding of the value of building an organization of people who do three things: use the products or services, share them with others, and find others who will do the same. It takes a lot of people, each doing a little bit, to make it all work. But for many today, as in the early days of the industry, there is confusion over whether to place your emphasis on product sales or on building an organization. The answer lies in deciding what you want out of your business.

Home parties, clinics, and retail sales create immediate, short-term cash in hand. Building an organization of distributors who use and share the products and duplicate this process produces long-term residual income. With some exceptions, such as medical doctors, most professionals entering the networking scene today prefer the passive residual income from organization building over the immediate gratification of product movement. Even those who come into our industry unaware of anything but the ability to sell products, like scholar athletes Steve and Jeanette Baack, will often inadvertently discover the longer-range value of building an organization. But they aren't alone.

It was November of 1979 when Jan Ruhe first learned about Multi-Level Marketing. "I had a four-year-old daughter, Sarah, and a two-year-old son, Clayton, and was invited to a product demonstra-tion. I wanted to join the day I attended. But the company rep told me that she wasn't going to be associated with the company any more and that I would have to call her upline. I called that next person and left her message after message. She finally called me back and told me to stop annoying her. She then informed me that our company was very new and they had stopped letting people become sales reps until the following March.

"On the first day of that month I called the local sales rep in Dallas, Texas, who told me I could stop by the church where she was working to pick up a form—she didn't want to 'mess with' getting it to me. I joined while I was pregnant with my soon-to-be-daughter, Ashley. We had no money—I was sick of being broke and sick of always asking my husband for a little money. I never really thought in terms of wanting financial independence; I just wanted to have some extra money. I was thirty years young and not willing to live like a pauper for the rest of my life. My husband had no desire to be financially successful, and I felt captive with three children—not being able to earn any money without leaving them. I called my mother and asked her for the start-up kit deposit but she discouraged me, certain that these kinds of home parties were not for me. She said I should 'stay home, be a mother, and let my husband's income provide for us.' I was disgusted with her attitude and called her mother, my grandmother, who said, 'Honey, I will be happy to invest in you. I am going to stake a claim in your future.'

"That day I knew I had found the perfect vehicle. It seemed perfect—a real business that allowed me to be with my children and sell a product out of my home. I just didn't know yet that it was network marketing. The day I joined, my local upline associate quit, and my next upline associate was located in California. I was the only sales rep for my company in the entire south of the United States. No training, no meetings, no support. Oh well, I was determined to be the best salesperson I could be. At my first home party, twenty people were there and I sold $75 in product. Wow! Someone actually bought from me! I was thrilled. I booked a few parties and my business took off. As I showed the products in private home parties, people lined the hallways to buy from me and some even asked how they could sell and become involved.

"Well, I had no idea, so I told them that they couldn't join me, that I was the only one who could represent this product to the public in Dallas. Can you believe that? I didn't understand about recruiting, but I had booked more parties than I could handle. About six months into the business, I decided to take a look at the small company manual in the bottom of a box in my garage. It said that my company was an MLM business and that I was to recruit others to sell the product. Well, blow me away! I had no idea and had never kept the names of the many who had asked to join me! I am still looking for those people today!" This moment of discovery created such a wonderful visual for us—just thinking about her rummaging around in her garage and being "blown away" when she read her manual made us laugh until we cried.

"The next six weeks," she continues, "I focused on recruiting and found thirteen people who also wanted to sell. At that point, my California upline associate called me. In fact, everyone called me! In 1980, those thirteen distributors made me the top recruiter in the history of the company! One of the recruits told me that she only wanted to do parties and that she would not recruit. I had booked the coming Fall with home parties almost every other night, which represented more than half my business. I remember that I had baby Ashley in my arms when that newest frontline called to inform me that she was quitting (the same day she joined) because she had called all of her friends to book parties and they had already committed to come to mine. I made one of the hardest and, as it turned out, most significant decisions of my career. I told her she could have the home parties that I had booked.

"Through those parties, she became the top seller that year in our company. And though I was pretty bitter at first, it gave me more time to be with my three babies, all under four years old. In spite of herself, she ended up recruiting six people, whom I trained and supported. As my organization grew, I set up a tiny office in a corner of the playroom so that I could work and supervise my children at the same time. I got on the phone prospecting and following up for hours each day. Even with the care of the children, I made at least twenty calls a day. I was driven by the money. Everyone else in my entire company was mission-oriented—save-the-world-type people. Not me. I wanted to make money. I figured out that if I made my mission helping enough others make money, then I, too, would eventually make money. And it worked.

"I also took my three babies to the zoo and to parks every other day. They had a great time while I prospected! I was determined and driven. I would do whatever it took to get some extra money. I was propelled to success because I wanted the money to put Sarah and Clayton into a private school in Dallas. The day I 'gave away' my parties to my new recruit and focused on finding others who wanted to recruit or do parties—that's when my business took off. I focused on getting a lot of people doing a little bit. By the end of that year, I had twenty-four people in my group and had earned about $5,000. By the following January, almost everyone quit. I just started all over again. I can't believe I stuck it out. My children and my business were my entire world. They both flourished, but my marriage did not. I'm sure none of you can relate to that.

"I survived divorce, mega-debt, single parenting, the death of my grandmother, the death of my upline, miscarriages, along with the ups and downs of being the head of a growing MLM organization. I thank God every day that someone recruited me into MLM. My parents have moved from Texas and now live close by. My mother became one of my sales reps! My children have turned out to be wonderful young adults; two have now completed college. I got to stay home and now my family and many others in my downline are reaping the rewards."

Today, eighteen years later, Jan is happily married, living with her second husband in a mansion on the top of a mountain in Aspen, Colorado. Through network marketing, she has become a millionaire with over 7,000 people across the

We elevate ourselves by lifting up others.

nation selling almost $10 million a year. She is the author of three bestselling books in MLM. The "Working at Home" September 1997 issue of *Success* magazine featured her rags-to-riches story! Her motto in those early years was "Lead me, follow me or get out of my way." It is still her motto today!

Many distributors come into this business because they fall in love with the line of products and want to make money telling everyone about them. Organization builders, particularly those who understand business, love to have retailing distributors as part of their group. But we owe it to everyone to make sure they know that the option is always there for them to elevate their goals through duplication. The day Jan "gave away" her home parties to one of her frontline associates is the day her business began to take off. Why? Because Jan accidentally blundered into one of the cornerstone principles of Multi-Level Marketing: We elevate ourselves by lifting up others. And it is interesting to us that it all began when an unselfish grandmother refused to accept mediocrity for her granddaughter

and chose to invest in her future. God bless that darling lady.

Building a Network Organization Full-Time

HAVING left the world of traditional business behind, the first challenge to a networker who was formerly a "big biness man," as Mark is fond of saying, is the loss of his pride. A lowered self-image is the greatest challenge to former corporate people. Even though they were overworked and/or underpaid and/or laid off or about to be, still, in their former life, they were "somebody" . . . with a title and a fancy office to prove it. Now, they are at the bottom of the rung and have to prove themselves through productivity, and that can be scary. The first step in sponsoring and training corporate executives or businesspeople is to be sensitive to the fact that they are probably at the most vulnerable place in their lives. They may still have the old bravado in their talk, but don't be fooled by it. They need you right now.

Show them your strength and lead them through the steps to be successful, pointing out the blatant differences between the world of network marketing and their former world of traditional business. Encourage them with your every word.

As product manager for a major Wall Street investment firm, Jay Primm supervised fifty-six branches throughout California. Although he was given a great deal of independence as the only manager in his firm on the West Coast, he can still recall the adjustments he had to make as he transitioned into full-time network marketing.

In January of 1989, when Jay signed up with his company, the stigma of MLM was much greater than it is today. As Jay explains, "It was really tough, and I took a lot of heat from my friends, who thought I was crazy. My father continually dropped hints, in those early days, about my getting back to a real job." Jay left the glamour of the TransAmerica building in San Francisco for a bedroom office in his home. On a bad day, even he questioned what he was doing. Even if he was miserable in corporate America, he could hide behind the prestige of a job that at least looked wonderful.

"Then," as Jay describes, "there was the urgency. I had allowed myself exactly one year to replace a six-figure income. I was sick of being battered by corporate

America. The more I did, the more they expected. Now I was running my own show and I was excited. I was accountable only to myself and no one else. I had to deal with all of the usual preconceived notions about this industry. I thought of myself as being a resource for people. Basically, I just looked for prospects who saw this business the same way I did—as a major global opportunity.

"I was driven to succeed. I thought nothing back then of putting in ten to twelve hours a day six, and sometimes seven, days a week. We lived and breathed this business. I worked closely with my upline associate, Marc Barrett, and we were recruiting machines. I was in one room on the phone setting appointments, and he was in the other doing his part of the presentation to my people.

"The biggest problem most corporate people experience in making the transition into network marketing is the total lack of structure. I was accustomed to being fairly self-reliant, but many new distributors miss not having someone tell them what to do. Marc handled this by throwing corporate types, like me, to the wolves. Since my previous position was as a trainer, he played off my strength. By the first week, I was doing presentations before I even felt like I knew what I was doing. It was baptism by fire and it was the best way for me. The busier I was, the happier I was, while caught up in the frenzy of those early, desperate days."

One year later, Jay had replaced his income; six months after that he had multiplied it five times again. Today, Jay lives just outside of Boulder, Colorado, with his wife, Betty, and their two children, Jason and Ashley. He and Betty travel extensively to Asia, and other parts of the world, to support their downline. He works from home, in an environment where his children have never known it any other way. They've grown up with the misguided notion that most dads work from home and spend most of their time with their family. What a concept! We're certain that when Jason or Ashley find out that other dads go to offices and write memos all day, they will have a similar response to Jan Ruhe: "Well, blow me away!"

Building a Network Organization Part-Time

BUILDING a part-time network marketing organization while holding down a full-time job presents many challenges. Part-timers must often deal with their bosses' negative reactions, their spouse's skepticism, all the while maintaining an equilibrium throughout the process. Any one of these is enough, all by itself, to destroy the possibility of success.

Sandy Elsberg describes her doubts about her husband's initial pursuits in MLM. "One evening, my husband, Bill, told me to get all dolled up because we were going to a hotel. I decked myself out in my highest heels with ankle straps, adorned my hair with oleanders and off we went. When we arrived, he waltzed me into a room full of 300 people, right up to a front seat on the aisle where a guy in plaid, polyester pants and a dark brown polyester jacket with white topstitching told me I could make $28,000 a month working part-time.

"Instinctively, I folded my arms, crossed my legs, and closed my mind. After growing up in a city project and working long hours for ten years as an elementary school teacher, I couldn't even imagine the seemingly obscene numbers this guy was throwing at me. I leaned over to Bill and said, 'Look, buster, the Brooklyn Bridge is sold. We just opened our own clinic, and now you want me to waste my energy on this?'

"But Bill said, 'Honey, I want to do this. If you're not going to support me, at least don't resist.' And he added, 'Just be positive for six months.' So for six months I barely saw my husband. My father used to call every few days and ask how we were doing, and Bill was never around.

When the first check came, and it was a little over $100, my father declared, 'Follow him, he's got a girlfriend.' But I kept my promise and the next month wasn't much better (just over $300).

"The month after that, the check was up to $500, but he was still spending all of that and more getting the business off the ground, and he was still gone every night and weekend. I accused him of ruining our marriage; he reminded me about the six-month deal. The next check was $1,100, then $2,200. At the end of six months, it was up to $3,800 and he was still doing it part-time, putting in full days at the clinic.

"In all the years I taught school, I'd never taken home more than $1,000 a month. At this point, I started to get ideas. 'Honey,' I said, 'I could write a little training program for you so you wouldn't have to keep repeating the same thing over and over and people could make a fast start. And, let's make a nice little handbook, just like I do for my first-graders. That way everything will be simple and easily duplicated.'

"And you know what? In ninety days our check doubled! When we made $7,000 in one month, suddenly I could see how $28,000 a month could be possible. That's when I got it! That is what it took for me to become a believer. I had to experience the process firsthand. I had to hold my skepticism at bay long enough to allow success to happen. I will always be grateful that Bill held me to my promise to reserve judgment for those six months. And as promised, MLM 'showed me the money.'"

In many cases, people with full-time occupations can start slowly by making smaller sacrifices. This is what Tony Neumeyer chose to do and he has definitely reaped the benefits.

"Real estate provided a very good living; however, I had time poverty and was always at the beck and call of others. I was working twelve to fourteen hours a day, six or seven days a week, and my time was not my own . . . my job was running me. In order to make time for my network marketing business, I had to make some real choices. I decided to get up an hour earlier each day to get some of my real estate paperwork out of the way. I also chose to put some of the activities I loved—particularly baseball and golf—on hold for a while.

"Getting up an hour earlier five days a week was a simple decision. I knew I would gain over twenty hours a month or a full work week every two months. I knew the leveraging and compounding of time would pay huge dividends in a relatively short period. The key was to use that time effectively. Within a few months, my organization had developed across three time zones. Since I was already awake at 5:00 A.M., my time, I was able to phone people on the east coast where it was 8:00 A.M. This proved very effective in spurring growth.

"Choosing to put my social activities on the 'back burner' for a couple of years proved the most difficult of my choices. Sports were my outlet to maintain sanity. Fortunately, my wife was extremely supportive. We had a toddler of twenty-one months and a two-month-old infant when I started with my network marketing company. Kate kept the house running and our personal family matters in order so that I could devote my time to getting ahead. She was and is amazing. I truly felt that by working hard for a few years we would be set for life, and now that has proven to be absolutely true! Just one hour a day and a few sacrifices have changed our lives forever!"

By using this steady, methodical approach, Tony Neumeyer has achieved the honor of being the top Canadian distributor in a large network marketing company.

Building a Network Organization As a Single Woman

THERE are hundreds of thousands of single women like Jan Ruhe in network mar-keting. Their struggles to build an organization while accepting their other responsibilities—as wives, mothers, and female executives—have been valiant. Today, there are just as many flocking in from corporate America. As president of a company, while still in her twenties, Carmen Anderson was responsible for the sale of a chain of restaurants and the accompanying real estate. She put in sixteen-hour days and seven-day weeks with employees, FICA, overhead, food costs, paperwork, and meetings, meetings, meetings!

As Carmen describes her experience, "After completing my projects with this company, I had the good fortune to have an entrepreneurial friend who knew me during my tenure as an executive. She told me there was a better way: Find the right vehicle, work hard for a few years, and create leverage so you will be paid whether you work or not. I'd always worked very hard at any job I'd had anyway. So, I went to a meeting. Wow! My first impression was these people are happy. And they are earning incredible money. I was definitely open to the opportunity and decided to try the company's products. In two days, the products had relieved some serious concerns and discomfort I had been experiencing. I looked and felt better. Immediately, all my friends who had the same concerns were introduced to the products. I was sharing, not selling them, and felt really good about being able to help my friends. Next thing I knew, I was off to Hong Kong sharing the products and business with people there when our company expanded internationally, then Australia, then New Zealand.

"In Hong Kong I met the man who later became my husband and he finally got me back to America. We now have two babies: a boy and a girl just more than a year apart. And guess what? I have a global business based in my home here in Alabama while I take time to enjoy my children throughout the day and spend quality time with my husband. I'm happy and fulfilled—life just doesn't get any better." Carmen and her husband, Joel, live with their children in Sheffield, Alabama, and keep a condo in New York. They also have a marvelous yacht in Boca Raton where we welcomed in a memorable New Year with them.

Sandy Elsberg's experience, once she was left on her own to build an organization, epitomizes that of so many women in our industry today. "After some moderate success with our first MLM company, our fortunes took a decided turn for the worse. Bill developed a chronic debilitating illness that prevented him from working the business. Then we discovered that the MLM company in which we'd in-vested so much of our energy and hopes and dreams had let us down. About seven years after starting our first MLM business, we'd reached a serious crisis.

"I was forty-one years old and nine months into a high-risk pregnancy with a four-year-old child in tow. My ankles had swollen to the size of thighs, Bill was still very sick and we had no health insurance. We were worse than broke—broke would have been easy. With our credit ruined and over $250,000 in debt, we didn't even have enough cash to buy a large package of diapers at the supermarket. Talk about scared? If I'd seen a light at the end of the tunnel, I'd have thought it was an oncoming train. But, like Mary Pickford said, 'Failure is not in the falling down, but in the staying down.'

"Just in time, a friend introduced me to another networking opportunity, and I set out in my beat-up Volkswagon van—without heat, air conditioning, or a radio—driving up and down the 405 interstate doing home parties. When it was cold, I put on a pair of woolen booties to keep my feet warm while I drove. When it was blistering hot, I kept my make up in a little ice chest in back of the van to keep it from melting.

"I didn't have the money to run ads. I couldn't buy a fax machine. Heck, I couldn't even put more than $5 worth of gas in the car at once. But I knew from previous experience that this industry delivered; I was willing to go into the gold mine with my pick and shovel and dig as long and hard as I must in order to succeed. And guess what? After that first month, I'd earned a bonus check of $7,000 (which arrived the day after the baby!). What's more, I also pocketed about $4,000 in cash from retail sales.

"Having lived this story allows me to understand, at a gut level, what it feels like to be a discouraged welfare mother; or a laid-off, middle-aged corporate manager; or a retiree eating oatmeal three times a day at the end of the monthly social security check. I know what desperation feels like. But I also know that, with the eye of the tiger and the willingness to do whatever is necessary, we each have the ability to create our own success. It's not luck. It's not magic. It's what's inside us."

We have known Sandy for several years now, and this is the message she delivers so sensitively to women audiences. There is not a single woman with reasonable skills and serious drive who cannot pull herself out of her plight and achieve greatness. Sandy and Bill Elsberg live in Dove Canyon, California. Sandy has gone on to become a major advocate for the industry and a much sought after speaker among network marketing companies nationwide.

As an upline associate to Sandy Elsberg, Jerry Rubin had these kind words to say about her: "Sandy is a veteran of network marketing, but every day she approaches the business like it's the first day of the rest of her life. She is emotionally and intellectually involved in the business and comes to it from the depths of her soul. She's a product of her mentors, and her life's experience, and she works harder than anyone I know. She's one of the best teachers in the business because she understands how she got where she is. If you understand how you got where you are, then you will be able to teach others how to get there too."

You may remember Jerry Rubin for his Chicago Seven anti-capitalism protests in the '60s. By the '90s, he had dramatically changed his thinking. He and Mark were working on a book together called *The Capitalist Manifesto* when Jerry met with an untimely death. Most of the world remembers Jerry Rubin as a radical who dared to smoke pot during an interview on national television. But we remember him sitting in our living room in Reno just a few months before his death, moved by the quietness of our environment, so contrasting to his own. The real Jerry was a sensitive man who had become a caring capitalist. He was prepared to do whatever it took to help others rise to their full potential through the very system of capitalism that many of us ridiculed in the '60s. We miss him dearly.

Single women are pouring into the network distribution industry because it is the last bastion of free enterprise. Whether you are coming from the corporate world, because, like Terry Hill, Jay Primm, or Carmen Anderson, you found a better alternative to corporate America; or you're a homemaker, like Jan Ruhe, who is sick and tired of being broke and dependent on her husband; or your back is against the wall, like Bill and Sandy Elsberg—you can build a networking business. All of these success stories have two things in common: (1) they went the extra mile in the early stages to make it work, (2) when it stopped working, as life deals us all setbacks from time to time, they "put their make up on ice" and started over.

Supplanting Executive Attitudes

WITH more and more defectors leaving traditional businesses and corporate positions to follow the call of network marketing, we should all do our best to keep the typical executive attitudes from carrying over into the network distribution industry.

Seek Personal Development over Monetary Gain

It seems fair to say that most executives are preoccupied about how much money they are making, where they stand in the income structure among their peers, and, in most cases, worried that wherever they are isn't high enough. They are often distressed about the many side effects of their profession: sixty-hour weeks, stress-induced coronaries, layoffs, mergers, and hostile takeovers. Network marketing has had a transforming effect on many business men and women in this regard.

Gary Leeling, of Temecula, California, had been a dentist for twenty-seven years. He describes his own transformation. "Dentistry was initially good to me but, about 1987, things started to change. HMOs, OSHA, liability problems (I was virtually practicing law to keep from getting sued)—all started to make life difficult. I stuck my head in the sand. After all, dentistry would never fail me; dentists are supposed to make big bucks. It continually became harder to make ends meet and I finally began to look for something else to do. But every business out there looked like built-in failure to me. Network marketing wasn't even in my vocabulary. I would never stoop to that.

"In August of 1995, while I was attending a dental seminar, one of the other dentists there mentioned a network marketing company to me. That definitely wasn't for me, but when I heard they had dental products, I thought maybe I could sell them. Ultimately, I came to love the products and agreed to go to one of the company's leadership seminars. By December of that year, I found myself not only selling the products, but also enrolling several of my colleagues in the company. With great difficulty, I managed to sign up thirteen others but, by February, all of them had quit. I was batting zero.

"Out of desperation, and fortunately for me, I attended another company-sponsored leadership seminar and one of the leaders in my upline volunteered to coach me. It was from that moment forward, at the ripe old age of fifty-two, that I started to discover an entirely new life philosophy. Network marketing was first and foremost about personal growth and development. Through a number of seminars and the cultural influence of my fellow networkers, today I am a different person. My business is exploding; my relationship with my wife, Dixie, and my family is at an all-time high; and my outlook on life has changed from pessimistic to optimistic. Although I still practice dentistry part-time, I no longer feel like a dentist with all the worries and preoccupations that go with being one. I now feel like a network marketer with an opportunity that can benefit everyone. I have a great outlook on life and am doing what I enjoy with an enthusiasm that I never knew was possible."

Exalt Others Instead of Ourselves

Without passing judgment on all executives, there is a tendency among them to demonstrate an egotistical disposition: "We are great. Those who work for us are inferior to us. All of this success is due to our brilliance." But in network marketing, it is just the opposite demeanor that makes this business work. Pat Hintze and Steve Schultz, partners in their network marketing business, discovered the real secret to MLM success. This is a story you may find yourself repeating over and over as you build your business. It accurately describes the real nature of our industry as well as any we've read. We hope you enjoy sharing it as much as we have.

As Pat and Steve tell it, "Our story is definitely not one of overnight success. The truth is we have simply outlasted most of the others in this industry. For three and a half years, we worked this business with so little results it's almost embarrassing to discuss. We went through every possible negative human emotion. We asked ourselves repeatedly, 'Why won't this work? What are we doing wrong? Why is everyone growing faster and bigger than we are? Will this ever really work for us?'

"We went to every rally, every function possible. But even those seemed to be more depressing than exciting because all we ever heard were the tremendous stories of success about other people. Just once, we would have loved someone to stand up and say, 'I drove three hours last night and got stood up!' Now that would have made us feel great! (If there is one thing we have learned about this business, it's how easy it is to put yourself down. Just compare your success to the success of others. There will always be others who are experiencing more success than you are at any given time.) But we kept going because we thought we might find 'the secret' to the business.

"We lasted long enough to do just that. We traveled eight and a half hours to a rally intent on finding 'the secret.' We knew that the top money earner in the company was going to be there. We got there early so we could find out from him the key to making this business work. We found him and started asking a barrage of burning questions: How do you do this? How did you make it work? What is the secret? His answer was a bit surprising.

"He said, 'I really didn't do it. I've got good downline people; they have actually done it. Why don't you ask them.' So we did. But they said, 'We really didn't do it, we have good downline people, they have actually done it. Why don't you ask them.' So we did. But they said, 'We really didn't do it; we have good downline people.' So we came away from that meeting understanding that *no one* actually does this business. It's just something you give away to other people! So we went home and tried to find some other people we could give it to. And it worked!

"The law of large numbers will rescue the persistent. We kept trying long enough to eventually find others to whom we could give it—people who knew what they were doing. They were actually making their organizations grow. We got excited and started exalting them, telling everyone about their success. Then they found others to give it to, who started having more success than they were. Incredible! We started pointing to their success and others got inspired by what they were seeing. Over the last three and a half years, all we have managed to do is stumble across a few others to whom we have given this opportunity and they were able to do the same.

"Today, we have thousands of people across the country trying to give this business away as a gift to others. Oh, we get the chance to stand up in front of many people and take credit for it, but really . . .

In the words of Ignatius Joseph Firpo of Truckee, California, "What we have done for ourselves dies with us. What we have done for others remains, and is immortal."

we didn't do it!" Steve is a former teacher and Pat is a former sales rep for a paper company. Today, after seven years, they are among the very top income earners in their company—we are talking millions and millions of dollars a year! During the early years before it all started working for them, though they never seriously considered quitting, they developed a philosophy about starting over that they explain in this way: "Even today, we continue the practice of starting over again as if we had no one in our downline. It helps us stay focused on what really makes this business work: *persistence.* The one thing we've learned is that failure cannot handle persistence."

First-year distributors, in particular, must avoid the temptation to follow the high-powered systems brought to our industry by former corporate executives during the Executive Explosion. Be sure to show empathy toward those leaving the corporate world in droves to join our industry. Despite outer appearances, many of them are scared and vulnerable. By leaving behind the "security" of titles and structure, they are faced for the first time with the awesome responsibility of self-reliance. Give them straight answers to their questions, teach them the system of duplication like you teach everyone else, and, if the timing is right, they will do it. Or, rather, they will not do it, but give it away to others who will do it . . . and in turn will give it away to others. In the words of Ignatius Joseph Firpo of Truckee, California, "What we have done for ourselves dies with us. What we have done for others remains, and is immortal."

SUMMARY

- The Executive Explosion refers to the huge influx of corporate executives joining our industry, bringing with them the same management styles that led to low productivity and unjustifiably high incomes in their former careers.

- These executives face two challenges as they enter the field of network distribution:

  1 An unmistakable desperation stemming from their loss of prestige and sudden withdrawal of benefits, company cars, and income.

  2 A misguided conviction that they can transfer their management strategies from traditional business into network marketing, an industry without managers.

- Most upline distributors have a high regard for the education, experience, and expertise of corporate executives and are naturally inclined to listen to what they have to say.

- In light of the respect they carry, former corporate executives pose two obvious challenges to our industry:

  1 As high achievers with great egos, they often intimidate the very distributors who sponsor them.

  2 Even though many of the tools they used in traditional business are simply not applicable to our industry, they try nevertheless to introduce management styles and high-tech approaches into our business, which can sidetrack both their upline and downline associates.

- Even if you have a blue-collar work background, don't make the mistake of assuming that some "corporate big hitter" knows more about our business than you.

- When teaching former corporate executives, take control in your training and teach them how different our MLM business is from traditional business.

- Given the fact that many former corporate execs are discouraged after their departure from traditional business, your task is merely to sift out those who seriously desire change and are at the right time in their lives to join MLM.

- The quicker you can provide corporate people or business professionals with information about the upside potential of our business, the faster they can do their research and make one of three decisions:

  1 They are ready to get started (a positive step).

  2 The time is not right (a positive step—use the card-file system to follow up).

  3 This business is not for them (ask for referrals).

- New distributors, especially from corporate America, must be taught from day one that product usage, prospecting, and recruiting are what lead to success.

- Memos and meetings are time-wasters, as are the creation of slide shows, presenters, overheads, and charts.

- While traditional business encourages people to emphasize their strengths and past successes, network marketing teaches people to also share their vulnerabilities—the circumstances that lead them to MLM—in order to break down the walls of resistance.

- It is generally this "down" experience that opens the door to network marketing. Telling your personal story is what makes other people relate to you—they want to hear why you've chosen this industry as a solution to your former problems.

- Unlike "passing the buck" in traditional business, executives who want to build a large organization in network marketing must leave behind their habits of delegating responsibilities and begin leading by example.

- Do not qualify your prospects, but rather make room for the widest possible cross-section of people.

- Home parties, clinics, and retail sales create immediate, short-term income; however, building an organization of people who use and share the products, and then teaching others how to duplicate this process, produces long-term residual income.

- A lowered self-image is the greatest emotional challenge for those who leave the corporate world and enter full-time into network marketing.

- Many part-time networkers worry about their bosses' negative reaction and their spouse's skepticism, while maintaining a positive outlook throughout the early stages of the process.

- There are hundreds of thousands of single women in network marketing struggling to build organizations while meeting all their other demands as wives, mothers, and female executives. But there is not one with average skills and strong drive who cannot achieve greatness.

- Network marketing can have a profound effect on many businesspeople after they discover that, first and foremost, our profession is about personal growth and development.

- Unlike the corporate work environment, there are no threats to an executive's position in network marketing if he exalts his downline.

- A profound truth about our industry is this: Possessive clinging will never lead to success; only by giving the business to others will you ultimately receive huge rewards in the remarkable world of network marketing.

CONCLUSION

FOR THE FIRST HALF OF OUR CAREERS, prior to meeting, falling in love, and becoming husband and wife, each of us was dedicated to building our respective organizations in the only company either of us has ever represented. For the past six years, we have striven diligently to be good-will ambassadors for the entire network marketing industry. Our colleagues understood our desires to elevate the stature of our profession—even our company president has encouraged us in this endeavor.

We've been honored to speak at a number of conventions. Other MLM company presidents, such as Richard Brooke, have allowed us to coach their best leaders. Many of the very top money earners of our industry have attended our college certification course, which was founded at the University of Illinois at Chicago by Dr.

and Mrs. Charles King and us several years back with the cooperation of their innovative dean of business, Dr. Paul Uselding. It's now being taught internationally. As industry-wide consultants and advocates, we've learned much from those with whom we work.

Recruiters in traditional business are called "head hunters," but we learned early on that network marketers must be "heart hunters." Attempting to build this business by stealing distributors from other companies is patently wrong, given the structural integrity of the network distribution industry. Our philosophy has always been to find a good company and stick with it—don't become an MLM junkie. Not once have we solicited any single distributor away from another company, although many unknowing distributors have asked if they could join us. If a networker has joined a solid company with a proven track record, then we strongly encourage him or her to remain with that company.

We feel blessed to have stumbled into this profession many years ago. Not only did it give us the time and financial freedom to do exactly what we want, but it also enabled us to meet each other and build a life together. Our professional goals for the coming decade include writing books beyond our industry. Mark has several book projects underway, including one on achieving self-wealth, updating one of his father's previously published works with modifications for today's audiences, and, his most prized project, a love story. Rene has been working for over a year on a self-help book based on various aspects of her own life experiences. However, it is within the MLM industry that we intend to continue to place our greatest energy. We hope to further elevate the stature of our profession through public appearances, major convention speeches, consultations, and education through books, tapes, and the media.

In light of this, we would like to ask you to join us in converting our remarkable industry from a job into a profession. There are a few things you can do to help us make this happen.

First, let's all resolve to stop badmouthing each others' companies. We are all in this together and yet we seem to be the only profession in which, whenever there's a danger or a challenge, we circle our wagons and fire *inward*. Networkers often cooperate with regulators and journalists in an investigation of one of their competitors, and rejoice in their demise. In some cases, MLM corporate leaders actually testify as government witnesses against their competitors . . . and, sadly, some are not guilty of being pyramid scams. It's merely a way of hurting the competition. Distributors sometimes act as if by denigrating others they somehow elevate themselves. But that isn't the result. So first and foremost, we ask you to please join us in adopting a simple philosophy: We refuse to bad-mouth our colleagues, other distributors, and other companies in the field of Multi-Level Marketing. If you won't write it down and sign your name to it, then don't say it.

The other side of the coin, and there always is one, is to quickly report any pyramid scam, as soon as you have legitimate proof that people are being ripped off, to the Direct Selling Association and the Federal Trade Commission. And if the concern you have is with your own company, don't just sit back. Take action. Contact the top leader in your upline. If you can, call the president of your company. Do everything in your power to stop unethical activity wherever you find it.

Try to replace the problem with a solution that will make you proud to represent your company. And if all else fails, walk away.

Once we understand that success stems from uplifting our own companies and products rather than destroying the reputations of our MLM competitors, that is when our industry will become the most lucrative in all of free enterprise. One of the outcomes of our university course, in which representatives from many companies spend a long weekend together, is that our students realize that those companies they may have been denigrating are made up of real people, *special* people, with whom they have just shared a very meaningful experience. In that environment we've seen hundreds of networkers resolve to stop reputation-slamming practices.

Second, create your own short presentation specifically designed to educate audiences about the obvious differences between illegal pyramid scams and legitimate network marketing corporations. Then, go to your local chamber of commerce and obtain a list of all clubs and organizations. Make an appointment each month to speak to at least one local club or association as an ambassador for our profession. Not only will you help the industry change its image through education but, in the process, you will obtain numerous prospects for your own down-

line. The general public simply doesn't understand our industry, and most journalists and media broadcasters do not cover stories about the positive truth of network marketing, because only sensationalism and negativism sell newspapers and increase ratings. In their own words: "Good news is no news!"

Third, purchase everything you can through MLM companies whenever possible. If your own company does not yet sell a product you need and want, find out which network distribution company distributes it and contact them. If you don't know a distributor personally, be sure to call their corporate headquarters or you'll have to endure a recruiting pitch. However, we've found that once you make your intentions clear, once they realize you are only interested in representing your own company, they will respect your decision. Let's all stop buying inferior products and services at stores and through catalogs, and start utilizing our own distribution channels.

As one of our contributions to the industry, we have also begun a closing and motivation line that you or your prospects can reach by calling 1-900-PROSPER. Instead of spending $3.99 a minute for recorded astrology, psychic messages, and dubious sexual conversations, why not invest $1.49 a minute in your future success. Any prospect who calls this line and doesn't sign up immediately on your front line is brain-dead. And any despondent distributor who's on the verge of quitting and calls this line will probably give it another good year. Some of the folks who called our previous 900-line once a week were so upset when we cancelled it that we opened this new one permanently. We may update it periodically, but it will basically remain the same and will simply be there for you whenever you need it for yourself or your prospects. It's the only MLM motivation line that is generic and actually turns around the negatives for the most ardent cynics. Proceeds fund our prisoner reform program.

Finally, just go out there and make us all proud to be in network marketing. We have the opportunity to make a difference in our world. And the beauty of network marketing is that it doesn't have to happen in grandiose ways; it occurs one by one by one as we touch the lives of other people. Because of the exponential growth of our industry, before we know it, we will have transformed the spirits of hundreds of millions of people.

If you have enjoyed this book, please give it away to a few people you know and maybe they will pass it along to a few more people. And before you know it, we may find ourselves in an industry that is capturing the largest global share of the personal care, household, nutrition,

health, telecommunications, environmental, educational, and personal development markets of our world, just to mention a few. Network marketing is here to stay, and we predict that over the next decade, and well into the twenty-first century, our industry will be noticed for two things: (1) for its sound marketing strategies and (2) for the sensitivity and integrity that people within the field show toward one another.

Dee Hock, the founder of Visa, had a vision that led to his success in the trillion-dollar credit card industry. Similarly, network marketing is on the brink of explosive growth in the next century. To quote Dee Hock, whom we so admire: "We are at that very point in time when a 400-year-old age is dying and another is struggling to be born—a shifting of culture, science, society, and institutions enormously greater than the world has ever experienced. Ahead is the possibility of the regeneration of individuality, liberty, community, and ethics such as the world has never known, and a harmony with nature, with one another, and with the divine intelligence such as the world has never dreamed." We believe that network marketers will help to make this dream a reality, and we consider this book merely a first step in that direction. In fact, as we literally edited these final words, the ink hardly dry, we were introduced to a new concept that is the culmination of decades of research into human empowerment and peak performance. Leaders in the cognitive sciences like Dr. Albert Bandura, president emeritus of the American Psychological Association, and Steven Pinker, director of the Center for Cognitive Neuroscience at M.I.T., have documented the fact that human destiny knows no limits. This bold, new world of highly technical, academic research suggests that the key to unlocking the inherent potential within everyone may lie, not in the mere acquisition or competency tools similar to the ones presented in this book, but in a more cognitive, personal change. These visionaries suggest that self-efficacy (i.e., having the power to produce certain effects within oneself) combined with competency development (i.e., promoting the specific skills necessary to accomplish a given task) may be the true key for unlocking the power within us all. And according to them, both proficiencies can be learned and duplicated.

Although we have but scratched the surface of these cutting-edge techniques, we have been sufficiently intrigued to join with other leaders from several countries in the formation of a synergistic, think tank consulting firm called 21st century Global Trust. Together, we are meticulously exploring this body of evidence in order to create a blueprint for enhanced performance, with the goal of helping millions of network marketers rise to their fullest potential. For we believe our industry, in which the barriers to individual greatness and personal empowerment have been lifted, is the last bastion of free market capitalism. We are an infant industry, and the only reason we still exist, given the challenge empowered individuals pose to big government, is that we developed our profession too rapidly for the professional ruling class to seize control, though many of us have suffered from their past attempts. As an industry, we must not only quadruple our membership in the next decade, but also employ strategies that will empower grassroots participants to prosper as meaningfully our top 3 percent—those of us who have achieved the financial and time freedom first envisioned by our founders. We believe that empowerment giants like Lou Tice and Dr. Bandura are absolutely correct in their assessment of the positive benefits of techniques that combine mastery of task performance with exercises in self-efficacy, and we intend to create and launch programs that will capitalize on these new mental applications.

We all stand at the dawn of a fresh millennium, caretakers of a bold, new, limitless profession, one that can bolster economic freedom throughout the world and create a beautiful and worthy future for our grandchildren. But we must demonstrate in the twenty-first century that a much larger percentage of people who join the ranks of network marketing have an equal chance to prosper in our profession, and we now believe that the tools needed for such widespread prosperity are within our grasp. Currently, 3 percent of the MLM population earn over $93,000 per year, and 56 percent earn less than $6,000 per year. It is the middle 40 percent that we believe we can and must reach. Our commitment to you as industry advocates and leaders is to continue to research, analyze, and simplify the newest scientific and academic advances in human potential enhancements, then implement easily duplicated strategies designed to unleash the peak performance of those who would entrust their futures to network marketing. For too many years the human outcome has been mediocrity, but we believe that network marketing, given its lack of boundaries and limitations, affords each of us an exhilarating future of unprecedented opportunities.

We are incurable optimists, and you can rest assured that you haven't heard the last from us . . . because, as we all know, *Your First Year of Network Marketing* is only the beginning.

INDEX

Q

Qualification of leads, avoidance of, 125–127, 236–237

R

Realistic expectations, 85–91, 105–109

Real volume, vs. promotional volume, 43–45

Recognition, as benefit of network marketing, 62

Recruiting meetings, 187–191
local, 211–213
long-distance, 209–211

Recruiting system
focused approach, 145–149
follow upline advice, 149–150
myths, 83–111
switching organizations during, negative effects, 150–154
technology and, 184–185
wide focus as key to, 36–39

Recruits
number needed to succeed, 91–98
qualification of, 236–237
successful, factors behind, 33–36

Rejection
dealing with, 18–20, 22–23
effects on network marketing, 1–26
factors behind, 1–9
as positive motivation, 22–23
preparing for, 9–14

Relationship marketing, 113, 136

Restaurant meetings, 183–184

Retailing products, 26
versus organization building, 237–241

Retail sales, and success, 107

Retirement, early, as unrealistic recruiting tool, 103–105

Rogow, Mark, 16–18

Rose, Steve and Cynthia, 78

Rubin, Jerry, 247

Rubino, Joe, 146–147

Ruhe, Jan, 238–241, 245, 248

S

Sales, versus organization building, 237–241

Sales volume, 105–107

Scatter bomb marketing
checklist, 166–168
as unfocused approach, 143–168

Scharp, Bob, 70–71

Schultz, Steve, 249–251

Schumacher, Patrick, 135–136

Secrets of Building a Million-Dollar Network Marketing Organization, 147

Self-confidence, as key to warm marketing, 118–124

Self-doubt, xvii

Self-esteem
effect on warm marketing, 120–121
role in network marketing, 15–18

Self-sufficiency, among associates, creation of, 27–51

Silent Unity, 60

Single women, and organization building, 245–248

Sledge, Steve and Caroline, 124, 131, 188

Spouses
as obstacles to network marketing, 1–4

Staubach, Roger, 231

Storytelling, importance, 234–235

Stress reduction, 61

Structure, role in successful downline distributors, 159–162

Success
among downline distributors, 33–36
emotional energy and, 53–54
impact of faith on, 74–77
key elements for, xiii–xiv
managing vs. supporting as key to, 27–28
number of recruits necessary for, 91–98
perseverance as element in, 77–80
planning for, 85–87
for recruits, factors behind, 33–36
requirements for, 88–111
retail sales and, 107
role of structure in, 159–162
time required for, 98–100, 109
warm lists as fundamental to, 113–142

About the Authors

Mark Yarnell is an accomplished author, speaker, and international businessman, and serves as a key field leader in Legacy USA. He has 12 years of applied network marketing experience and has built a successful network marketing organization of more than 200,000 representatives worldwide.

Mark has delivered lectures throughout North America, Europe, and Asia, and has authored and published several books about network marketing including *The Wall Street Journal* and *Business Week* bestseller *Your First Year in Network Marketing*. As a respected advocate of the industry, Mark served as contributing editor to *Success Magazine*, and contributed ten articles to this well-known publication. The Yarnells and Dr. Charles King created the first certification course in network marketing at the University of Illinois, Chicago.

Mark has been honored and recognized internationally with numerous awards in the industry, including the American Dream Award from the Howard Ruff Company (1989), the Leadership Award (1992) and Distributor of the Year Award (1995) from the Multi-Level Marketing International Association, and the Greatest Networker in the World award by *Upline* magazine. Mark has been inducted into the Network Marketing Hall of Fame by the International Directory of Network Marketing (1997).

Mark founded both The Eagles, a literary and self-help organization for penitentiary inmates, and the School of Sobriety, the only free treatment program in Nevada for alcoholics and addicts, which is endorsed and utilized as a resource by many Northern Nevada judges. Mark also helped establish, along with Vice President Albert Gore and former Soviet leader Mikhail Gorbachev, the International Green Cross, which focuses on worldwide environmental preservation.

Mark's newest book, *Self-Wealth*, coauthored with Valerie Bates and Dr. John Radford, is now available at Amazon.com and all major bookstores. Currently, Mark is at work on his 7th book, *90 Days to Self-Wealth, 100 Anecdotes, Witticisms & Affirmations to Live By*, scheduled for release in the year 2000.

You may reach Mark at:

markyarnell@home.com

www.self-wealth.com

250-995-2644

Rene Reid Yarnell is a well-loved international speaker, writer, and consultant for the network marketing industry. Having built a successful organization with her partner of more than 200,000 marketing representatives worldwide, she has been heavily involved in helping shape the Network Marketing industry for well over a decade.

Formerly a Catholic nun with an M.A. in Theology, Rene has dedicated much of her life to the field of education, beginning in the classroom in the sixties and expanding to include hosting both talk radio and television shows. Today, she is a regular host on Freedom Radio, the Net's only Network Marketing broadcast.

A member of the Network Marketing Hall of Fame, Rene is considered one of the country's most successful and sought-after authorities on network marketing and personal development. A prolific writing career, which includes the national best-seller *Your First Year in Network Marketing* and *Power Multi-Level Marketing*, (both coauthored with Mark Yarnell) has become the focal point of her passion for helping people create the life of their dreams. Her manual, *The Encyclopedia of Network Marketing*, is used as part of the University Certificate Seminar she co-founded and teaches in the U.S. and abroad. Having recently released another book on the subject, *The New Entrepreneurs: Making a Living – Making a Life in Network Marketing*, Rene introduces the industry to professionals leaving the corporate world. A great prospecting tool, this book has a companion program in both audiocassette and MP3 formats.

Mark and Rene's impact on the world of network marketing has garnered a litany of awards and distinctions, including being named "Greatest Networker in the World" by *Upline* magazine. They co-founded the International Green Cross with vice-president Al Gore and former Soviet prime minister Mikael Gorbachev to address worldwide environmental preservation issues.

From 1989 to 1993, Rene served in the elected position of County Commissioner in her hometown of Reno, Nevada, where she has lived for 20 years. She founded and serves on the local board of Project Restart, a program committed to assisting the homeless in Northern Nevada. Rene has two grown children: a son, Chris Grove, and a daughter by marriage, Amy Yarnell.

You may reach Rene Reid Yarnell at:
www.yarnell.com
rene@yarnell.com
800-300-1489

To order her books and training materials:
www.yarnell.com
888-285-6316 (U.S.)
801-225-9520 (outside U.S.)

The New Face of Network Marketing

Every year, thousands of men and women leave established, lucrative careers to pursue new opportunities in the booming network marketing industry—an industry that is now attracting former doctors, CEOs, and others seeking independence and financial rewards. Inside *The New Professionals,* you'll meet people—just like you—who have exceeded the income and prestige of their previous careers and are now living the American dream.

"A must-read for anyone interested in being the architect of their destiny."

—FRANK J. KEEFER, president and CEO, *Network Marketing Lifestyles* magazine

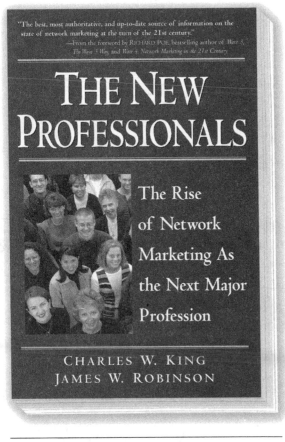

ISBN 0-7615-1966-1 / Paperback / 352 pages
U.S. $15.95 / Can. $23.95

THREE RIVERS PRESS

Available everywhere books are sold.
Visit us online at www.crownpublishing.com.

The Bestselling Guides to Network Marketing

In the *New York Times* bestseller *Wave 3,* award-winning journalist Richard Poe examines the revolutionary trend that offers freedom from salaried drudgery. Network marketing offers people like you the chance to start your own business, work comfortably from home, and—maybe—achieve wealth beyond your wildest dreams. In *The Wave 3 Way to Building Your Downline,* Poe shows savvy network marketers how to build their downline wide and deep, for lucrative payments that will extend far into the future.

The Wave 3 Way to Building Your Downline
ISBN 0-7615-0439-7 / Paperback
256 pages / U.S. $14.95 / Can. $22.50
Also Available on Audiocassette!
ISBN 0-7615-0757-4
U.S. $18.95 / Can. $25.95

Wave 3
ISBN 1-55958-501-3 / Paperback
288 pages / U.S. $14.95 / Can. $22.95
Also Available on Audiocassette!
ISBN 0-7615-0673-X
U.S. $18.95 / Can. $25.95

**Available everywhere books are sold.
Visit us online at www.crownpublishing.com.**

THREE RIVERS PRESS

Network Marketing for the New Millennium

Millions of people around the world are dreaming of starting their own business. In *Wave 4,* bestselling author Richard Poe shows how network marketing can help you achieve exciting financial goals in the 21st century, detailing how the marriage between the Internet and people-to-people sales will revolutionize the industry of direct selling. In *The Wave 4 Way to Building Your Downline,* Poe reveals the secrets to becoming an effective multilevel marketing leader, including valuable insights into network marketing strategies.

Wave 4
ISBN 0-7615-1752-9 / Paperback
336 pages / U.S. $15.00 / Can. $22.00

The Wave 4 Way to Building Your Downline
ISBN 0-7615-2213-1 / Paperback
224 pages / U.S. $15.95 / Can. $23.95

THREE RIVERS PRESS

Available everywhere books are sold.
Visit us online at www.crownpublishing.com.